# CULTURAL PROFICIENCY

## SECOND EDITION

*To*
*Hermon Lindsey for his wit and wisdom*
*Winston H. Robins for setting high standards*
*William Terrell for his encouragement and unconditional love*

# CULTURAL PROFICIENCY
## A Manual for School Leaders

### SECOND EDITION

## Randall B. Lindsey
## Kikanza Nuri Robins
## Raymond D. Terrell

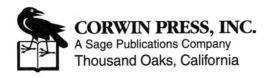
**CORWIN PRESS, INC.**
A Sage Publications Company
Thousand Oaks, California

*For information:*

Corwin Press, Inc.
A Sage Publications Company
2455 Teller Road
Thousand Oaks, California 91320
www.corwinpress.com

Sage Publications Ltd.
6 Bonhill Street
London EC2A 4PU
United Kingdom

Sage Publications India Pvt. Ltd.
B-42 Panchsheel Enclave
New Delhi 110 017 India

Printed in the United States of America

**Library of Congress Cataloging-in-Publication Data**

Lindsey, Randall B.
Cultural proficiency : a manual for school leaders / Randall B.
Lindsey, Kikanza Nuri Robins, Raymond D. Terrell.— 2nd ed.
    p. cm.
Includes bibliographical references and index.
ISBN 0-7619-4643-8 (Cloth) — ISBN 0-7619-4644-6 (Paper)
    1. Multicultural education—United States—Case studies. 2. Educational sociology—United States—Case studies. 3. Educational leadership—United States—Case studies. I. Robins, Kikanza Nuri, 1950- II. Terrell, Raymond D. III. Title.
LC1099.3 .L555 2003
370.117'0973—dc21                                              2002154045

This book is printed on acid-free paper.

03  04  05  06  07  08  7  6  5  4  3  2  1

| Acquisitions Editor: | Rachel Livsey |
|---|---|
| Editorial Assistant: | Phyllis Cappello |
| Production Editor: | Julia Parnell |
| Copyeditor: | Cheryl Adam |
| Typesetter/Designer: | Christina Hill |
| Indexer: | Pamela Van Huss |
| Cover Designer: | Tracy E. Miller |
| Production Artist: | Janet Foulger |

# Contents

Foreword to the Second Edition      xi

Foreword to the First Edition      xiii

Introduction to the Second Edition      xv

Preface to the First Edition      xix

About the Authors      xxiv

## Part I    Understanding Cultural Proficiency

### 1. What Is Cultural Proficiency?      3

*Cultural proficiency is not an off-the-shelf program. It is an approach; it provides tools and help for an increasingly diverse world with an increasing number of well-intentioned and fearful people.*

Going Further      22

Reflection      23

Structured Exercises:

Response Sheet 1.0.1: The Culturally Proficient
Professional      25

Activity 1.1: Diversity Lifeline      26

Activity 1.2: Identifying Shared Values for Diversity      28

Response Sheet 1.2.1: Definitions for Shared Values      30

Activity 1.3: Cultural Proficiency Consensus      31

Response Sheet 1.3.1: Cultural Proficiency Consensus      33

Response Sheet 1.3.2: Cultural Proficiency Consensus
Preferred Responses      34

Activity 1.4: Journaling      36

### 2. The Historical Context for Cultural Proficiency      38

*People of goodwill have been trying to respond to these issues for a long time. Race relations, human relations,*

3654

106949

*multiculturalism, desegregation, and integration have all been*
*approaches that have helped—but not enough.*

| | |
|---|---|
| Going Further | 53 |
| Reflection | 54 |
| Structured Exercises: | |
|     Activity 2.1: Storytelling | 55 |
|     Activity 2.2 : Simultaneous Storytelling | 57 |
|     Activity 2.3: Pick a Cell | 59 |
|     Response Sheet 2.3.1: Evolution of Equity Policies | 61 |
|     Activity 2.4: Discussion Questions About U.S. History | 62 |
|     Response Sheet 2.4.1: Discussion Questions About U.S. History | 64 |
|     Response Sheet 2.4.2: Answers and Commentary | 66 |
|     Activity 2.5: Cultural Perceptions | 67 |
|     Response Sheet 2.5.1: Cultural Perceptions | 69 |
|     Activity 2.6: Circle of Stereotypes | 70 |
|     Activity 2.7: Personal Stereotypes | 72 |
|     Activity 2.8: Cultural Stereotypes | 74 |
|     Activity 2.9: Ethnic Perceptions | 76 |
|     Activity 2.10: Group Stereotypes | 78 |

## Part II   Using the Tools of Cultural Proficiency

### 3.  The First Tool, Descriptive Language: The Cultural Proficiency Continuum   83

*People need a way to talk about individual behaviors and*
*organizational practices that will keep the conversation open.*
*Calling someone a bigot or declaring that an organization is*
*racist does not invite change. Pointing out where the behavior*
*or action falls on the continuum does.*

| | |
|---|---|
| Going Further | 91 |
| Reflection | 93 |
| Structured Exercises: | |
|     Activity 3.1: The Cultural Proficiency Continuum | 94 |
|     Response Sheet 3.1.1: The Cultural Proficiency Continuum | 97 |
|     Response Sheet 3.1.2: The Cultural Proficiency Continuum Chart | 101 |
|     Activity 3.2: Circle of History | 102 |
|     Activity 3.3: Human Relations Needs Assessment | 105 |

Response Sheet 3.3.1: Human Relations Needs
    Assessment Instrument                107

## 4. The Second Tool, Behavioral Competencies: The Essential Elements of Cultural Proficiency 110

*The continuum describes behavior and practices broadly. The
elements set standards for deep structural change at the positive
end of the continuum. These behavioral competencies can be
used as a measuring stick for individual and organizational
development.*

Responsibilities of Culturally Proficient School Leaders:
    Table 4.1        119
Going Further        122
Reflection        123
Structured Exercises:
    Activity 4.1: Exploring Behaviors Along the
        Continuum        124
    Response Sheet 4.1.1: The Essential Elements of
        Cultural Proficiency        126
    Response Sheet 4.1.2: Behaviors Along the
        Continuum        128
    Activity 4.2: Understanding the Essential Elements    129
    Response Sheet 4.2.1: Culturally Proficient Practices    131
    Response Sheet 4.2.3: Activities to Reinforce the
        Essential Elements of Cultural Proficiency    133
    Activity 4.3: Essential Elements of Cultural Proficiency    137
    Activity 4.4: Planning With the Five Essential Elements    139
    Activity 4.5: Performance Competencies and the
        Essential Elements    141
    Response Sheet 4.5.1:Performance Competencies
        and the Essential Elements    144
    Response Sheet 4.5.2: Words Used to Describe
        Oppressed and Entitled Groups    145
    Activity 4.6: Intercultural Communication    146
    Activity 4.7: Managing Conflict With Our Core Values    148
    Response Sheet 4.7.1: Managing Conflict With Our
        Core Values—Example    150
    Response Sheet 4.7.2: Examining Your Core Values    151
    Activity 4.8: Cultural Competence Self-Assessment    152
    Response Sheet 4.8.1: Cultural Competence
        Self-Assessment    154

5.  The Third Tool, Underlying Values:
    The Guiding Principles of Cultural Proficiency          157

    *Healthy organizations have strong core cultures; people with*
    *integrity have a clear sense of their own values. The underlying*
    *values of cultural proficiency are the principles. One cannot not*
    *have culture; dominant cultures affect dominated groups in*
    *interesting and sometimes unexpected ways.*

    Approaches to Diversity: Figure 5.1                        158
    Going Further                                             165
    Reflection                                               166
    Structured Exercises:
        Activity 5.1: Guiding Principles Discussion Starters    167
        Response Sheet 5.1.1: The Guiding Principles of
            Cultural Proficiency                             169
        Response Sheet 5.1.2: Cultural Proficiency
            Discussion Starters                              170
        Response Sheet 5.1.3: Guiding Principles Discussions    171
        Activity 5.2.1: My Work Values                       173
        Activity 5.3: Demographics                           175
        Activity 5.4: Assessing Your School's Culture         177
        Response Sheet 5.4.1: Assessing the Culture of
            Your School                                      179
        Activity 5.5: Examining Your Organizational Values    181
        Response Sheet 5.5.1: Examining Our Organizational
            Values                                           183


Part III   Overcoming the
           Barriers to Cultural Proficiency


6.  Culturally Proficient Leadership:
    Formal and Nonformal Leaders                             187

    *Creating a culturally proficient school or district requires*
    *culturally courageous leadership. Leaders come with and*
    *without titles.*

    Going Further                                             204
    Reflection                                               205
    Structured Exercises:
        Activity 6.1: The Great Egg Drop                      206
        Response Sheet 6.1.1: The Great Egg Drop              209

Response Sheet 6.1.2: Analyzing the Great Egg Drop     210
Activity 6.2: Seven-Minute Day     211
Response Sheet 6.2.1: Seven-Minute Day Roles     214
Response Sheet 6.2.2: General Instructions     215
Response Sheet 6.2.3: Seven-Minute Day Data Sheet     216

## 7. The First Barrier: Unawareness of the Need to Adapt     217

*In an open, inclusive, relational organization, everyone changes. Becoming culturally proficient is making a commitment to change oneself.*

Myths About Change: Table 7.1     221
Phases of the Change Process: Table 7.2     223
Going Further     228
Reflection     230
Structured Exercises:
Activity 7.1: The Process of Personal Change     231
Response Sheet 7.1.1: The Process of Personal Change     233
Activity 7.2: Seven Dynamics of Change     234
Response Sheet 7.2.1: Seven Dynamics of Change     237
Figure 7.1     238
Activity 7.3: Differences That Make a Difference     239
Activity 7.4: Paradigms     241
Response Sheet 7.4.1: Assessing Your Paradigms     243

## 8. The Second Barrier: The Presumption of Entitlement     244

*Institutionalized oppression allows people in the dominant culture to accrue privilege and benefits they may not even recognize. People from historically oppressed groups may unknowingly or unwittingly continue the policies and practices that flow from these privileges and benefits.*

Types of Minority Status: Table 8.1     250
Words Used to Describe Oppressed and Entitled Groups:
Table 8.2     258
Stages of Racial Consciousness: Table 8.3     270
Going Further     271
Reflection     272
Structured Exercises:
Activity 8.1: Stand Up     273
Activity 8.2: Line of Privilege     275
Activity 8.3: Entitlement Survey     277

Response Sheet 8.3.1: A Survey of Privilege and
    Entitlement       279
Activity 8.4: Starpower       281
Activity 8.5: Barriers to Cultural Proficiency       283
Response Sheet 8.5.1: Barriers to Cultural Proficiency       285

## Part IV   Making the Commitment to Cultural Proficiency

### 9.  Cultural Proficiency: A Moral Imperative       289

*Cultural proficiency presents us with a moral imperative to make our communities and our world a place where justice and harmony are the norms.*

Going Further       295
Reflection       296
Structured Exercises:
    Activity 9.1: Introductory Grid       297
    Activity 9.2: Totems or Crests—Getting to Know You       300
    Activity 9.3: Name Five Things       302
    Activity 9.4: Who Are You?       304
    Activity 9.5: Who Am I?       306
    Activity 9.6: Cultural Portrait       308
    Activity 9.7: Exploring Your Cultural Roots       310
    Activity 9.8: Observation Activity       312
    Response Sheet 9.8.1: Observation Questions       314
    Activity 9.9: Strength Bombardment       315

### 10.  The Case: One Last Look       318

*Here are the collected stories of the characters that illustrated the points in each chapter.*

Going Further       333
Reflection       334
Structured Exercises:
    Activities Organized by Topic       336
    Activities Organized by Expertise of Facilitator       337
    Activities Organized by Readiness of Group       339

Bibliography       341

Index       353

# Foreword to
# the Second Edition

In the fall of 1968, I left a Roman Catholic seminary and walked into Dominguez High School in Compton, California. As a rookie school-teacher, I knew nothing about the forces of cultural diversity shaping the school and the history of inequitable school policies and practices in that district that had caused all manner of chaos, including racial tension, riots, bomb threats, and assaults. What I did know is that students, teachers, administrators, and parents couldn't get along and that their disagreements were impeding both teaching and learning.

Thirty-four years later, as I retire this fall as the longest-serving urban superintendent in the country, it's a real pleasure to discover a book for school leaders that offers a systematic approach to addressing problems and challenges that have impeded teaching and learning in so many classrooms, schools, and districts for such a long period of time. I would add that the problems and challenges today are not as obvious as those I encountered as an emergency permit teacher in that tumultuous year of that tumultuous decade. They are, in fact, much more subtle and below the surface, but their ability to impede is in some ways much stronger and more problematic.

This is a book that is grounded first and foremost in respect for people and institutions as they struggle with the important issues of diversity, equity, and fairness. It provides leaders with a profound understanding of the importance of cultural proficiency as a guide to long-term improvement in schools and classrooms, where differences should never be ignored in our haste as school administrators to maintain positive public relations at all costs. It challenges school leaders with a moral imperative and a bias for action that puts the importance of leading the change process as the defining factor in their daily work lives.

Those who are looking for quick fixes, magical cures, and short-term spikes in student achievement will be disappointed by this second edition. The case studies are rich, the practical applications are relevant, and the exercises are designed to force thinking in new ways that profoundly challenge the status quo. Such activities provide a real guide to long-term thinking about new policies, programs, and practices that offer genuine hope in creating a bright future for all those students who have been left behind in school systems everywhere.

This is the beauty of the moral imperative and urgency that these authors capture better than most in the literature on this subject. It goes without saying that our failure to act and to understand the importance of these concepts will lead to continued handwringing about an achievement gap that couldn't be closed in 1968 and won't be closed in this new century.

Carl A. Cohn
*University of Southern California*

# Foreword to the First Edition

For years, education work that went under the label *multicultural* was well intentioned and appropriate in orientation but superficial. *Culture* was undefined. Rarely was there any grounding in the study of culture. Even as anthropologists were brought into the picture, our understanding of diversity was not enhanced much given the extremely wide range of cultures that are a part of the American mosaic.

Not only was cultural understanding superficial, but our understanding of pedagogy (especially valid pedagogy) was not much better. Even now, it is hard to have a coherent dialogue about valid pedagogy. It is hard to separate the trivial from the substantial. It is hard to see how valid pedagogy makes a difference in everyday work. Yet powerful general approaches to teaching and learning exist and are well documented, and many demonstrations can be seen (e.g., Eakin & Backler, 1993; Ladson-Billings, 1994; Sizemore, 1983; Suzuki, 1987).

Valid pedagogy shows that, given a high quality of teaching and nurture, all children succeed in spite of IQ, poverty, crime- and drug-ridden neighborhoods, and other issues. Simply put, ordinary teachers who are well prepared, motivated, and dedicated produce high-achieving students. This production is not rocket science. With reasonably hard work and an appropriate focus, success is certain for all children (e.g., Sparks, 1997).

Culture can be understood, and powerful pedagogy is within the grasp of well-prepared teachers. So why does success elude us, especially for so many poor "minority" students? Simply put, a third factor complicates and obscures our view of both culture and pedagogy. It is politics. Teaching and learning in schools are the sites for power struggles. These sites are the places where hegemonic agendas are played out (e.g., Freire, 1970; Kohn, 1998; Kozol, 1991; Oakes, 1985). The intersection of these three things is the context within which teaching and learning take place. No understanding of school success and failure is possible in ignorance of how these things interact.

A sophisticated understanding of each of these three components separately and in interaction with each other is necessary to raise the level of professional dialogue, analysis, and professional practice.

This book is one in a small number that presents clear voices on these matters. These authors plumb the deep structure of the diversity issue in education. They provide precise definitions of such things as culture and oppression. Moreover, they offer a wide array of anecdotal examples that have the ring of authenticity to them. The anecdotes alone are a rich source of stimulating materials guaranteed to launch meaningful dialogue. The anecdotes bring to life what would otherwise be dry and perhaps irrelevant talk about abstract things, things that are also likely to be decontextualized. Yet the authors weave these anecdotes skillfully into the text, giving it a robustness seldom found in educational literature.

As if this were not enough, the authors provide many activities suitable for staff development. Even veteran staff development leaders will find activities here to enrich their repertoires of best practice.

Culture is real and is a major element in all human interactions. Those who are blind to cultural diversity are blind to reality. Teaching power is also real. Those who are blind to that must improve their own competency. Above all, power and hegemony, the desire by some to dominate vulnerable groups, are alive and well. The ugly history of American apartheid (segregation) is but one example of how hegemony plays out in education and becomes embedded in structures of schooling, root and branch, from ideology to methodology to curriculum to assessment.

The theory and practice described and presented here challenge all to offer at least as much quality as the authors have shown.

This book is a major contribution to the education literature on diversity and pluralism in education. Cultural proficiency, as discussed here, contributes to the language of empowerment.

Asa G. Hilliard, III
*Georgia State University*

# Introduction to the Second Edition

We are delighted to be writing together again, and we are honored that Corwin invited us to write a second edition to *Cultural Proficiency*. When we began to respond to the issues that arise in diverse environments using the tools of cultural proficiency, we knew that it was the best approach that we had seen. Since 1990, we have introduced cultural proficiency to our clients across the country, and we are still convinced that cultural proficiency provides the most effective tools for organizations and individuals to respond to the diversity in their lives.

Our readers have been wonderfully responsive, and we have sought to use their comments and their suggestions in this second edition. This second edition reflects our continued use of cultural proficiency; these tools have helped us to go further in our personal development and in the organizational development of our clients. Our readers have shared with us how they have used the book to make a difference in their organizations. We say "organizations" because our readers are in schools, hospitals, government agencies, not-for-profit organizations, private industry, and churches. They have demonstrated over and over that cultural proficiency is an approach that works when people are committed to systemic change regardless of the nature of their business.

There are a number of things that we have changed in this second edition. First, the organization is different. We start each chapter with a vignette from the case, which describes the work of a suburban school district and an inner-city school district. The case has a stronger story line and fewer characters, so it will be easier to follow the characters as they interact throughout the book. The entire case is in the last chapter, so that you can use the case as you study leadership and diversity in other contexts. As in the first edition, we intersperse vignettes from the case to provide examples and illustrations of the information we present to you.

In the spirit of cultural proficiency, we have changed our language. We refer to cultural proficiency as an *approach* to responding to the issues that emerge in a diverse environment, and we talk about the *tools* of cultural proficiency. This is important because we want to emphasize that cultural proficiency is not a theory, nor is it an off-the-shelf program that you add to your agenda. It is a way of being that involves the use of tools for both individual and organizational development. Instead of *white people*, we use the term *European American*, which is parallel to the words used to describe other ethnic groups. We have learned that people whom we have called Native Americans prefer to be called People of the First Nations. They remind us that most people who were born in the United States consider themselves "natives" of this country. We capitalize Gay and Lesbian because our friends who are part of these groups have asked us to. We also speak of a larger group that is marginalized in U.S. society: GLBT, or Gay, Lesbian, Bisexual, and Transgendered people. We never liked the term *minorities* and, in the first edition, we used *people of color*. We continue to use this term and have added *emerging majorities* to describe the ethnic groups in many areas of the United States that are emerging as the majority group. In our ongoing quest to be culturally proficient, we recognized that when we use the terms *oppressed* or *historically oppressed groups*, images of victims and martyrs emerge for many people. So we are using *dominant* and *dominated*. Our hope is that our readers will understand that we are not laying blame but rather are seeking to describe social constructs.

The format of the text is simpler, with fewer charts and tables. We have expanded the material on the continuum, the elements, and the principles of cultural proficiency. This is a reflection of our increased understanding and appreciation of these tools. We have added new material on change and leadership, and we have acknowledged standards as a new trend in the ever-evolving field of education. Each chapter ends with questions that will take you further into the topic. There is also space for you to write your reflections as you respond to the questions.

We have added a few more activities, and we have moved them from the back of the book and arranged them topically after each chapter. These activities will help you as you work with your colleagues to better understand the concepts we present and to use the tools of cultural proficiency in your particular situations. As educators, you know that any one activity can be used to reinforce many different points, and every activity cannot be used in all environments. For that reason, we have provided charts that list the activities so that you can quickly review them topically or select them according to the readiness level of your group or your expertise as a facilitator. The activities are listed in the table of contents, and we have placed charts at the end of the book that organize the activities by topic, readiness of the group, and expertise of the facilitator.

The worksheets and handouts we have created for you are presented as *response sheets* that will be easy for you to duplicate. Although *handout* is a commonly used term in our field, for many people it carries a negative connotation, so we sought to find a word that was a bit more dignified—hence response sheet. Each response sheet requires some type of response from you—sometimes written, sometimes verbal, and, we hope, always in your thinking. Although we provide instructions or suggestions for your use, at the same time, we encourage you to be creative in how you use the materials. If you develop variations to our activities or create new activities that you find particularly effective, please contact us and tell us about your experiences at **culturalproficiency@earthlink .net**. We would like to share your stories and your ideas with our clients and our readers.

The resources we provide include an extensive bibliography and web pages when appropriate. We have, of course, listed all of the works to which we refer in the text; additionally, we included those books that inform and influence our work. We sincerely hope that you will add a number of these references to your professional libraries. Another book that we hope you add to your collection is *Culturally Proficient Instruction* (Nuri Robins et al., Corwin Press). We think it will make a wonderful companion to this book, and for those of you who are more interested in how cultural proficiency relates to the curriculum, you will find many of the answers to your questions about instruction in a diverse environment.

We could not have made any of these changes without the help of a wonderfully supportive community. First, we appreciate those who purchased and read our books. We also appreciate every professor who required his or her students to buy our books. We are humbled by your enthusiastic reception of our work. We are awed by our many clients who translated school language to organizational language as they applied the concepts to their work in arenas outside of education. We are grateful for the invitation of Corwin Press to produce this second edition. We are delighted that, once again, we have been able to work with Rachel Livsey, our editor, coach, and cheerleader, and with Phyllis Cappello, whose intuitive diplomacy kept us on track and out of trouble. We appreciate the other members of the production team who made room for us at their table. Thanks also to Shari Hatch for lovingly pushing us out of her nest and to Cheryl Adam for grace and clarity under pressure. Finally, as coauthors and friends, we bow to one another—*Namaste*.

Randall B. Lindsey
Kikanza Nuri Robins
Raymond D. Terrell

# Preface
# to the First Edition

As educators, we are used to trends. Every three to five years, something new is presented that is supposed to be the answer to all our professional nightmares. Some educational innovations truly work; others simply make more work. About 30 years ago, educational sociologists and curriculum specialists began writing about urban schools and the special demands presented by students in our urban centers. Of course, *urban school* was a euphemism for a school whose population was not white middle-class or better. The poor, the oppressed, the outcasts, and the castoffs lived in the urban cores of the United States. Teachers and other educators needed to deal with them. Today, the buzzword for this country's minorities, the women and men who are the poor, the people of color, the Gays and Lesbians, and the disabled, is *diversity*.

It has become politically correct to talk about issues of diversity. Anything that used to be labeled deprived, disadvantaged, or different is now called diverse. In some schools, not much has changed except the labels. We propose to talk not about how to deal with diversity, but rather about how school leaders can respond to issues arising from working with diverse populations. Diversity is as real as the chair in which you are sitting or this book that you are holding. We do not need to discuss whether diversity is an issue. Diversity is a neutral descriptor that lets you know that the people around you are not all like you. What we propose to do in this book is to help you develop positive and productive responses to the diversity in your school and community.

Cultural proficiency is a relatively new approach to diversity developed for work in mental health agencies. The cultural proficiency model provides a framework for individual and organizational change, both of which are necessary for systemic change. Cultural proficiency is the policies and practices of a school or the values and behaviors of an individual that enable the person or school to interact effectively in a culturally diverse environment. We introduce the cultural proficiency model to school leaders with examples relevant to school settings. This approach to the topic of diversity is easy to internalize. It provides a non-threatening, comprehensive, systematic, and systemic structure. Its application is behavioral, focusing on individual performance as well as on organizational policies and practices. Many schools and people have an aversion to dealing with their own issues related to equity, affirmative action, and diversity. We wrote this book because cultural proficiency provides a nonthreatening, comprehensive, systemic structure for school leaders addressing these issues.

Government agencies, including schools, continue to battle ineffectively with programs called affirmative action, multicultural curriculum projects, and diversity. Rarely do they deal with the underlying issues of class, caste, and culture that make diversity an issue in our country. As our society becomes increasingly diverse, so do our schools. In schools, the issues are complicated by student populations that change far more rapidly than the demographic profiles of the educators responsible for teaching them. Urban schools are heavily populated with students who historically have been underserved—African American, Latino, Caribbean, Native American, and students from low-income families. For these and many other related reasons, it is important for schools to address proactively the issues caused by the diversity of their communities with approaches and programs designed not to fix but to change a system so that it is appropriate and responsive to the changes that have taken place among faculty, staff, students, and families. This book provides a structured and theoretically sound process for systematically addressing diversity in terms that enhance the educational opportunities of all students.

We are indebted to the work that others have done before us. John Ogbu, James Banks, Paolo Freire, Henry Giroux, Asa Hilliard, Christine Sleeter, and Carol Gilligan have inspired us. Many other scholarly works remind us of all that can and cannot be presented in one volume. In this book, we therefore focus on the application of theory by contextualizing a model that has worked for the school practitioner in a variety of settings. This book is for formal and nonformal school leaders. It serves as a guide to analyzing schools and oneself as you plan, implement, and assess change. If we are going to create culturally proficient schools, the leaders at the school level must create them. In addition to the practitioner, students in schools of education will find that the book complements their study of educational change, and emerging issues in education.

*Cultural Proficiency* uses examples from our work over the past 10 years in teaching school leaders how to adapt the cultural proficiency model to their unique situations. Our goal is to provide the reader with a strong conceptual understanding of cultural proficiency and to give specific, practical, field-tested applications of those same concepts. After reading *Cultural Proficiency*, you will have a model for assessing behavior and programs in schools. You will have a framework for implementing change within classrooms or schools or throughout districts. Additionally, you will have a comprehensive case study and structured exercises to use with your colleagues and staffs for helping them analyze and address the issues caused by diversity in schools.

We have adapted the theories of Terry Cross for use in schools and other agencies. In *Toward a Culturally Competent System of Care* (Cross, Bazron, Dennis, & Isaacs, 1989), he illustrates appropriate ways to meet the needs of culturally diverse mental health clients.

Within the chapters of this book is an ongoing case study. In Chapter 2, we respond to the question, *What is cultural proficiency?* We define cultural proficiency in the context of guiding principles and essential elements that facilitate its application to the individual person as well as to the school setting. We then provide a historical context for the evolution of modern social policy and equity issues so you can better understand the dynamics of intergenerational issues among school faculties and between other groups. In Chapter 3, we describe the culturally proficient leader after summarizing the theories of leadership and organization that support systemic change in schools. In Chapters 4 and 5, we confront the reality that whenever there is change, there also exists the resistance to change. We discuss the change process in Chapter 4 and present activities for school leaders who are engaged as change agents. We devote Chapter 5 to understanding entitlement as a barrier to change. This type of change is the moral choice that informs personal responsibility and initiative.

We recognize that there is no magic formula or silver bullet for improving schools. The magic (if there is any in this book) will happen when faculty use the cultural proficiency model to guide inquiry and response to the issues caused by diversity within themselves and within their schools. This book

- Provides readers with guidelines for examining the school's policies and practices and their own values and behaviors using the principles of cultural proficiency

- Provides readers with a tool for categorizing a range of responses to differences—the cultural proficiency continuum

- Provides readers with performance-based criteria, the essential elements of cultural proficiency, to guide in planning for personal, professional, and curricular development

- Provides readers with descriptions of our work in schools in the form of a case study to illustrate each of the concepts we present

We recognize that some people will pick up this book and begin looking for quick solutions for their immediate problems, or for a step-by-step process guaranteed to work in any setting. They will be disappointed and will fail no matter what they try. Cultural proficiency is not a program supplement, nor is it a plug-and-play model. Schools that adapt the cultural proficiency model for responding to the issues of diversity make a commitment to change the culture of the school. The individual and the organization must grow and change to be culturally proficient. For that reason, it is important that we say what this book is not:

- It is not a collection of structured activities for random use in a staff development session. We do not recommend that readers skip the text and proceed to the activities in the Resources. Successful use of the activities is predicated on a thorough understanding of the underlying concepts in the cultural proficiency approach to diversity.
- It is not a collection of boilerplate school policies and practices such as those that regulate attendance, suspension, expulsion, and the identification of students for special services. We believe that schools are better served when school personnel and community members gather policies on their school, examine them along with the corollary practices, and recommend changes together, using the principles and essential elements of cultural proficiency as their guide.
- It is not a magic formula, a silver bullet, or a panacea. You have to do the work. Schools have been designed for some students to be successful. It will take great effort and hard work to make schools places where all students can be successful.

We are deeply grateful to several people who influenced this work. First, we thank Terry Cross (1989) for his conceptualization of cultural proficiency. His pioneer work gave us the model by which to organize our experiences. It is the cultural proficiency model that has best supported school leaders as they design and implement programs that effectively serve all students.

Second, as authors, we are individually appreciative of each other. This book is an important benchmark in our 30 years of friendship, during which each of us has, in turn, been a teacher to and a learner from the others. Our friendship has become deeper and dearer during the creation of this book. We truly appreciate the love, friendship, and strong support from Delores Lindsey, who knew there were important lessons in this book project. We are deeply indebted to Shari Hatch, whose loving friendship nourished us as she blended our three voices into one with her editorial magic. We extend sincere gratitude and appreciation to our many students and clients who provided the data for our case study, who trusted us over the years as we introduced this model to them, and who proved over and over again that it is possible to create culturally proficient organizations. We are also grateful for the support of our editor, Alice Foster, and the comments from Francesina Jackson and Gwen Turner, whose suggestions were both pointed and pragmatic.

# Acknowledgments

Corwin Press gratefully acknowledges the contributions of the following reviewers:

Stephanie Graham
Consultant for Equity and Student Achievement
Los Angeles County Office of Education
Downey, California

Festus E. Obiakor
Professor
Department of Exceptional Education
University of Wisconsin-Milwaukee
Milwaukee, Wisconsin

Nancy E. Law
Educational Consultant
Former Director of Research, Sacramento City Schools
Elk Grove, California

Susan Fettchenhauer
Educational Consultant
Leadership Options
Los Gatos, California

# About the Authors

**Randall B. Lindsey,** PhD, is Distinguished Educator in Residence at Pepperdine University. Prior to his position there, he served as chair of the Department of Educational Administration and Counseling in the School of Education at California State University, Los Angeles. He has served as a junior and senior high school teacher of history and as an administrator in charge of desegregation and staff development programs. He has worked extensively with school districts as they plan for and experience changing populations. Randy lives a short distance between the mountains and the ocean in Orange, California, with his wife Delores, where they enjoy the unique pleasures of southern California.

**Kikanza Nuri Robins,** EdD, MDiv, is an organizational development consultant who specializes in leadership, change, diversity, and spirituality. For more than 20 years, she has served individuals and organizations whose bottom line includes the quality of their service and compassion for the communities they serve. She facilitates groups as they wrestle with and reconcile their conflicts, coaches managers as they make the internal shift to become leaders, serves as a change agent for people and organizations that seek to transform themselves from the inside out, and mentors institutions that are adjusting their systems and structures to improve their effectiveness. She lives in Los Angeles, where she is the caregiver of two Chartreux cats—Manifest Justice and Munificent Concordance.

**Raymond D. Terrell,** EdD, is the Distinguished Professional in Residence in the Department of Educational Leadership at Miami University in Oxford, Ohio. He has served as an elementary school principal in Hamilton, Ohio, after retiring as a professor of educational administration and dean of California State University's School of Education. He began his career as a public school teacher and administrator and has more than 25 years of professional experience with diversity and equity issues. Ray lives in Woodlawn, Ohio, with his wife Eloise. He serves as a member of his local village council.

The authors work together as The Cultural Proficiency Group. They can be reached at **culturalproficiency@earthlink.net**.

# Part I

# Understanding Cultural Proficiency

# What Is Cultural Proficiency?

*That is what leadership is all about: staking your ground ahead of where opinion is and convincing people, not simply following the popular opinion of the moment.*

—Doris Kearns Goodwin

Rolling Meadows Unified School District has been getting some bad media coverage. One of the few black parents in the district, Barbara Latimer, an attorney, has accused some of the high school teachers of racism. Superintendent Hermon Watson is concerned and privately incensed. He has provided leadership for this district for the past 15 years, and he is not happy to have this kind of press coverage so close to his retirement. One of the reasons people live in this bedroom community is that, historically, it has been a stable, safe, family-oriented neighborhood in which to raise kids. It has been a place where people move because the schools are good and people don't have to deal with the issues caused by integrated schools and neighborhoods.

Although Rolling Meadows has its own business and civic center, the majority of the population make a long commute into the urban center for work. The trade-off is a community that is not fraught with urban problems. Today, the paper is quoting parents as saying, "We came out here to get away from these people. Now all they are doing is moving here and stirring up trouble."

Hermon shudders as he imagines his board members reading this over their morning coffee. "We have handled every single incident that has occurred in this district. We don't have racist teachers, and we certainly are not a racist district," Hermon says as he reviews the *Tribune* article with his cabinet.

"No one is perfect, and we have had only a few isolated incidents. We handled them discreetly, involving as few people as we can, and once handled, we don't speak of them again. My goal is that when we look at the faces in a classroom, or out across the commons area at lunchtime, we don't see colors, we just see kids."

Later in the day at an emergency cabinet meeting, Winston Alexander, the assistant superintendent for business, clears his throat. "I'm not sure, Hermon, but do you think that we ought to hire a consultant? It might look good right now to bring in some outside experts so they can tell the press what a good job we are doing."

"That's a fabulous idea," exclaims Holly Kemp, the assistant superintendent for curriculum and instruction. "We just finished the Regional Association of Schools and Colleges (RASC) accreditation review, so the documents describing our programs and students are in order. We could hire consultants to provide a cultural accreditation of some sort. We are not bad people—surely they will know that."

His cabinet rarely lets him down, Hermon muses. That is why they have been honored as a nationally distinguished district three times in the past 10 years. Aloud he says, "A cultural audit. Good idea. Winston and Holly, can the two of you put together a request for proposal (RFP) this week? Ask our attorney friend, Barbara Latimer, to give you a hand. That should quiet her down for a while, and it will also let her know that we really mean to do well by her people.

"Winston, what kind of money can you find for this? We may need to dig deep to climb out of this hole."

✎

## Cultural Proficiency: The Next Wave

In 1989, Terry Cross, executive director of the National Indian Child Welfare Association in Portland, Oregon, published a monograph that changed our lives. *Toward a Culturally Competent System of Care* provides several tools for addressing the responses to diversity that we have encountered in our work in schools and other organizations. Although Dr. Cross addressed the issues of difference in mental health care, his seminal work has been the basis of a major shift in responding to difference in organizations across the country.

We like this approach for several reasons: It is proactive; it provides tools that can be used in any setting, rather than techniques that are applicable in only one environment; the focus is behavioral, not emotional; and it can be applied to both organizational practices and individual behavior. What makes our book different from other books on diversity is that we use cultural proficiency as the foundation for addressing the issue of differences in schools. Most diversity programs are used to explain the nature of diversity or the process of learning about or acquiring new cultures. This book is an approach for responding to the environment shaped by its diversity. It is not an off-the-shelf program that supplements a school's programs. It is not a series of mechanistic steps that everyone must follow. It is a model for shifting the culture of the school or district—a model for individual transformation and organizational change.

## ■ The Four Tools

Cultural proficiency is a way of being that enables both individuals and organizations to respond effectively to people who differ from them. Cultural competence is behavior that is aligned with standards that move an organization or an individual toward culturally proficient interactions. There are four tools for developing one's cultural competence:

1. **The Continuum:** Language for describing both healthy and nonproductive policies, practices, and individual behaviors
2. **The Essential Elements:** Five behavioral standards for measuring, and planning for, growth toward cultural proficiency
3. **The Guiding Principles:** Underlying values of the approach
4. **The Barriers:** Two caveats that assist in responding effectively to resistance to change

## ■ The Continuum

There are six points along the cultural proficiency continuum that indicate unique ways of seeing and responding to difference:

**Cultural destructiveness: See the difference, stomp it out.**
The elimination of other people's cultures.

**Cultural incapacity:** *See the difference, make it wrong.*
Belief in the superiority of one's culture and behavior that
disempowers another's culture.

**Cultural blindness:** *See the difference, act like you don't.*
Acting as if the cultural differences you see do not matter, or not
recognizing that there are differences among and between cultures.

**Cultural precompetence:** *See the difference, respond inadequately.*
Awareness of the limitations of one's skills or an organization's
practices when interacting with other cultural groups.

**Cultural competence:** *See the difference, understand the
difference that difference makes.*
Interacting with other cultural groups using the five essential elements
of cultural proficiency as the standard for individual behavior and
school practices.

**Cultural proficiency:** *See the differences and respond
positively and affirmingly.*
**Esteeming culture, knowing how to learn about individual and orga-
nizational culture, and interacting effectively
in a variety of cultural environments.**

■ The Essential Elements

The essential elements of cultural proficiency provide the standards for
individual behavior and organizational practices.

**Name the differences: Assess culture**

**Claim the differences: Value diversity**

**Reframe the differences: Manage the dynamics of difference**

**Train about differences: Adapt to diversity**

**Change for differences: Institutionalize cultural knowledge**

■ The Guiding Principles

These are the core values, the foundation on which the approach is built:

- **Culture is a predominant force; you cannot NOT be
  influenced by culture.**

- **People are served in varying degrees by the dominant culture.**
- **It is important to acknowledge the group identity of individuals.**
- **Diversity within cultures is important; cultural groups are neither homogeneous nor monolithic.**
- **Respect the unique cultural needs that members of dominated groups may have.**

## ■ The Barriers

- **The presumption of entitlement**
- **Unawareness of the need to adapt**

Systemic privilege or **the presumption of entitlement** means believing that all of the personal achievements and societal benefits that you have were accrued solely on your merit and the quality of your character. Resistance to change often is the result of an **unawareness of the need to adapt**. Many people do not recognize the need to make personal and organizational changes in response to the diversity of the people with whom they and their organizations interact. They believe, instead, that only the others need to change and adapt to them.

# Just Another Education Trend?

Every few years, some new process, concept, reform, or innovation is touted as the magic cure-all that will remedy whatever ails the profession—followed by disappointment that many ailments continue to plague us. Educators are often as baffled by—and perhaps impatient with—these perpetual shifts and their accompanying array of dazzling new terminology, as are members of the wider community. Recently, one of our presentations on cultural proficiency was marketed as "The Next Wave" in diversity training. Malcolm Gladwell describes what he calls the *Tipping Point* in his book by the same name. New ideas are often with us for a while before they gather the momentum or are accepted by a critical mass of people. Then, it seems as though, overnight, everyone is accepting and supportive of the new idea. In 1984, Ken Keyes, Jr., wrote *The 100th Monkey: A Story About Social Change*, a small book warning people about the horrors of nuclear war. In it he tells about the Japanese monkey, *Macaca fuscata,* which had been observed in the wild for more than 30 years:

❧

In 1952, on the island of Koshima, scientists were providing monkeys with sweet potatoes dropped in the sand. The monkeys liked the taste of the raw sweet potatoes, but they found the dirt unpleasant. An 18-month-old female named Imo found she could solve the problem by washing the potatoes in a nearby stream. She taught this trick to her mother. Her playmates also learned this new way and they taught their mothers too.

This cultural innovation was gradually picked up by various monkeys. Between 1952 and 1958, all the young monkeys learned to wash the sandy sweet potatoes to make them more palatable. . . . In the autumn of 1958, a certain number of Koshima monkeys were washing sweet potatoes—the exact number is not known. Let us suppose that when the sun rose one morning there were 99 monkeys on Koshima Island who had learned to wash their sweet potatoes. Let's further suppose that later that morning, the hundredth monkey learned to wash potatoes.

Then it happened! By that evening almost everyone in the tribe was washing sweet potatoes before eating them. The added energy of this hundredth monkey somehow created an ideological breakthrough!

❧

Keyes's story dramatically tells us that there is a point at which if only one more person tunes in to a new awareness, a field is strengthened so that this awareness is picked up by almost everyone. When we began writing our book, not many people had heard of *cultural competence.* Most people who had heard the term thought that it was a euphemism for diversity and did not know that it referred to specific tools developed by Terry Cross. Now, we see that cultural competence has been adopted as a standard of behavior in many mental health care organizations and by health care professionals—particularly nurses. Diversity consultants are starting to use the term. When Kirk Perucca, the president of Project Equality,[1] speaks of cultural proficiency being the next wave in diversity work, he implies that we are nearing Ken Keyes's proverbial hundredth monkey. It is our hope that our books (this one and *Culturally Proficient Instruction,* Corwin 2001) will provide the tipping point, or the momentum, to mobilize the metaphorical monkey that will make a difference for all educators and all children.

# A Historical Perspective

This work that we do has been called a number of things:

- Desegregation
- Integration
- Race relations
- Human relations
- Antiracism
- Teaching tolerance
- Cultural competence
- Multicultural transformation

Each term represents changing responses to issues of diversity. Societal response to diversity has changed a lot in the past 50 years. Each decade has spawned new social policies in response to the current issues of concern. Schools have responded to these changes as well. To fully understand the forces of policy evolution and the multiple factors that have led to policy shifts in U.S. society, particularly in schools, one must track the development of social policies related to the issues of diversity, the major movements in schools, and the concomitant resistance to these changes. We invite you now to reflect on your knowledge of the major social movements, and the terms used to describe them, that affected schools and school policies over the past 50 years:

Before 1950s: Segregation
1950s: Desegregation
1960s: Integration, equal access, equal rights
1970s: Equal benefits, multiculturalism
1980s: Diversity
1990s: Cultural competence
2000s: Cultural proficiency

## ■ Prior to the 1950s: Segregation

Before the 1950s, legal separation of cultural and racial groups in the United States was the norm. In the southern United States, legal forms of segregation included slavery and Jim Crow laws, which defined racial groups, mandated the separation of those races in public settings (e.g., schools, buses, and restaurants), and dictated extremely different ways of treating individuals based on the physical characteristics that identified their ethnicity. The oppression of people of African descent through slavery and Jim Crow systems were based on legislative decisions by southern states and upheld by state and federal court review.

The remanding of people of America's First Nations, Native Americans, to reservations is another example of actions taken by federal and state legislatures, courts, and chief executives. As further denigration of First Nation people, people of northern European descent uprooted many and moved them to even less desirable locations when they discovered valuable mineral deposits or otherwise coveted property occupied by the First Nations. Beginning with the Mexican Cession of 1848 (though the encroachment had been under way for well over a century), native residents of what is now the southwestern United States were often excluded from the political and economic mainstream and increasingly marginalized as European Americans immigrated into that area.

The Chinese Exclusion Acts of 1882 and 1902 were federal legislative acts supported by the executive and judicial branches of the U.S. government. These acts of Congress were specifically designed to control and minimize immigration once the Chinese were no longer needed in labor-intensive projects such as building railroads throughout the western United States. Another example of legally sanctioned segregation is Executive Order 9066, initiated by President Franklin D. Roosevelt and supported by Congress and the U.S. Supreme Court, which herded U.S. citizens of Japanese ancestry into relocation camps during World War II.

## ■ The 1950s: Desegregation

The 1954 *Brown v. Topeka Board of Education* decisions that ended segregation in public facilities had its genesis in countless legal initiatives. Eight years before the Brown decisions, President Harry S Truman issued an executive order to desegregate the military. As many people know, it has taken the half-century since Truman's order to desegregate the military. Even now, there is a compelling argument that although the command structure has been desegregated, African Americans, Latinos, and other people of color and people of low socioeconomic status are overrepresented among the front-line combatants who receive the greatest casualties during conflict.

Throughout the history of the United States, disenfranchised groups have used the courts and the legislatures to seek redress of their grievances. The *Brown* decisions are widely acknowledged to have been the civilian apex of those efforts. Though the *Brown* decisions officially ended de jure segregation, actual, de facto segregation did not end. To this day, de facto segregation—segregation practices that are not the result of legal mandates—continues. Nonetheless, the *Brown* decisions provided the legal and political leverage by which segregation policies and practices that permeated every region of this country could be legally dismantled.

The process of school desegregation has been fraught with problems from the very beginning. Despite many successes in which children have benefited from school desegregation (Hawley, 1983), public attention has chiefly been focused on cases of resistance and failure. In southern states, private academies quickly emerged to offer segregated alternatives to European American students. Throughout the country, families have fled to the suburbs to escape unwanted assignments to schools in urban areas. In some cases, these parents did not want to have their children attend a school outside their neighborhood, but in many cases, parents simply wanted to isolate their kids from children with cultural backgrounds different from their own. Often, they viewed different children as genetically or culturally inferior to themselves. In response, the children and parents who were the targets of these reactions were alienated from the dominant culture.

## ■ The 1960s: Integration for Equal Access and Equal Rights

The shift from desegregation to integration was monumental. The 1960s was the decade of domestic revolutions. There were sit-ins, love-ins, bra burnings, freedom rides, and insurrection in the urban centers. It was a period of activism for social justice, with the push for civil rights expanding from the southern states and broadening to include women and other cultural groups. Although the focus was on the tension between black and white people, in the western and southwestern United States, Latino and First Nation children were included in the desegregation programs.

In schools, the push to desegregate had two consequences. First, voluntary and mandatory school desegregation efforts were designed to provide children of color the same opportunities that white children were receiving. Second, the expansion of entitlement programs (e.g., Title I of the Elementary and Secondary Education Act and the Emergency School Assistance Act) led to many children of color being placed in programs for the culturally and economically disadvantaged. The unintended consequence of these programs is that the labels became permanently associated with the ethnicity, and students in desegregated schools continued to receive substandard educations. It was during this time that educators became aware of the effect of teacher expectations, gender bias, and second-language acquisition on the quality of instruction.

## ■ The 1970s: Equal Benefits and Multiculturalism

During this period, people of color in the U.S. were striving to extend the legal gains won during previous decades to broader societal contexts, such as the workplace. As educators engaged with more and more children of diverse cultures in their classrooms, they needed new approaches, strategies, and techniques for teaching them. Thus, the educational emphasis on multiculturalism was spawned. Multiculturalism represents a departure from the assimilationist, or melting pot, model, which had worked well for eastern and southern Europeans but did not work as well for people of color. Additionally, many educators questioned the appropriateness of assimilation as the goal for every cultural group. During this period, women's issues entered the multiculturalism discussion in many schools. In the broader society, Gay Men and Lesbians also began to claim their rights to equal opportunities and benefits in society.

## ■ The 1980s: Diversity

During this era, corporate America discovered that it was good business to address diversity-related issues. Many companies began offering diversity training for managers and other employees, and others began developing distinctive marketing strategies to target various sectors of society. As with most things, however, businesses did not uniformly embrace diversity throughout all companies or even throughout all industries. For example, the banking and the automobile sectors have recognized the money to be made in these new markets, but the technology sector still appears to be lagging far behind. Similarly, while the leaders in some companies bristled at the mere suggestion of diversity training, others enthusiastically embraced it. During this period, the aspects of diversity included in this training were also expanded from ethnicity, language and gender to include issues of sexual orientation, disability, and age.

■ The 1990s and Beyond:
   Cultural Competence and Cultural Proficiency

The essential elements of cultural competence provide basic behavior standards for effectively interacting with people who differ from one another. Cultural proficiency is a way of being that enables people to successfully engage in new environments. The work of Comer (1988), Levin (1988), Sizer (1985), and Slavin (1996) appears to be consistent with the basic tenets of cultural proficiency. They believe that all children can learn, and they demonstrate that children from any neighborhood can learn well, if they are taught well. Although the national debate over school desegregation has not ended, it now focuses on the equitable distribution of human and capital resources. One of the many contemporary trends in education focuses on finding ways to appreciate the rich differences among students. Many educators wonder how—or even whether—the previous decade's focus on multiculturalism really differs from the next decade's emphasis on diversity.

This shift is not merely a superficial change in terminology but a much-needed, profound change in perspective. Unlike the trend toward multiculturalism, which focused narrowly on students' ethnic and racial differences, the shift toward diversity responds to societal trends urging us to take a broader approach to addressing equity issues, encompassing a wide range of differences, including race, culture, language, class, caste, ethnicity, gender, sexual orientation, and physical and sensory abilities among students.

# Beyond Political and Cultural Correctness

Cultural proficiency is an approach to addressing diversity issues that goes beyond political correctness. In fact, political correctness yields only superficial changes rather than profound ones because the underlying intentions of such an outlook are always sincere. Culturally proficient responses may appear similar to politically correct ones at first glance, but on closer inspection, they reveal greater depth of knowledge, introspection, and sincere intent than may be found in politically correct responses. The sincere belief that a culturally proficient response to diversity is both necessary and good belies the difference between being politically correct and culturally correct.

*Culture* involves far more than ethnic or racial differences. Culture is the set of practices and beliefs that is shared with members of a particular group and that distinguishes one group from others. Most people think of culture as relating to one's race or ethnicity. We define culture broadly to include all shared characteristics of human description, including age, gender, geography, ancestry, language, history, sexual orientation, and physical ability, as well as occupation and affiliations. Defined as such, each person may belong to several different cultural groups. An ethnic group is defined by shared history, ancestry, geography, language, and physical characteristics. Individuals may identify most strongly with their ethnic group, and who they are is influenced by the ethnic group as well as the several other groups with which they identify.

Culturally proficient educators demonstrate an understanding of the cacophony of diverse cultures each person may experience in the school setting. Although they accept that they will not necessarily have intimate knowledge about each of the cultures represented in a classroom, school, or district, they recognize their need to continuously learn more. They develop a conscious awareness of the culture of their communities, districts, or schools, and they understand that each has a powerful influence on the educators, students, parents, and community associated with that school or district. By incrementally increasing their awareness and understanding, they begin to find the harmony within the diversity.

## What's in It for Us?

Cross, Bazron, Dennis, and Isaacs (1993) noted that a number of shifts had taken place in society that gave rise to a cultural imperative: shifting population demographics, shifting in a world or global economy, shifting the social integration and interaction paradigm, and shifting the goal from assimilation to biculturalism. Educators must respond to these and other issues of diversity because effective responses to diversity target several mutually interactive goals that educators care about deeply. Effective responses to issues that emerge in a diverse environment

- Enhance students' ability to learn and teachers' ability to teach
- Prepare students to find their own places in the global community they will enter when they leave their school communities
- Promote positive community relations
- Prepare students for outstanding citizenship

- Foster effective leadership

## Learning and Teaching Effectively

Addressing the many complex issues associated with diversity is tough under any circumstances. Such issues become even more complex in school settings with large numbers of students whose experiences reflect diverse ethnicities, socioeconomic classes, languages, genders, and sexual orientations. Sometimes, the challenge may seem so daunting as to be impossible. Educators must rise to the challenge, however, if they are to teach their students effectively. For students to learn what their teachers have to offer, they must feel fully appreciated as individuals, within the context of their own distinctive ethnic, linguistic, and socioeconomic backgrounds, and with their own particular gender, sexual orientation, and sensory and physical abilities. Educators need to address the issues that arise in the midst of diversity and respond sensitively to the needs of students in ways that facilitate learning. Additionally, educators need to address issues of diversity to provide mutual support to one another so that every educator feels understood and respected for who he or she is and to the groups to which they belong.

## Living in a Global Community

Over the past 10 to 15 years, it has become increasingly apparent that issues of diversity play a vital role in the economic and political life of the United States. The ability to understand and appreciate diverse peoples both within and across U.S. borders profoundly affects one's ability to flourish in the global economy and the world political community. Educators must prepare learners to function well and to interact effectively with the richly diverse peoples of their worlds. To do so, educators can start by helping students to address issues of diversity in each of their school and home communities.

Educational leaders who are successful in creating culturally proficient learning communities will enable students to play vital roles wherever they go in the global community. Technology has made the world much smaller. As the business community has learned, this nation's economic and political well-being depends on the ability of educators to foster an appreciation of diversity. If educators are to prepare future adults for this challenge, they must commit themselves to addressing effectively issues that arise in diverse environments.

## ◼ Participating in the Community

Educators play a key role in enhancing the relationship between the school and the community, both as individuals and as participants in schoolwide and districtwide decisions. As you respond to issues of diversity, you can change policies and practices that may negatively affect community members whose ethnicity, gender, age, sexual orientation, language, or ability differs from those of school leaders. A wholistic approach to issues that emerge in diverse environments provides tools for examining the school and the district to eliminate inappropriate policies, procedures, and practices that create negative outcomes for many students. If teachers and administrators have not been prepared to teach, lead, or work with people who differ from them, then the educational leader must take the initiative and create a learning community so they can master these skills on the job.

## ◼ Providing Leadership

Through a successful approach to diversity, you can improve staff and student morale by improving the effectiveness of communication, reducing complaints, and creating a more comfortable and gratifying climate for people in the school. As an educational leader, you can learn concepts and skills that you translate into new initiatives, curricula, programs, and activities that will enrich school life for all students and staff. As greater awareness and understanding develop in schools, so too will the awareness and understanding of the larger community be expanded. Very few educators intend to hurt their students or their colleagues. An effective approach to issues of diversity provides everyone with the information and skills that educators need to avoid unintentional slights or hurts and to improve the quality of life for school and home communities.

# The Case

We have worked with many school districts across the country and have spent our careers eavesdropping on conversations among educators. We present snippets of those conversations along with our observations of the people with whom we have worked. We hope that you will find the stories to be sources of enlightenment and encouragement. In each chapter, we use vignettes from the case we developed from these stories—at the beginning of the chapter, and sometimes integrated into the chapter—to illustrate the points that we make.

To help you use the stories and not have them be an impediment to your learning or moving through the text, we are presenting a description of the two school districts in our fictionalized county as well as the characters you will meet throughout the text. These are the people you will meet as you read the vignettes from the case that introduce each chapter and are used to illustrate the points we make in the text. The entire case is presented in the last chapter of the book.

There are two school districts in the case: Rolling Meadows Unified School District is a suburban district serving a largely professional, European American student population. The Coolidge Unified School District is an urban district with a diverse ethnic population. Both districts are moving toward cultural proficiency, at different paces and with mixed results.

✍

## Rolling Meadows Unified School District

Rolling Meadows is a bedroom community that has its own business and civic center, and the majority of the population makes a long commute into the urban center for work. The district is growing; it currently has about 15,000 students in three high school clusters, a continuation high school, and an adult school. Ten years ago, 82% of the student population of the district was white, with 4% Asian and Pacific Islanders, 6% Latino, 2% African American, and 1% First Nation students. Five years ago, the percentage of white students had declined to 52%, while the Asian and Pacific Islander, Latino, African American, and First Nation student populations had increased proportionately. In contrast to the changing student demographics, the teaching force has been relatively stable for the past 10 years. Ten years ago, 90% of the teachers were white; today, the percentage has decreased by only 5%.

✍

Hermon Watson, the superintendent, decides to hire consultants to conduct a cultural audit of the district. As you read, the text you will meet his cabinet and some of the teachers as they respond to the idea of an audit.

✍

| TABLE 1: | Rolling Meadows Unified School District |
|---|---|
| **District Administrators** | |
| Hermon Watson | Superintendent |
| Winston Alexander | Assistant superintendent for business |
| Holly Kemp | Assistant superintendent for curriculum and instruction |
| **School Administrators** | |
| Dina Turner | First African American high school principal |
| **Teachers** | |
| Bobby | A consistently unhappy high school social studies teacher and counselor |
| Celeste | A seasoned high school teacher of mixed heritage |
| **Parents** | |
| Barbara Latimer | An attorney, one of the few black parents in the district. She is on the high school site council and is also on the board of the Citizens Human Relations Council, which deals with issues throughout the county. She is known in both school districts. Her daughter, Kim, attends school in Rolling Meadows. |

## Coolidge Unified School District

On the other side of the county, Coolidge Unified School District serves the families that live in the urban center where many Rolling Meadows parents work. Coolidge High School continues to be among the schools in the county that earn top academic honors. The advanced placement classes have less than 10% African American and Latino students. In the past five years, the Title I population has increased from 5% to 35%. In that same time period, the English as a Second Language (ESL) classes have increased from serving less than 2% of the student population to serving slightly more than 35% of the student population.

| TABLE 2: | Coolidge Unified School District |
|---|---|
| **District Administrators** | |
| Bill Fayette | Superintendent |
| Leatha Harp | Director of credentialing and certification |
| James Harris | A diversity consultant who began his career as a social studies teacher |
| **School Administrators** | |
| Steve Petrossian | Elementary school principal |
| Richard Diaz | Middle school principal |
| Grace Ishmael | High school principal |
| **Teachers** | |
| Brittney | A naïve, second-year middle school teacher who is working with a provisional credential |
| Derek | A seasoned and effective middle school social studies teacher who is a friend of DeLois |
| DeLois | Middle school teacher with a big heart who will do anything to make certain that all of her students learn |
| Harvey | A jaded middle school teacher |
| Lane | A middle school teacher who is Harvey's friend |

There have been two resulting effects of these trends. The first has been decreased sections of honors classes and a dramatic increase in remedial and heterogeneous classes. The heterogeneous classes in English and social studies were created to overcome criticism about the negative effect of tracking; however, placement in mathematics and science classes has served to stratify the English and social studies classes, despite their alleged heterogeneity. The second effect of the demographic changes has been that the school's standardized test scores have steadily declined and have given the impression to the local media that the quality of education at the school has deteriorated. Teachers still have an interest in a traditional academic approach to curriculum. They also place a high value on a tracked system, in which the highest achievers are allowed to move at an accelerated rate.

The extracurricular programs of the school, except for football and basketball, tend to be associated with cultural groups. Though the sports program is nominally integrated, swimming is perceived to be a European American sport, wrestling a Latino sport, track an African American sport, and tennis a sport for Asians and Pacific Islanders. Student government represents the demographic profile of the school, but most of the clubs and other organizations are dominated by one ethnic group. Of the major ethnic groups at the school, Latino students participate least in clubs and other organizations. In recent years, there has been tension between the groups. Some fights and retaliatory attacks have received wide coverage in the newspaper.

&.

Bill Fayette, the superintendent of the Coolidge district, recently hired a diversity consultant, James Harris, to provide training for faculty on cultural proficiency. As you read, you will be able to listen to conversations among these characters.

# Structured Activities for Developing Culturally Proficient Leaders

We have used the activities in this book as we have helped schools and other organizations move toward cultural proficiency. The activities are not designed to be used alone to make changes, nor are they designed to be used as the only intervention in a diversity program. They are designed for use as part of a comprehensive plan for approaching diversity issues in your school or district. Some of these activities will help you build trust among the members of the planning group. Others will help you introduce and reinforce the guiding principles and essential elements of cultural proficiency. The remainder of the activities will help you explore the concepts that we have presented in the book, or they will help you to facilitate the planning necessary to embrace cultural proficiency as an approach for a school or district.

Although each chapter ends with a number of activities that we feel are appropriate for reinforcing or exploring the concepts in that chapter, do not limit yourself. Most of the activities have several variations and in different contexts will be useful for teaching more than one idea. Never conduct an activity simply as a space-filler. Always relate the activity to something that the participants are learning and to concepts you want to reinforce. If you have new activities or variations on the activities we have provided, please contact us so that in future books, we can share your ideas with others who are on the road to cultural proficiency. You can contact us at **culturalproficiency@earthlink.net**.

# Read the Text First

With so many activities for getting people to think about issues of diversity and to reflect on their own developing cultural competence, you may be tempted to skip the text and to proceed to these activities. We do not recommend that; each of these activities is directly linked to the text and the portion of the case study found in each chapter. Reading the text and discussing the case study will provide a context for these activities.

Base your decisions to use a specific activity on its purpose, the skill of the facilitator and the maturity of the group. Before conducting an activity, assess the readiness of the group and the expertise of the facilitator in working with groups on issues of diversity. We have rated each activity so that you can see the minimum level of experience and readiness we recommend for the activity to be successful. In the last chapter of this book, you will find lists of the activities organized by readiness and expertise levels. Readiness is determined by the experience the group members have in doing the following:

- Effectively responding to conflict situations
- Openly discussing difficult issues
- Honestly articulating their feelings
- Comfortably interacting with people who strongly disagree with them
- Willingly examining their own values and behavior
- Candidly examining the school's policies, procedures, and practices for benign discrimination

The expertise of facilitators is determined by:

- The work they have done on their own issues related to diversity
- The amount of time and variety of experiences they have had facilitating groups as they address issues of diversity

- The experience they have had working with hostile or reticent groups
- Their sensitivity to the dynamics of group process
- The skills they have in focusing and supporting groups ready for change
- Their recognition that debriefing is the most important part of a structured activity
- The skills they have for eliciting and integrating insights and conclusions during debriefing sessions

If you would like to develop your skills as a facilitator, consider taking a course in training for trainers from your local chapters of the American Society for Training and Development (www.ASTD.org) and the National Organizational Development Network (www.ODNetwork .org) or a course that will help you process your own diversity issues from the National Training Labs (www.NTL.org).

### Notes

1. In 2002, Project Equality in Kansas City, Missouri, adopted cultural proficiency as its approach to issues that emerge in diverse environments.

2. Specific issues of instruction are addressed in our book *Culturally Proficient Instruction* (Corwin Press, 2002).

## Going Further

At the end of each chapter, we include questions or activities that will take you farther along the path toward cultural proficiency. You may want to spend some time with these questions now.

1. When did you begin working in the field that is now call diversity?
2. What was it called when you started?
3. Have you heard the terms *cultural competence* or *cultural proficiency* before reading this book? In what context?
4. What are your personal goals for doing the work in this book?

# Reflection

_____

_____

_____

_____

_____

_____

_____

_____

_____

_____

# Structured Exercises

On the following pages and at the end of each chapter, you will find the directions and handouts for follow-up activities. In most workshops, the papers that are distributed to participants are called *handouts*. In this book, we label any material that is intended for distribution as a *response sheet*. The responses that these sheets elicit may be different for each sheet and each group in which you use them. Some have directions, others provide information, and some invite you to complete them with your own ideas and reflections. Most are tied to an activity. You have our permission to duplicate these pages as they are printed, with copyright notice intact, for work within your school or organization.

**Response Sheet 1.0.1:**

# The Culturally Proficient Professional

*This is a description of the culturally proficient behavior of someone who works using the five essential elements of cultural proficiency. As you read it, think about how you would describe specific culturally proficient behaviors of someone in your profession.*

- **Assesses culture.** The culturally proficient professional is aware of her own culture and the effect it may have on the people in her work setting. She learns about the culture of the organization and the cultures of the clients, and anticipates how they will interact with, conflict with, and enhance one another.

- **Values diversity.** The culturally proficient professional welcomes a diverse group of clients into the work setting and appreciates the challenges diversity brings. He shares this appreciation with other clients, developing a learning community with the clients.

- **Manages the dynamics of difference.** The culturally proficient professional recognizes that conflict is a normal and natural part of life. She develops skills to manage conflict in a positive way. She also helps the clients to understand that what appear to be clashes in personalities may in fact be conflicts in culture.

- **Adapts to diversity.** The culturally proficient professional commits to the continuous learning that is necessary to deal with the issues caused by differences. He enhances the substance and structure of his work so that all of it is informed by the guiding principles of cultural proficiency.

- **Institutionalizes cultural knowledge.** The culturally proficient professional works to influence the culture of her organization so that its policies and practices are informed by the guiding principles of cultural proficiency. She also takes advantage of teachable moments to share cultural knowledge about her colleagues, their managers, the clients, and the communities from which they come. She creates opportunities for these groups to learn about one another and to engage in ways that honor who they are and challenge them to be more.

---

**Activity 1.1:**

# Diversity Lifeline

■ Purpose

- To have participants analyze and share the significant events in their lives that have affected their perception of diversity
- To aid participants in understanding that diversity is a dynamic that has been and will be ever present in their lives

■ Skill of Facilitator

Moderate

■ Readiness of Group

Intermediate

■ Time Needed

90 minutes

■ Materials

Chart paper for each participant
Markers for each participant
Masking tape
Tables or floor space for participants to draw their lifelines
Enough wall space for all participants to hang their lifelines and discuss them in small groups

■ Briefing

Think about your life: How have you been affected by your diversity? When did you become aware of the diversity around you? On the chart paper, draw a graph of your life marking the significant points that reflect your awareness of diversity.

## ■ Process

1. Distribute markers and chart paper to each person.

2. Organize the participants into groups of two or three people. Encourage the participants to diversify their small groups. It is important to keep the groups small so that each person can share extensively. It is also important that people in the small groups are comfortable with each other.

3. Allow about 20 minutes for participants to draw and hang their lifelines.

4. Allow about 15 minutes per person to describe his or her lifeline.

5. Reorganize the small groups into one large group, allowing time for participants to view all of the lifelines.

## ■ Debriefing

1. What did you feel, think, or wonder as you started the assignment?

2. What did you notice about yourself as you drew?

3. What did you learn about yourself from this process?

4. What did you notice about your group members as they spoke or listened to the other members in the group?

5. What did you learn about your group members?

6. What did you learn about diversity?

7. How will you use what you have learned?

## ■ Variations

1. Use the lifeline process to have participants tell their stories without emphasizing any particular aspect of their lives.

2. Cover the wall with chart paper. As a group, draw a lifeline for the organization.

3. Allow participants to draw their personal lines to indicate where their lives intersect with the life of the school.

**Activity 1.2:**

# Identifying Shared Values for Diversity

■  Purpose

- To identify the values that participants share regarding diversity
- To begin the conversation about the convergence and divergence of values
- To compare the shared values of the school with the principles of cultural proficiency

■  Skill of Facilitator

Extensive

■  Readiness of Group

Intermediate

■  Time Needed

1-2 hours

■  Materials

Prepared chart or Response Sheet 1.2.1 with definition of value, shared value, and the example of a shared value

Chart paper

Marking pens

■  Briefing

We are going to identify our personal values about diversity and see if there are any values that we share.

■  Process

1. Post a chart in front of the room with this information, which can also be found on Response Sheet 1.2.1.

*Value:* A strongly held belief that influences behavior

*Shared value:* A strongly held belief shared by two or more people

*Example:* Persons of all racial, ethnic, gender, socioeconomic, religious, and sexual orientation backgrounds should be treated with respect.

*Clarify:* A value statement is not what you believe in, but a description of what you believe. A value statement is a sentence, not a word.

*Not:* We believe in honesty.

*But:* We believe that honesty in relationships creates the foundation for conflict resolution.

2. Encourage participants to say precisely what they mean when they use words such as *respect* and *honesty* so the group members are certain they are talking about the same thing.

3. Divide participants into small groups of 3-5 people.

4. Have participants brainstorm a list of their individual values for diversity on chart paper or a blank transparency.

5. Place a check mark beside those values on the list that everyone holds in common.

6. Ask each group to share its common values with the whole group.

7. Work to identify and build a consensus around the values that the entire group shares.

■ Debriefing

1. How difficult was it for your group to identify your shared values related to diversity?

2. What did you learn about your colleagues during the process?

3. How might the differences in values affect your relationships? Your planning?

4. What might we do with the shared values?

■ Variation

Use the shared values as the basis for examining work performance standards.

**Response Sheet 1.2.1:**

# Definitions for Shared Values

**Value**: A strongly held belief that influences behavior

**Shared value**: A strongly held belief shared by two or more people

**Example**: *Persons of all racial, ethnic, gender, socioeconomic, religious, and sexual orientation backgrounds should be treated with respect.*

**Clarify**: A value statement is not what you believe in, but a description of what you believe. A value statement is a sentence, not a word.

**Not**: We believe in honesty.

**But**: We believe that honesty in relationships creates the foundation for conflict resolution.

**Activity 1.3:**

# Cultural Proficiency Consensus

■ Purpose

- To develop with participants a common language and understanding of cultural proficiency
- To provide participants an opportunity to discuss issues and concerns about cultural proficiency

■ Expertise of Facilitator

Extensive

■ Readiness of Group

Intermediate

■ Time Needed

45 minutes

■ Materials

Response Sheet 1.3.1: Cultural Proficiency Consensus
Chart paper
Markers

■ Briefing

A consensus is a decision that each person in the group understands
and can support. This activity will help you to clarify and share your
perceptions of cultural proficiency by building consensus.

■ Process

1. Distribute copies of Response Sheet 1.3.1: Cultural Proficiency Consensus.

2. Divide participants into groups of four and ask them to arrive at consensus decisions for each item. Encourage them to avoid conflict-reducing techniques such as majority vote, averaging, or changing one's mind just to reach decisions.

3. Chart the consensus decision of each small group.

4. Lead a discussion of the responses by asking the spokesperson of each group to share his or her group's rationale for its answer.

5. Once each group has given its response, give the preferred response and accompanying rationale on Response Sheet 1.3.2.

■ Debriefing

1. What was your initial reaction to the activity?

2. What were your experiences in the small group discussion?

3. Describe your levels of comfort in discussing your answers with people who had similar views and with those who had dissimilar views.

4. How did your group deal with conflict?

5. What did you learn about the concepts and values associated with cultural proficiency?

6. How will you use this information?

**Response Sheet 1.3.1:**

# Cultural Proficiency Consensus

Please indicate whether you believe the following statements to be true or false.

_____ 1. Cultural proficiency recognizes that each individual is worthwhile and unique.

_____ 2. Culturally proficient education recognizes that each individual has dignity and integrity.

_____ 3. Skin color, language differences, sexual orientation, and other physical marks of difference are unimportant.

_____ 4. Students in U.S. schools need to learn to speak, write, and read standard forms of English.

_____ 5. School curricula should deal directly with the differences among people.

_____ 6. Educators should be taught to understand the cultural diversity of our society.

_____ 7. Parents and community people should help in planning and implementing a culturally proficient curriculum.

_____ 8. Schools should correct the differences found among students so that everybody in the United States learns to behave the same way.

_____ 9. Members of distinct cultural groups (e.g., ethnic, gender, sexual orientation, and occupation) have the same attitudes and values.

_____ 10. Education that values cultural proficiency serves only to divide people who are different.

**Response Sheet 1.3.2:**

# Cultural Proficiency Consensus Preferred Responses

1. **True.** In the United States, the goal of culturally proficient education is to recognize that each individual is unique and worthwhile. Although some so-called multicultural curricula may not achieve this goal, it is the goal of culturally proficient education and one toward which, we believe, all educators should be working.

2. **True.** This statement is an outgrowth of and consistent with statement 1. Though current curriculum and instruction may not achieve this goal, it does not detract from the need to respect the dignity and integrity of all students and their families.

3. **False.** Marks of difference may be unimportant to those who do not have them. Such people may think they judge others independent of these marks of difference. These marks of difference are important to those who have them, however. Not only do these marks of difference influence one's self-identity, but they also are often the basis of stereotyping or discrimination.

4. **True.** To have equity of opportunity in schools, business, or society in general, people must be able to speak, read, and write standard forms of English. This statement in no way detracts from the need for bilingual or multilingual skills or bi-dialectal. Every child who comes to school speaking a language or dialect other than standard English deserves to be respected for that language difference and to receive instructional support for maintaining that language and using it and standard English appropriately. Likewise, native English-speaking children should learn an additional language.

5. **True.** This statement is a corollary to statements 1 and 2. Of course, the statement does not deny the appropriateness of dealing with people's similarities.

6. **True.** To achieve the goals of a culturally proficient education, administrators, teachers, and school support personnel need to learn about diversity in their communities and society at large.

7. **True.** Parents and community members can be valuable resources in setting school goals that embrace culturally proficient values. They can also assist in developing guidelines for the implementation of goals and in evaluating those goals.

8. **False.** This may have been a hoped-for goal for those touting the assimilationist melting pot myth. Educators who value culturally proficient education understand that there is strength in diversity and that the appreciation of differences is an important goal for U.S. citizens.

9. **False.** An obvious stereotype. There exists the same degree of heterogeneity within groups that exists among groups. This becomes an important point of discussion when examining the compounding effects of class and caste.

10. **False.** Quite the contrary; cultural proficiency is not adversarial. A major goal of culturally proficient education is to support people in recognizing and appreciating their similarities and differences and learning from both.

**Activity 1.4:**

# Journaling

■ Purpose

To record your thoughts and feelings during a change process. During any change process, it is useful to record, in a systematic way, one's feelings and reactions. We have found journaling to be a welcome activity during intense, multiday training sessions.

■ Skill of Facilitator

Low

■ Readiness of Group

Beginning

■ Materials

A blank book or a special notebook for journaling; the book should be small enough for easy carrying. Invite participants to bring their own journals if they are already journalers.

■ Briefing

You are going to be hearing and experiencing things over the next few days, weeks, or months that will affect you profoundly. We want you to honor those feelings by reflecting on the experience in writing. This will give you an opportunity each day to give 100% attention to yourself.

■ Process

Give participants these guidelines for their writing:

Each day of the training, make an entry in your journal. This is a time for you to reflect on what has happened during the day and to think about how you will make use of the experience. You may want to organize your entry as follows:

- What happened today? Specify activities, exercises, or insights that stimulated new ways of thinking—"aha's."
- How do you feel about what happened? Based on what you say at first, what are your feelings about it? Was it a disturbing, energizing, positive, or negative experience?
- What are you going to do? Based on what you said happened and how you feel about it, what actions are you going to take? Consider both the short and the long term—tomorrow, in a few weeks, and several months from now in your work environment.

■ Debriefing

1. At the beginning of each time the group meets, ask participants to share something (not everything) from their journal entries with one other person. They may choose a different person each time.
2. How did you feel about being given time to journal?
3. How many have journaled before?
4. Have you ever kept a journal on a work-related process?
5. What was it like to share portions of your writing?
6. In what other setting might journaling be useful?

■ Variations

1. Encourage people to journal, but do not require that they share their thoughts with anyone.
2. Allow time at the end of each session for journaling.

# 2

# The Historical
# Context for
# Cultural Proficiency

*The fact that change is a prerequisite of progress may be axiomatic; but the fact that change should take place first at a deeper and perhaps subtler level than the conscious level was one I had established as a basis of action.*

—Anwar El Sadat

As the demographics in Rolling Meadows changed, this very insular district, which rarely hired administrators from outside the district, hired the district's first woman and first African American high school principal, Dina Turner. She had served as an assistant principal in another state, but this is her first principalship.

In the first two years, there was little evidence that anyone mentored her or showed her the "Rolling Meadows way of doing business." Another pressure on Dina was that last year Rolling Meadows was given only provisional accreditation from the regional accrediting agency, a blow to the egos in the district and the community. It was only after a consultant spent six days on campus interviewing teachers, students, aides, administrators, and parents and issued a report of his findings that faculty confronted the fact that the mission of the school had changed. It had been a school that "prepared students for college"; now it is a school that also has to prepare students to become citizens of this country.

✇

In our experience, the most effective and productive approach to addressing cultural diversity within schools is *cultural proficiency*. A culturally proficient environment acknowledges and responds to both individual and group differences. In a culturally proficient school, the educators and students know they are valued, and they involve community members in the school to facilitate their own cultural understanding. The culture of the school promotes inclusiveness and institutionalizes processes for learning about differences and responding appropriately to differences. Rather than lamenting, "Why can't *they* be like *us*?", teachers and students welcome and create opportunities to better understand who *they* are as individuals while learning how to interact positively with people who differ from themselves.

# An Inside-Out Approach

Cultural proficiency is an inside-out approach that focuses first on those who are insiders to the school, encouraging them to reflect on their own individual understandings and values. It thereby relieves those identified as outsiders, the members of the excluded groups, from the responsibility of doing all the adapting. The cultural proficiency approach to diversity surprises many people who expect a diversity program to teach them about other people, not about themselves. The commitment to become culturally proficient results in a way of being that acknowledges and validates the current values and feelings of people, encouraging change without threatening people's feelings of worth.

The cultural proficiency approach prizes individuals but focuses chiefly on both the school's culture, which has a life force beyond that of the individuals within the school, as well as the values and the behavior of individuals. This focus removes the need to place blame on individuals and to induce feelings of guilt. The process involves all members of the school community in determining how to align policies, practices, and procedures to achieve cultural proficiency. Because all the participants are deeply involved in the developmental process, there is broader-based ownership, making it easier to commit to change. This approach attacks the problems caused by the diversification of students, faculty, and staff at a systemic level.

## What It Takes

Building cultural proficiency requires informed and dedicated faculty and staff, committed and involved leadership, and time. Educators cannot be sent to training for two days and be expected to return with solutions to all the equity issues in their school. For instance, this approach does *not* involve the use of simple checklists for identifying culturally significant characteristics of individuals, which may be politically appropriate but socially and educationally meaningless. The transformation to cultural proficiency requires time to think, reflect, assess, decide, and change. To become culturally proficient, educators participate actively in work sessions, contributing their distinctive ideas, beliefs, feelings, and perceptions. Consequently, their contributions involve them deeply in the process and make it easier for them to commit to change.

If you are truly committed to embracing diversity and effectively responding to the issues that emerge from a diverse environment, you can use the cultural proficiency tools to transform your classroom, school, or district at a systemic level. The culturally proficient school district closes the door on tokenism and stops the revolving door through which highly competent, motivated people enter briefly and exit quickly because they have not been adequately integrated into the school's culture. Culturally proficient educators can confidently deliver education knowing that their students genuinely want it and can readily receive it without having their cultural connections denied, offended, or threatened. Culturally proficient educators can also be sure that their community perceives them as a positive, contributing force that substantively enhances the community's image and the school's position in it.

Important to understanding how to use these tools is to recognize that cultural proficiency is not an off-the-shelf program that is implemented in all schools and districts in the same way. Rather, each classroom and each district that has embraced cultural proficiency as a goal will do so differently. The standards for a culturally proficient hospital or culturally proficient university will be different from those for a culturally proficient school. A culturally proficient suburban school that is predominantly European American will have different standards than an urban school serving communities of color.

# What Is Culture?

Early anthropologists defined *culture* as that complex whole which includes knowledge, beliefs, art, law, morals, customs and any other capabilities and habits acquired by a member of society. Every diversity trainer has definitions for diversity and culture. Some are quite complicated, whereas others are very simple. In this book, we define *culture* as everything you believe and everything you do that enables you to identify with people who are like you and that distinguishes you from people who differ from you. Culture is about groupness. A culture is a group of people identified by their shared history, values, and patterns of behavior.

Culture provides parameters for daily living. The purpose of a culture is to assist people who are members of a group in knowing what the rules for acceptable behavior are and to provide consistency and predictability in everyday actions. These rules, a reflection of the covert values, are called *cultural expectations*. The cultural expectations for a group assist in screening outsiders and controlling insiders, thus providing the basis for a group to sustain itself. When people think of culture, they often think only in terms of *ethnic culture* and the behaviors associated with people who look different from themselves.

Ethnic culture is related to ancestral heritage and geography, common history, and, to some degree, physical appearance. Ethnic cultural groups are commonly called *racial groups*. *Race* is a concept developed by social scientists that was misinterpreted and popularized by eugenicists and social Darwinists in the 19th century in an attempt to characterize people by their physical features and to use those differences in society to justify the subjugation of people of color and perpetuate the dominance of the white race. To become culturally proficient, you may need to expand your conceptual paradigm for culture to encompass everything that people believe and everything that they do that identifies them as members of a group and distinguishes that group from other groups.

Furthermore, organizational, occupational, and social cultures shape people's values and affect their communications. For example, *social cultures* are groups of people who share a common interest or activity (e.g., jogging, volunteer work, and arts and crafts). *Occupational cultures* are based on involvement in a common vocation (e.g., teachers, administrators, lawyers, and accountants—each group evokes an image). Dress, language, and beliefs are all aspects of occupational culture. People who work for the same school or district are members of an *organizational culture*. They share values of the larger district but differ from educators in other schools and offices in the district.

The culture of each organization—whether the organization is your family or your school—is what distinguishes it from other organizations. Each culture develops its own set of formal (overt) and informal (covert) processes to function. When you walk into a school building for the first time, you immediately get a sense of what type of school it is: whether it is a positive, healthy place for children; whether the administrator cares about what is going on; and whether someone will notice that you don't belong there. That feeling is your experience of the school's culture. You can go into several second-grade classrooms, and each one will feel different; those distinctions reflect the culture of each classroom. Harrison (1992) calls this cultural milieu the school's "climate."

The culturally proficient leader will understand that the overlay of school climate, student cultures, and professional cultures provides a unique mix that will affect each of the groups at the school in a different way. Your success as a culturally proficient leader is in part determined by the culture of your school or your district. The culturally proficient leader ensures that cultures within the school are identified, articulated, and taught to increase understanding.

To most people, diversity connotes racial and ethnic differences. *Racial and ethnic cultures* are tied to a common history, ancestry, language, and geographic origin. Additionally, each of us identifies with the culture of our own gender and sexual orientation; these are influenced by the wider culture's expectations and roles for each gender and sexual orientation, as well as by the aspects of these cultures that are self-determined. In a society in which there are several ethnic cultures, one is usually dominant and consequently sets the norms for language and cultural expectations.

The dominant culture has disproportionately greater political and economic power in a society. Professional, school, and social cultures are additional types of culture that affect the power relationships of people in a school environment. These types of cultures are important to recognize because people usually identify with several cultural groups. Therefore, each person in the school is represented by several types of cultures. It is from this amalgam of culture types that the dominant cultural patterns emerge within the school. As the school culture's dominant pattern emerges, it either embraces or marginalizes educators, parents, and students of dominated cultural groups.

⮝

The opinions of the faculty and administration at Rolling Meadows High School reflect the range of views in the community. Many believe that the school can be organized to provide a high-quality education for all students. A smaller and very vocal group, however, continually decries any changes that appear to lower standards and accuses the school and district administration of not supporting the school by getting tough with troublemakers. Members of this group believe that if the school returns to a well-defined tracking system that creates a vocational level for students who are not interested in learning, the needs of everyone will be served. They also believe that senior teachers should be given first choice for teaching courses. This vocal minority among the veteran faculty continues to protest loudly the many changes occurring at the high school.

Annoyed, Celeste, a teacher at Rolling Meadows High School, circled *sex* on the needs assessment form sent out from the district administrative offices. Beside it, she wrote, "As often as possible." Then she wrote *gender* on the form, carefully drew a small box next to it, marked it, and wrote "*female.*" Further down on the form, she was asked to indicate her race or ethnicity. "Ayy," she groaned, and turned to her friend, Bobby, who was completing the same form. "I hate these forms. I am so tired of being forced into boxes that don't fit."

"Just fill out the form," Bobby yawned. "It doesn't really matter. And besides, these are the categories that the U.S. Census uses."

"I don't care about the U.S. Census Bureau. They are wrong! Where is the box for me on this chart? I am not African American. My cultural identity is Brazilian."

"Well, you are Black Hispanic, aren't you?"

"No. I am a U.S. citizen of African descent. I was born in Boston and moved with my parents to Brazil as a child. My first language is Portuguese. My father is Brazilian and my mother is from Panama; they met when they were studying at Tufts University. I speak Spanish, but I am not Hispanic because Brazil was not colonized by the Spanish. I look black and I relate most strongly to people from Central and South America."

✖

# What Happened to Race?

If you came of age in the 1960s, you may be most comfortable with the classification of people called race. *Race* is a false classification of people created in the 17th century by people seeking to describe and categorize the physical differences of humans in order to affirm the presumed superiority of Caucasians, or, more specifically, people of northwestern European descent. Anthropologist George Armelagos (1995) said that "[W]hile biological traits give the impression that race is a biological unit of nature, it remains a cultural construct. The boundaries between races depend on the classifier's own cultural norms" (p. 68). Race is a term that is used by the federal government, which is in turn used as a model for many other forms and applications. It is the most commonly used term, but not necessarily the most accurate one.

In this book, we use the term *race* to denote the large groups of people distinguished from one another by their physical appearances. These groups are people of African descent, people of European descent, Asians, Pacific Islanders, Native Americans, and Hispanics or Latinos/ Latinas. Clearly, these groupings exclude a large number of ethnic groups and cultures. Such groupings do not speak to the widespread migration and miscegenation that has created what are sometimes called mixed-race, biracial, or multiracial groups. For instance, what should one call the people of African descent who live in Central and South America and who speak Spanish? Are they Hispanics of African descent? What about white South Africans? Are they Africans of European descent?

Racial terminology inadequately names the different racially defined ethnic groups. Rather than seeking to name the various groups of people, it might be more effective to develop ways of identifying, interacting with, and responding to anyone who differs from you in ways that demonstrate a value for human dignity. In this book, we use the term *ethnic group* or *ethnicity* to describe groups of people with shared history, ancestry, geographic and language origin, and physical type. Although race is a shorthand term that most people understand, in our efforts to move toward cultural proficiency, we choose to use terms that are more descriptive. When possible and appropriate, we use the name of a specific ethnic group. At the same time, we will continue to use the term *racism* when alluding to the social construct or describing the form of oppression that is based on the castes created by the physical appearance of people.

Does it really make much of a difference what names people call one another, whether they use racial, cultural, or other kinds of names? Yes. To grasp this importance, simply think about your own name and the names of your children or other family members. Each one has several names that are meaningful to him or her. A person may be Bob to his friends, Robert to his staff, Mr. Jones to his students, and Robbie with his family. Clearly, names mean a great deal to everyone. U.S. citizens are not alone in attaching deep meaning to names: Across cultures, the naming process has great significance. In regard to personal names, many cultures have naming ceremonies for their children, at which time it is believed the soul enters the body of the child. Almost every culture has traditions and rituals for the giving of names. Choosing, adopting, or changing one's name is sometimes part of a rite of passage. For example, most U.S. and European women, and increasing numbers of men, change their names on marriage.

Because names connect people to their history, their families, and their culture, naming can be an act of dominance and a symbol of psychological and sometimes physical control of one person or group over another. (You may recall the scene in *Roots* when Kunta Kinte was forced to relinquish his African name to become "Toby.") Humans are objectified by assigning them names or labels for their particular behaviors or characteristics (e.g., *schizophrenic, blind, classy, girl*). By naming these ideas, we reify them and dehumanize the people to which we attach the labels.

Dominant groups, the groups in power, do not name themselves; they name other people. The others are named in relationship to the dominant group. When the first white explorers arrived in the territory called Alaska and asked the inhabitants what they called themselves, the people replied, "Eskimos," which means "people." Because the Eskimos were the only people around, they didn't need to name themselves in relationship to anyone else. The explorers, however, needed to distinguish the Eskimos as others, so they called them "Eskimos." In this book, we use names for the various racially defined ethnic groups in the United States that our clients have told us they preferred:

- African American
- Asian
- Pacific Islander
- European American
- Hispanic or Latino/Latina
- People of the First Nations

For other cultural groups, we use the terms for which our client populations have stated a preference, including

- Differently abled or physically challenged
- GLBT: Gay Men, Lesbians, Bisexual, and Transgendered people
- Older Americans
- Women
- Men

## Labels for Historically Oppressed People

A list of labels that have been ascribed to the emerging majority groups in our society includes

- Genetically inferior
- Culturally inferior
- Deprived
- Disadvantaged
- Deficient
- Different
- Diverse

These labels reflect the power of dominant groups to define others in relation to the norms set by the group in power and to name them in such a way that their otherness is reinforced. Historically oppressed people, for example, women, people of color, Gay Men and Lesbians, the aged, and the differently abled, move through a progression of stages in reaction to both the social policies of the time and their current and historical position in society.

Note the progress from social Darwinist attributions of inferiority, deprivation, disadvantage, and deficiency to a recognition of difference without the negative connotations. The social Darwinist attributions are classic labels that blame dominated people for their lot in life, even though these groups of people have been legally, educationally, and economically discriminated against. All disenfranchised and oppressed groups move through this system of being reclassified by the dominant society.

Across time, each cultural group has been assigned the same labels from the dominant society. In each case, the group labels were pernicious, and the societal response by each group was feelings of alienation from the dominant society. Prior to the 1950s, slavery and Jim Crow laws gave widespread sanction to the belief that African Americans were genetically and culturally inferior, despite the numerous instances of free blacks making significant academic and economic accomplishments throughout U.S. history. During this period, the dominant society also commonly segregated black communities from white ones.

Similarly, most First Nation people were confined to reservations either by legal mandate or through economic disincentives for leaving the reservations. Though many Native Americans have built strong, independent lives separate from or within the dominant society, the vast majority has been treated by the dominant society as culturally and genetically inferior. As with African U.S. citizens, the labels of inferiority are often cloaked in seemingly beneficent terms describing (and treating) them as exotic. Although society is generally too sophisticated to use such terms as *noble savage* any more, it is not unusual for schools to invite First Nation people to dance and tell folk stories, with little regard for learning the societal and spiritual similarities and differences among cultural groups.

For Latino groups in general and U.S. citizens of Mexican and Puerto Rican ancestry in particular, state laws that forbade children from speaking Spanish in schools heightened Latinos' alienation from the dominant society. Similarly, the various Asian groups that immigrated to this country were segregated from dominant society. By prohibiting the immigration of their compatriots, the dominant society continuously reminded Asians of their second-class status. Clearly, African American, First Nations, Mexican American, Puerto Rican, and Asian American feelings of alienation from the dominant society are not difficult to recognize and understand in this context of legally sanctioned segregation and exclusion.

During the 1950s, 1960s, and 1970s—periods of great social change— the labels for historically oppressed groups subtly shifted from *inferiority* to *deficiency*. Inferior people were easy to provide for. They were perceived as simple, and incapable of being like members of the dominant society. They were encoded as deviant, stupid, hostile, docile, childlike, or just plain backward. However, as these groups moved closer to emerging as majorities in the social mainstream, different ways of experiencing them had to be developed.

Though referring to a person as *deficient* is hardly positive, it acknowledges a potential member of society. In fact, if it were not for a deficiency or two, these deficient persons could be just like members of the dominant society. Throughout this country, schools and other social agencies began to take the approach that because they were going to have to work with these groups, they had to figure out what was wrong with them and provide what they needed. It was widely held that the unidentified deficiencies could be cured through remediation via public education.

Unfortunately, this perspective led educators to self-fulfilling prophecies; they asked, "How could those people with such insurmountable deficiencies possibly be educated?" The educational tracking system became the vehicle by which inordinate numbers of African Americans, Latinos, and other people with low socioeconomic status were placed into lower-ability groups and continuously exposed only to basic curriculum. Throughout this period, few policymakers ever asked themselves: Why do some children of color, girls, and low-income children throughout the United States succeed in schools, and what conditions contributed to their success? The few policymakers who did ask often surmised, unfortunately, that success stories are meaningless anomalies.

Finally, during the 1980s and 1990s, educators began to use the terms *different* and *diverse*, which acknowledged a common valuing of one another as fellow humans. Perhaps in the 21st century, educators will use terms such as the Mayan expression, *en la Kech*, which signifies that "you are in me and I am in you" and projects a high level of humanity into the discussion of policy and equity. To paraphrase a provocative question asked by Joel Barker (1996), a futurist: What seems impossible to do today, but, if we could do it, would radically change how we create equity across cultural groups? In 1950, the vast majority of people in this country probably could not have envisioned the changes that were to be made in human rights. Perhaps by the 2050s, people will accept as commonplace matters of equity beyond our imagination now.

                                                                 ॐ

Winston Alexander, Rolling Meadows' assistant superintendent for business, is reviewing the proposals he has received in response to the request for proposal (RFP) and is learning a lot. He gets some information from the specific responses to the questions the RFP team proposes, and the team gleans even more insight from the underlying values of the consultants. It is easy to discern what they believe from the way they present themselves and the extra materials they included. Right now, he muses over two ideas:

No nation has ever sought to provide universal education for as broad a spectrum of social classes and ethnic or racial groups as has the United States.

We are more successful at education than any other nation in the world today, but our development of a de facto caste system has created great inequities. We are at a point in history where we must heed the warning to avoid creating "two societies, separate and unequal" (Riot Commission, 1968).

                                                                  ॐ

# Effects of Discrimination

As the social policies, motivations, and labels changed over the decades, the attitudes, feelings, and beliefs of historically oppressed people changed in response. Prior to the 1950s, while isolated and segregated from the dominant culture, they experienced intense feelings of alienation. During this time, everyone in society agreed that there was an US and a THEM, and everyone knew to which group he or she belonged.

As society began to invite some dominated people to assimilate into the dominant culture, they were expected to disassociate themselves from all vestiges of their primary or native culture, so they felt dissonance. Within the dominant culture, they faced tremendous obstacles and difficulties, yet they were obliged to resist reliance on their native cultural resources to help them overcome these problems. They knew that to be accepted into the dominant culture, they had to abandon all traces of their native culture. Similarly, they were expected to adopt the dominant culture's view, disparaging their native culture and denigrating the people in their respective native cultural groups. Thus, they felt dissonance not only with members of the dominant culture and in settings reflective of the dominant culture, but also often with members of their native culture and in settings reflecting their native culture (Adams, 1996; Kovel, 1984; Locust, 1996; McCarthy, 1993; Ogbu, 1978).

Many U.S. citizens who had emigrated from Europe were able to overcome these obstacles as their distinctive native cultures melted into the dominant culture. Similarly, Gay Men and Lesbians were able to assimilate as long as they carefully avoided being open about their sexual orientation. Even some women were able to assimilate by accepting the dominant society's definitions of gender roles: If they wished to become chief executive officers (CEOs), they accepted that they must dress, speak, and act like CEOs—that is, like white men (Boyd, 1984; Gilligan, 1983; Weiss & Schiller, 1988).

The melting pot did not work for all people. Some people, no matter how thoroughly they abandoned their own native culture, were still not welcomed into the dominant culture because their physical appearance continued to distinguish them despite their best efforts at being indistinguishable. For instance, most women and people of color continue to look different from white men, even when they adopt the same values, attitudes, and behavior that white men show. Furthermore, much to the surprise of some members of the dominant society, many historically oppressed people rejected entirely the goal of assimilation: They did not want to have their differences melted away.

During the 1960s, many people outside the dominant culture experienced feelings of *marginality*: They knew two cultures but were not entirely accepted by members of either one essentially because they could function in the other culture. Among those who experienced marginality were children bused to schools where very few members of their primary group were present; once they learned to cope with and thrive in the dominant culture, they often felt marginalized on returning to their home communities. They no longer felt at home while at home. Similarly, Latino children forced to speak only English in school, to the point of forgetting or becoming developmentally disabled in their native language, often feel marginalized in Latino culture. First Nation children educated in the long-running Bureau of Indian Affairs boarding schools too often fit neither in the white culture for which they were educated nor in their home cultures from which they had been separated. In all these cases, the insult added to the injury was that these children continued to be marginalized in the dominant culture while being marginalized in their native cultures (Cummins, 1990; Duchene, 1990).

During the 1970s, many people were able to integrate successfully into a new culture while remaining comfortable in their native culture. Nonetheless, they felt unable to mesh the two worlds, so they experienced a sense of *dualism*. Unlike marginalized people, who live between two worlds, people who feel dualism live in the two worlds, moving back and forth yet never carrying one into the other. Many adults today experience a sense of dualism: They function successfully in corporate America yet continue to go home to a segregated community, where they socialize and worship with just the members of their native culture (Delpit, 1993; Fine, 1993; Sapon-Shevin, 1993). Closeted Gay Men and Lesbians experience dualism when they function in a straight business world in which most of the people with whom they work are straight, and never imagine that their colleagues live in another world outside of work that is very different from theirs.

During the 1980s, many people attempted to bring aspects of their marginalized culture into the world of the dominant culture. This process demanded that they negotiate for the acceptance of those in the dominant group. Members of the dominant culture assumed that they were inherently inferior and undeserving of the position in society they occupied. So they also had to negotiate for a respect and acceptance in the workforce by proving that they did have the skills and credentials to do the job for which they were hired. Finally, starting in the 1990s, people have begun to feel bicultural affirmation, functioning effectively in two cultural worlds in which the people in each cultural world know they are a part of the other and respect their biculturality. The difference between dualism and *biculturality* is that although both involve knowledge of the norms and values of two cultural groups, with dualism, one group knows nothing about the other. With biculturality, both groups know about the other and celebrate that their group member is part of both. These contrast with *marginality*, in which the person functions in two worlds and is accepted by neither. Perhaps in the 2000s, people will experience multicultural transformation, in which the norm for all people will be to know and function comfortably within several cultural groups and be changed for the better as a result (McCarthy, 1993; West, 1993; Willis, 1996).

In reviewing the changes across the past five decades, one can see historically oppressed people moving through a process of acceptance, internalization, and rejection of the labels given to them by others and moving toward self-determination and self-identification. Although this discussion suggests that these general trends apply to all cultural groups, in fact, each cultural group moves at its own distinct pace. Furthermore, the individuals within each group vary widely in terms of how they view social policies, social impetuses and motivations, and labels, as well as in their responses to discrimination. For instance, even today, Gay Men and Lesbians may experience feelings ranging from alienation to multicultural transformation. New immigrants from Guatemala may still feel alienation, whereas their U.S.-born cousins may experience bicultural affirmation.

What does this historical process mean to the culturally proficient educational leader? It means that the culturally proficient leader has to be adept at recognizing that a typical school faculty comprises teachers, aides, staff, counselors, and administrators who have had widely different life experiences. More importantly, the culturally proficient leader recognizes that the experiences of the school faculty and staff may be much different from the experiences of students and parents in the community served by the school. The culturally proficient leader recognizes that he or she must address issues of labeling in a way that helps people from the dominant culture to understand the pain caused by labeling and helps recipients of such labeling go beyond that pain to focus on self-determination and self-identification.

## Motivation and Social Impetus

As society moves from one social period to the next, it continues to include policies, attitudes, and practices from the previous periods. Many people may continue to be guided by outdated policies; hold attitudes acquired years ago; and implement long-standing practices in their work, home, and community interactions. Just as policies, attitudes, and practices are cumulative, so is the motivation to change any particular policy. The social impetus and motivation for a particular decade may appear isolated, yet closer inspection may reveal that the motivating forces from previous decades have also been influential. Moreover, each social policy era spawns awareness in groups that did not initiate the change to press for social reforms affecting them, too. For example, the modern civil rights movement of the 1960s struggled to gain rights for African Americans and later for other cultural minority groups. These struggles then helped to spawn the modern reconvergence of both the feminist movement and the Gay Pride movement.

Over the past 50 years, each decade has been characterized by a particular impetus for social policy. The social impetus for the changes leading from segregation prior to the 1950s to desegregation and integration in the 1950s and 1960s focused on obtaining legal equity. During the 1960s, the social impetus continued to focus on legal equity, such as the provisions of the 1964 Civil Rights Act. In the push for integration, equal access, and equal rights, however, legal changes alone did not suffice. To broaden the application of these legal measures, the social impetus shifted to activism for social justice. For instance, such activism included the development of programs to rectify inequitable distribution of resources such as nutrition, prenatal care, child care, and early childhood education.

During the 1970s, the impetus for multiculturalism was almost uniquely motivated by the widely acknowledged need for equity in education. Educators sought to teach language arts and social studies in ways that recognized and included the increasingly multicultural populations found in U.S. schools (Banks, 1994). During the 1980s, the motivation for social policies of diversity was primarily economic issues. The business community recognized the changing demographics of consumers and workers. Once businesspeople recognized that diversity has an economic payoff, they started to make many changes addressing this issue, for example, changes in TV programming, images in commercials, and languages used in automatic teller machines.

During the 1990s, educators and other community leaders began to view cultural proficiency as a moral imperative. This book is an outgrowth of this social impetus because we recommend social policies and school reforms that reflect cultural proficiency. For the 2000s and beyond, cultural proficiency is our vision of what this society will become.

# Going Further

1. Before reading this chapter, how did you define culture? What do you think now? How does your definition affect the lens through which you observe and understand your school or district?

2. Find someone who has lived through the Civil Rights Movement, attended a segregated school, rode with the Freedom Riders, or can tell you about some other significant time or event in this country's racial history. After talking with this person, write his or her oral history and your response to it.

3. The Social Policy column in Response Sheet 2.3.1, Evolution of Social Equity Policies, illustrates the evolution of equity policies as a result of societal forces. In that column, find the cell that best describes your focus and concerns today, or suggest a social policy describing your own focus and concerns.

# Reflection

_____

_____

_____

_____

_____

_____

_____

_____

_____

_____

**Activity 2.1:**

# Storytelling

■ Purpose

- To demonstrate the power of storytelling
- To get acquainted with each other
- To gain some insight into participants' leadership styles

■ Expertise of Facilitator

Low

■ Readiness of Group

Beginning

■ Time Needed

60 minutes

■ Materials

None

■ Briefing

This activity will give you a chance to get to know your colleagues in a deeper way.

■ Process

1. Divide the group into dyads, asking people to partner with the person whom they know least well.
2. Have each team member tell a story about himself or herself that reveals something about his or her personality or lifestyle that the partners may not know.
3. Have the dyads join with two other sets of partners so that they are in groups of six.

4. Have each person share his or her partner's story with the small group.
5. Have one member of the group synthesize the stories for the entire group.

## ■ Debriefing

1. What did you learn about yourself? Your partner? The other people in your group?
2. What conclusions can you draw about the members of your group?
3. What differences did you notice between the different groups?
4. What do the groups have in common?
5. How can you use this information in the work you will be doing?

## ■ Variation

Tell the story of when you

- Became aware of your culture
- First felt a need to serve the community
- Became an activist, pacifist, or something similar
- Decided to change your career
- Knew you were a leader
- Knew you didn't want to be a leader

**Activity 2.2:**

# Simultaneous Storytelling

■ Purpose

To help participants understand how it feels to not be listened to

■ Expertise of Facilitator

Intermediate

■ Readiness of Group

Moderate

■ Time Needed

20 minutes

■ Materials

None

■ Briefing

Think of a time when you did something that was hard for you and you were very proud of your accomplishment. This may be something that no one else knows about or that is easy for most people to do. Think of a time when you overcame a personal barrier. Prepare to tell this story to a member of your group.

■ Process

1. Ask group members to sit in groups of four or five.
2. After they are situated, thinking they will each have a turn to tell their stories, instruct them to tell their stories now, ALL AT ONCE.

■ Debriefing

When the last person has told his or her story, ask the following questions:

1. How did you feel when you got the assignment?
2. How did you select the story to tell?
3. How important was the story to you?
4. Have you ever told the story before?
5. How did you feel as you anticipated telling the story?
6. Did you expect the listeners to empathize with you and understand how important this experience was to you?
7. What did you think when you got the instructions to tell your stories simultaneously?
8. How did it feel to tell the story with everyone else talking?
9. Have you had an experience similar to this one in which you were talking but no one was listening?
10. Have you ever not listened when someone was trying to tell you something that was more important to them than it was to you? Often, a person is so intent on telling his or her story that he or she does not hear, and therefore can neither understand nor empathize with the stories of others.
11. What have you learned from this activity?
12. How will you use what you have learned?

**Activity 2.3:**

# Pick a Cell

■ Purpose

To examine the social issues and historical events presented in Response Sheet 2.3.1 from a personal perspective

■ Skill of Facilitator

Extensive

■ Readiness of Group

Intermediate

■ Time Needed

45 minutes

■ Materials

Copies of Response Sheet 2.3.1

■ Briefing

Let's take some time to talk about how the events presented in Response Sheet 2.3.1 have affected your own lives. This is a chance to make this chart come alive.

■ Process

1. Ask participants if there are any general questions about the chart. If they ask a question that you cannot answer adequately, for example, "What do you mean by culturally marginal?", check to see if there are members of the group who may be able to respond.
2. Organize the participants into small groups of 3–4 people.
3. Ask each person to select a cell in the chart that is particularly meaningful to him or her.

4. In turn, each person tells a story in response to the cell he or she chose, while the others listen, ask questions for clarification, or respond with stories of their own.
5. Allow 20-30 minutes for the small group interaction.

■ Debriefing

1. Summarize what happened in your small group.
2. What did you notice?
3. What did you learn about yourself?
4. How do you understand your colleagues differently now?
5. How do you understand this chart differently now?
6. How will you use this information?

■ Variations

1. Assign to each group a particular row to discuss.
2. Assign to each group a particular column to discuss.
3. Assign to each group a particular cell to discuss.

**Response Sheet 2.3.1:**

# Evolution of Equity Policies

| Relative Time Period | Social Policy | Cumulative Motivation | Label for Dominated People | Response to Discrimination by Dominated People |
|---|---|---|---|---|
| Before 1950s | Segregation | Legal Separation | Genetically and Culturally Inferior | Alienation |
| 1950s | Desegregation | Legislated Desegregation | Deprived | Dissonance |
| 1960s | Integration, equal access, equal rights | Activism for social justice | Disadvantaged | Marginality |
| 1970s | Equal benefits, multiculturalism | Education | Deficient | Dualism |
| 1980s | Diversity | Economic | Different | Negotiation |
| 1990s | Cultural competency | Moral | Diverse | Bicultural Affirmation |
| 2000s | Cultural proficiency | Ideal | *En la Kech*[1] | Multicultural Transformation |

*NOTE:* 1. *En la Kech* is a Mayan term that means, "I am in you and you are in me." We appreciate this contribution from our colleague Alberto Ochoa at California State University, San Diego.

**Activity 2.4:**

# Discussion Questions About U.S. History

■ Purpose

- To teach that issues of oppression have historical foundations in the history of our country
- This activity provides participants with the opportunity to understand seldom-discussed events in U.S. history and the effect they have on current intercultural relations.

■ Skill of Facilitator

Extensive

■ Readiness of Group

Intermediate

■ Time Needed

60 minutes

■ Materials

A facilitator with a good grasp of U.S. history
Copies of Response Sheet 2.4.1: Discussion Questions About U.S. History for each participant
At least one copy of Response Sheet 2.4.2, the answer sheet for the facilitator

■ Briefing

This activity will familiarize us with historical events in which U.S. citizens were treated with discrimination and the effect of these on our human relations today.

■ Process

1. Distribute one copy of Response Sheet 2.4.1 to each participant.
2. Ask participants to complete the questions as best they can.
3. Divide the group into small groups of 4-6 people. Ask them to select a recorder.
4. Ask them to arrive at a consensus on answers to as many questions as they can in 20 minutes.
5. Take each question and ask the groups what they thought the correct answers should be. Allow time for different perspectives. You will find that some members will argue with every minute detail; that is okay because dialogue is the order of the day.
6. Give the preferred responses to the factual questions and lead participants in discussions of the implications of the others using Response Sheet 2.4.2.

■ Debriefing

1. What were your feelings when you first received the questionnaire?
2. How did you react to the discussion in your group?
3. How do you feel about your knowledge of history?
4. What do you see as the effect of history on today?
5. What is the implication of this activity for you in your role at school?
6. What information or skills do you believe you need to do an even better job?

**Response Sheet 2.4.1:**

# Discussion Questions About U.S. History

The questions below are to be used as a discussion catalyst. Please read and mark whether you believe them to be true or false. Some of the questions are factual and call on your knowledge of U.S. history; others may be matters of perspective and call on your ability to make judgments. In a few minutes, you will be asked to discuss your answers with other participants and to arrive at consensus responses.

_____ 1. First Nation people have been remanded to reservations in the United States.

_____ 2. Columbus discovered the Americas.

_____ 3. African Americans were guaranteed full citizenship status with the enactment of the 14th Amendment to the U.S. Constitution in 1868.

_____ 4. Jacksonian democracy of the 1830s expanded voting rights to people who did not own land.

_____ 5. Women were granted the right to vote with the enactment of the 19th Amendment to the U.S. Constitution in 1920.

_____ 6. In the pre–Civil War United States, the only people who could vote in national elections were white men.

_____ 7. U.S. citizens of Japanese ancestry were confined to relocation camps during World War II.

_____ 8. History, as written in our textbooks, is factual and without bias.

_____ 9. Addressing issues of diversity is a process in which white men can have a responsible role.

_____ 10. In our country's history, the practice of hiring and promoting people usually has been predicated on selecting the most qualified person.

_____ 11. Racism and sexism are institutional practices that have served as barriers to people of color and women in our country.

_____ 12. Racism and sexism as institutional practices no longer exist in this country.

_____ 13. One of the consequences of institutionalized racism and sexism has been that people of color and women have been kept out of the workforce and white men have benefited.

_____ 14. The melting pot concept was an effective process by which many European immigrants within two or three generations were blended into the U.S. mainstream society.

_____ 15. Many states in our country enacted Jim Crow laws that denied people basic human rights based on their ethnicity.

_____ 16. *Backlash* is the angry and defensive reaction to programs and laws that promote a diverse society.

_____ 17. Some white men are angry and defensive about diversity programs because they believe these programs will cause them to lose their jobs.

_____ 18. Women and people of color have had to resort to legislative and judicial processes to have their voting rights assured.

_____ 19. Racism and sexism affect all people in this society.

_____ 20. Issues caused by diversity are historical phenomena rooted in the foundation of our country.

**Response Sheet 2.4.2:**

# Answers and Commentary

Questions that have factual responses:

1. **True.** U.S. history is replete with such examples. Many make the argument that today many people stay on reservations due to the inducements to do so.
2. **False.** There were millions of people in the Americas when he arrived.
3. **True.** That was the intent of the legislation, although it was usurped throughout the United States.
4. **True.** It applied, however, only to white males.
5. **True.** That was the intent of the legislation, though it, too, was usurped throughout the United States.
6. **True.**
7. **True.** Well over 100,000 U.S. citizens were denied basic rights of citizenship.
14. **True.** This was the genesis for the melting pot theory.
15. **True.** After the U.S. Civil War, states throughout the country devised ways to prevent African Americans from voting.
18. **True.** As indicated in the responses to questions 4 and 5, women and people of color have had to use legal means to gain the right to vote in this country.

The balance of the questions will promote interesting discussion among the participants.

Question 8 may appear to be false at first reading but the actual problem is the way educators and members of the community approach textual material.

Question 9 poses the moral dilemma referred to in the latter part of Chapter 5 and is a quite important topic.

Questions 10, 11, 12, 13, 16, 17, 19, and 20 ask a person to deduce from historical events the effects that these events or social forces had on the citizenry of this country.

**ACTIVITY 2.5**

# CULTURAL PERCEPTIONS

■ Purpose

To be used as an opening warm-up activity, as a way to test assumptions, and to introduce the concept of stereotyping

■ Expertise of Facilitator

Extensive

■ Readiness of Group

Beginning

■ Time Needed

20 minutes

■ Materials

Copies of Response Sheet 2.5.1: Cultural Perceptions

■ Briefing

This activity will test your intuition and perceptions.

■ Process

1. Have participants select as a partner someone they don't know well or they would like to get to know better.
2. Using Response Sheet 2.5.1, have the first partner share his or her perceptions of how the second partner would respond to each of the stems.
3. After the first partner shares his or her perceptions, the second partner gives his or her responses.
4. Switch roles and repeat the process.

■ Debriefing

1. Reassemble the group and ask for volunteers to share their experiences in learning about another person.
2. Which assumptions were accurate? Which were not accurate?
3. Ask how it felt to have the responsibility for making the perceptions; how it felt being on the receiving end of the perceptions; and, what insight this gives to the process of stereotyping.
4. Ask how this informs us of the stereotyping that may occur when we face new teachers, aides, students, and parents.
5. How are stereotypes helpful? How are they harmful?
6. If the school is large, how are these perceptions enacted with people we rarely see?
7. What was the most important thing you learned from this experience?
8. How will you use this information?

**Response Sheet 2.5.1**

# Cultural Perceptions

Select for your partner someone that you don't know well, or who you would like to know better. Use the list below to share your perceptions. Ask your partner to give you his or her responses. Then switch roles and have your partner share his or her perceptions with you.

- Country of family origin and heritage
- Languages spoken
- Interests or hobbies
- Favorite food
- Type of movies, TV programs preferred, if any
- Type of music preferred
- Pets, if any, or favorite animals

## ACTIVITY 2.6

# CIRCLE OF STEREOTYPES

■ Purpose

To identify common stereotypes used with children and to experience how it feels to interact through the filter of someone's stereotype.

■ Expertise of Facilitator

Extensive

■ Readiness of Group

Intermediate

■ Time Needed

40 minutes

■ Materials

Construction paper suitable for making crowns
Masking tape
Markers
Paper and pencils

■ Briefing

We are going to talk about how stereotypes affect our children. This activity is designed to have participants discuss how common stereotyping is in our everyday life and to realize the feelings often associated with the use of them.

■ Process

1. Divide the participants into two groups.
2. Give Group 1 the construction paper and tape. Ask it to make crowns for each member.

3. Ask Group 2 to generate a list of labels used to identify children, for example, *slow, very bright, nerd, teacher's pet, troublemaker, accident-prone, hostile.*

4. Have each person in Group 1 give his or her crown to someone in Group 2.

5. Have participants in Group 2 put one label on each crown, without showing the label to any members of Group 1.

6. Ask Group 1 to stand and form a circle facing out.

7. Ask Group 2 to form a circle around Group 1, with each member facing the person whose crown he or she is holding. Without showing the label, Group 2 crowns Group 1.

8. Members of Group 2 rotate one person to the right and talk to the person they are facing using language appropriate for the label on the crown the person is wearing. After a few moments, signal the members of Group 1 to rotate to the next person in the circle.

9. After each person in Group 1 has been addressed by each person in Group 2, have all the participants sit in a circle. Members of Group 1 continue to wear the crowns. They can see the labels of others but not of themselves.

■ Debriefing

1. Ask everyone in Group 1, individually, to talk about how they felt after listening to Group 2 speak to them, and to guess what label was on their crown.

2. Ask members of Group 2 to comment on how they felt when addressing members of Group 1 and to describe how members of Group 1 reacted to the prejudicial comments.

3. How realistic are the labels? How frequently do you see them used?

4. What is the relationship of the labels to the ethnicity of students?

5. Is there anything wrong with the positive stereotypes used?

6. What did you learn from this activity?

7. How are you going to use what you learned?

■ Variation

For mature groups, try putting the names of various ethnic groups on the crowns. Describe specific situations, such as "at a school social function" or "in a disciplinary interview," and rotate the circles.

**ACTIVITY 2.7**

# PERSONAL STEREOTYPES

■ Purpose

To identify the stereotypes associated with different kinds of people and to examine how stereotyping affects communication and self-esteem

■ Expertise of Facilitator

Extensive

■ Readiness of Group

Intermediate

■ Time Needed

30 minutes

■ Materials

Several large Post-it notes for each person

■ Briefing

This activity will help you see how everyone is confronted with stereotypes.

■ Process

1. Ask each person to make of a list of the socio-cultural groups to which they belong and with which they associate painful stereotypes.

2. On one Post-it note, each person writes the name of one group, for example, "fat people," and places it on his or her chest.

3. On another Post It, each person writes stereotypic comments associated with that group. For example if on one Post It, "fat people"

was written, the other Post It might have, "stupid, lazy, and un-healthy."

3. Ask participants to *silently* walk around the room, reading the labels that have been written.

4. After everyone in the group has had a chance to read all the labels, ask them to organize themselves into small groups, based upon what they have written on their labels. For example, if only one person wrote "fat people," but several wrote labels that were related to body size—"too thin," "skinny legs," "big butt"—they can sit together in a group.

5. Ask the participants to discuss their labels and the stereotypes associated with each of them.

■ Debriefing

1. How did you feel writing and wearing the sterotypic comments?
2. What was it like to talk to others who suffer from the same or similar stereotypes?
3. How did you feel reading the stereotypes of others?
4. How do stereotypes impede healthy human relations?
5. How do they affect self-esteem?
6. How are stereotypes helpful?
7. What was the most important thing you learned from this exercise?
8. How will you use the information?

■ Variations

Rather than wearing the Post-it notes, sit in a semi-circle. Ask each person to come to the front of the room and to state the socio-cultural group and then the stereotypes associated with it. Move through the semi-circle quickly and without comment until everyone has spoken. Then discuss the process, the feelings, and what was learned.

## ACTIVITY 2.8

# CULTURAL STEREOTYPES

■ Purpose

To identify the stereotypes associated with different groups and to examine how stereotyping affects communication and relationships

■ Expertise of Facilitator

Extensive

■ Readiness of Group

Advanced

■ Time Needed

60 minutes

■ Materials

Paper
Pencils

■ Briefing

We are going to explore the stereotypes associated with the various ethnic groups to which we belong.

■ Process

1. Ask group members to sit with the people with whom they have the strongest ethnic identity. Trust the group to sort itself out. People may be uncomfortable at first, but if you give them time and no options, they will form appropriate groups.
2. In the groups, ask members to make a list of the common stereotypes held about their group.

3. Then ask group members to discuss the truth that has been overgeneralized to create that stereotype and what they want others not in their group to know about the stereotype.

4. Ask group members to identify additional information that they want others to know about their group.

5. Ask small groups to share with the larger group the essence of their discussions and the information they wish to teach or share.

■ Debriefing

1. How did you feel when you articulated the stereotypes about your group?

2. What was your response to the explanations of the stereotypes you heard?

3. Are there other stereotypes about which you have questions?

4. How do stereotypes impede healthy human relations?

5. How are stereotypes helpful?

6. What was the most important thing you learned from this exercise?

7. How will you use the information?

■ Variation

Separate participants by role, for example, classroom teachers, resource teachers, school administrators, district administrators; parents, teachers, students; or students, teachers, administrators; and conduct the activity.

Have groups creatively present their "findings."

**ACTIVITY 2.9**

# ETHNIC PERCEPTIONS

■ Purpose

To help members of various ethnic groups identify and examine stereotypes held by group members and members of other ethnic groups

■ Expertise of Facilitator

Extensive

■ Readiness of Group

Advanced

■ Time Needed

3 hours

■ Materials

Chart paper
Break-out rooms for each group

■ Briefing

We are going to examine stereotypes that you hold about your group and about other groups.

■ Process

1. Ask participants to self-select into ethnic groups. Members of the group they choose to join can question a participant's choice; however, others, including the facilitator, cannot.

2. Each group gets two sheets of paper to describe themselves:
   How we see ourselves
   How we think you see us

Each group gets an additional sheet of paper for every other ethnic group represented:

Group name

How we see you

3. Allow 15 minutes for each question a small group has to answer. For example, if there are four small groups, each group will need 75 minutes for this step, 15 for your group and 15 minutes for each other group.

4. Provide each group with sufficient privacy to complete the activity in an open and honest manner.

5. Have each group return to the original meeting area and arrange chart paper panels by ethnic groups.

6. Participants are to mill around and read the work of all groups. This may take from 15 to 30 minutes depending on the size of the group.

7. Have each ethnic group meet again and discuss feelings, reactions, and observations about their own and others' data. Allow 10-20 minutes.

8. Have the total group reassemble and summarize reactions to the data about each group and other groups. Invite participants to ask questions to clarify. Allow 15 minutes per group.

9. Lead the group in discussing reactions, observations, and learning from the activity.

## ■ Debriefing

1. Example questions:
   a. What was it like to be in your ethnic-specific group?
   b. What issues were raised when you were asked to join an ethnic-specific group?
   c. What are your reactions to the way in which your own group viewed itself?
   d. What are your reactions to how similar or different your perceptions of your group compared with how other groups viewed your group?
   e. What do you see as differences or similarities among how groups are viewed?
   f. How will you be able to use this information in your school?

2. Invite participants to
   a. Write, in journal fashion, how this activity affected them

b. Engage in dialogue with colleagues about ways in which they may use this information

c. Discuss with colleagues the ramifications of these ethnic perceptions on interactions with parents, the community, students, and teachers

**ACTIVITY 2.10**

# GROUP STEREOTYPES

■ Purpose

To identify the stereotypes associated with different groups of people, and to examine how stereotyping impacts one's perceptions of others.

Recognize how often negative stereotypes are applied to every cultural group.

■ Skill of Facilitator

Extensive

■ Readiness of Group

Advanced

■ Time Needed

60 minutes

■ Materials

Several pieces of chart paper
Large Post-it notes, about 20 for each participant

■ Briefing

This activity will help you to see how we stereotype other people.

■ Process

1. Label each piece of chart paper with one of these group categories: White women, White men, Black women, Black men, Hispanic women, Hispanic men, Gay men, Lesbians, etc.

2. Hang the charts around the room.

3. Give each participant a small stack of large Post-it notes.

4. Ask them to write labels and stereotypes they have heard used about each group.
5. Silently have the participants affix the Post-it notes to the appropriate chart.
6. Mill around and read what has been written.

■ Debrief

1. How did you feel writing the stereotypes?
2. What did you think as you read what was written?
3. How did you feel as you read what was written?
4. What is your reaction to all these labels around the room?
5. What are the implications of this activity?
6. How will you use the information?

■ Variation

Instead of ethnic stereotypes, use the various roles in the school and district, e.g. teacher, administrator, support staff, gifted student, average student, etc.

# Part II

# Using the Tools of Cultural Proficiency

# The First Tool, Descriptive Language: The Cultural Proficiency Continuum

*All of the great leaders have had one characteristic in common: it was the willingness to confront unequivocally the major anxiety of their people in their time. This, and not much else, is the essence of leadership.*

—John Kenneth Galbraith

The teachers at Rolling Meadows Middle School have heard that the district is going to hire some consultants to assess their cultural sensitivity. They are neither impressed nor pleased. Sitting in the teachers' lunchroom, they speak wistfully about when their own children attended the district, failing to acknowledge that the demographics have been changing dramatically. Their comments about the children and the impending work with the consultants range in attitude from culturally destructive to culturally proficient.

In one corner of the room we hear:

"This is America, everyone should speak English; they should be adapting to us. This is reverse discrimination. We didn't do anything to those people, why do we have to change?"

"Our goal for examining our school policy on student grouping must be to enhance student achievement. If we get some good consultants in here, they can help us to disaggregate these test data. Then we can really understand student needs."

"Why are we trying to fix something that's not broken? When I walk into a classroom, I do not see color or ability or gender, I only see children."

"I believe that conflict is natural and normal; I'm glad we will be learning how to do things differently when conflict occurs."

Across the room, some teachers are discussing their students:

"I didn't know his father was gay. He doesn't look gay to me."

"She catches well for a girl."

"I can't believe my Japanese boys only scored in the 80th percentile!"

Over by the copier, some of the teachers are trying to be proactive:

"We need a Korean vice principal to help us with the Korean students."

"We celebrate Cinco de Mayo and Martin Luther King's birthday. What holiday can we use for American Indians?"

"Let's look at the school calendar to make sure we don't schedule our potlucks during Ramadan, Ridvan, or Yom Kippur."[1]

ᴀ

## The Continuum

Cultural proficiency is a way of being that enables one to effectively respond in a variety of cultural settings to the issues caused by diversity. A culturally proficient organization interacts effectively with its employees, its clients, and its community. Culturally proficient people may not know all there is to know about others who are different from them, but they know how to take advantage of teachable moments, how to ask questions without offending, and how to create an environment that is welcoming to diversity and to change. Culturally proficient individuals

---

[1]These are the holidays of the Muslim, Baha'i, and Jewish faiths, respectively, that require the faithful to fast during the day. Ramadan and Ridvan last for several weeks, so your Muslim and Baha'i colleagues and students may be at school while fasting.

use four tools for developing the cultural competence of their organizations or in themselves.

**The Guiding Principles** provide the underlying values of the approach. **The Five Essential Elements** are behavioral standards for measuring and planning for growth toward cultural proficiency. **The Barriers** are two caveats that assist in responding effectively to resistance to change individual behaviors. **The Continuum** provides language for describing both healthy and nonproductive policies, practices, and behaviors. There are six points along the cultural proficiency continuum that indicate unique ways of seeing and responding to difference:

> **Cultural destructiveness**—*See the difference, stomp it out:*
> The elimination of other people's cultures

> **Cultural incapacity**—*See the difference, make it wrong:*
> Belief in the superiority of one's culture and behavior
> that disempowers another's culture

> **Cultural blindness**—*See the difference, act like you don't:*
> Acting as if the cultural differences you see do not matter,
> or not recognizing that there are differences
> among and between cultures

> **Cultural precompetence**—*See the difference, respond inadequately:*
> Awareness of the limitations of one's skills
> or an organization's practices when interacting
> with other cultural groups

> **Cultural competence**—*See the difference, understand
> the difference that difference makes:*
> Interacting with other cultural groups using the five
> essential elements of cultural proficiency as the standard
> for individual behavior and school practices

> **Cultural proficiency**—*See the difference and respond
> positively and affirmingly:*
> Esteeming culture, knowing how to learn
> about individual and organizational culture, and
> interacting effectively in a variety of cultural environments.

| Cultural<br>▼Destructiveness | | Cultural<br>▼Blindness | | Cultural<br>▼Competence | |
|---|---|---|---|---|---|
| | ▲Cultural<br>Incapacity | | ▲Cultural<br>Precompetence | | Cultural▲<br>Proficiency |

Once people have been introduced to cultural proficiency and see that there is a continuum of behaviors, they often want a grade. As an educator, you may be inclined to give that grade. That is not how the continuum is best used. Certainly, because it looks like a measuring device, it could be used as such, but you will find it far more useful as a tool that provides language for describing the behaviors of people and the policies and practices of organizations. The infinite points on the continuum can represent every intercultural and intracultural interaction. When you assess your own assertiveness, you may determine that you are very assertive as a consumer, moderately assertive when talking with your boss, and a total wimp when trying to confront your mother. Assigning a particular point on an assertiveness continuum for each interaction is both more descriptive and more instructive than giving you an average score for assertive behavior. The cultural competence continuum works in the same way. A school may have a mission statement that embodies the guiding principles and have policies that reflect each of the essential elements, but the practices of the people in the school office may be culturally blind or even culturally destructive. On the other hand, you may have a teacher with an exemplary culturally competent classroom, functioning in a school that is rife with practices that can only be described as cultural incapacity.

Use the continuum when discussing a particular situation or a specific policy, or in articulating why someone's behavior is inappropriate. The continuum provides a perspective for examining policies, practices, and procedures in a school by giving reference points and a common language for describing historical or current situations. It will be easy to assign a point on the cultural proficiency continuum to events that have resulted in people being murdered, maimed, or exploited by dominant and destructive groups. Identifying how students' opportunities have been preempted, denied, limited, or enhanced, however, may be more difficult to categorize. So take the time to practice with your colleagues by describing situations, events, and policies as they arise.

**Cultural destructiveness** is any policy, practice, or behavior that effectively eliminates another people's culture; it may be manifested through an organization's policies and practices or through an individual's values and behaviors.

**Cultural incapacity** is the belief in the superiority of one's own culture and behavior that disempowers another's culture. It is any policy, practice, or behavior that subordinates all cultures to one.

**Cultural blindness** is any policy, practice, or behavior that ignores existing cultural differences or that considers such differences inconsequential. This could include people acting as if the cultural differences they see do not matter or not recognizing that there are important differences among and between cultures.

**Cultural precompetence** is reflected in people and organizations that are trying to use appropriate behaviors and practices and that recognize that they still have much to learn.

**Cultural competence** is awareness of the limitations of one's skills or an organization's practices when interacting with other cultural groups. It is any policy, practice, or behavior that consistently uses the essential elements of cultural proficiency as the standards for their interaction.

**Cultural proficiency** is a way of being. Culturally proficient people may not know all there is to know about others who are different from them, but they know how to take advantage of teachable moments, how to ask questions without offending, and how to create an environment that is welcoming to diversity and to change. A culturally proficient organization is an open and inclusive learning organization that also has a strong core culture that is clearly articulated to all.

## ■ Cultural Destructiveness

The easiest to detect and the most negative end of the continuum is represented by attitudes, policies, and practices destructive to cultures and consequently to the individuals within a culture. Extreme examples include cultural genocide, such as the U.S. system of enslaving African peoples and the westward expansion of American territory that resulted in the near-extinction of First Nations. Other examples of cultural destructiveness are the Bureau of Indian Affairs educational programs that took young people from their families and nations and placed them in boarding schools where the goal was to eradicate their language and culture.

Additional examples include the ethnic cleansings and holocausts in Europe and Africa. The Nazi extermination targeted Jews, Gypsies, Gay Men, and Lesbians, as well as others viewed as less than desirable by occupying forces. Other destructive acts have included the pogroms of Russia; the Turkish extermination of Armenians, Cypriots, and Greeks; and the killing fields of Southeast Asia, as well as the wars of Hutu and Tutsi in central Africa and the wars in the former Yugoslav Republic.

Elementary and high schools historically have been places where students were socialized for active participation as U.S. citizens and taught basic skills for functioning in the workplace. In the 19th and early 20th centuries, this process of acculturation involved socializing people from all parts of Europe into an emerging dominant European American culture. This melting pot approach to public school education was relatively effective within two to three generations for the European immigrants. Over the past 50 years, compulsory attendance requirements have brought into schools increasing numbers of Latinos, African Americans, First Nation people, immigrants from Southeast Asia, and European Americans from low socioeconomic groups.

Although some members of these groups have been successful in school, their acquisition of English proficiency and dominant society mores has not necessarily ensured their access either to higher education or to the dominant culture in the United States. The cultural destructiveness that these groups have experienced in schools is manifested in markedly lower achievement, higher dropout rates, and lower social mobility. Specific examples of cultural destructiveness in schools include English-only policies that prohibit students from using their native language at school, Bureau of Indian Affairs schools, dress policies that single out specific ethnic groups, and tracking programs that systematically allocate specific ethnic groups to low-achieving courses that limit students' opportunities.

## ■ Cultural Incapacity

The next point on the continuum describes organizational practices or individual behaviors that show extreme bias, belief in the superiority of a dominant group, or belief in the inferiority of subordinate groups. One example of cultural incapacity is believing that it is inherently better to be heterosexual than homosexual. Organizations or individuals exemplifying cultural incapacity are often characterized by ignorance as well as either a dislike or an unrealistic fear of people who differ from the dominant group. Cultural incapacity virtually guarantees limited opportunities and can lead to *learned helplessness*, which is people's belief that they are powerless to help themselves because of their repeated experiences of disempowerment.

Historical examples include the Oriental Exclusion Acts, which were restrictive immigration laws targeting Asians and Pacific Islanders, and the Jim Crow laws that denied African Americans basic human rights. Other examples include discriminatory hiring practices, generally lower expectations of performance for dominated groups, and subtle messages to people who are not members of the dominant group conveying that they are not valued or welcomed.

Cultural incapacity is also exhibited by window-dressing and tokenism, such as putting one or two members of a dominated group in highly visible positions to prove that the organization is open and inclusive. Individuals may respond to members of emerging majority groups based on stereotypic characteristics. Cultural incapacity assumes, for example, that all African American families are poor or that the Latina who has been hired recently would be a role model for Latinas, without recognizing that all children can profit from having role models from other cultural groups. Other examples include failing to hold accountable any members of minority groups who are not performing well or making rules against hate speech instead of having a curriculum that teaches the cherishing of history, cultures, and languages that are different.

～≈∿

At Coolidge Middle School, Derek effectively teaches children from diverse ethnic and socioeconomic backgrounds, but down the hall, Brittney, a second-year teacher, is unsuccessful with and unhappy about having to teach "that kind of child," referring to various children from the local community. DeLois, Derek, and several other teachers at Coolidge Middle School organize their students by reading levels, continuously moving children to the next highest reading level as they progress through the year. By June, their top groups are quite large. On the other hand, Brittney is among the many other teachers in the school who organize reading levels at the beginning of the year and keep the students in the same groups all year long, regardless of how much individual students progress.

～≈∿

## ■ Cultural Blindness

The third point on the continuum, cultural blindness, is paradoxical for some people. Cultural blindness is the belief that color and culture make no difference and that all people are the same. For many educators, that is the goal of a diversity program. The values and behaviors of the dominant culture are presumed to be universally applicable and beneficial. The intention of the culturally blind educator is to avoid discriminating—that is, to avoid making an issue of the differences manifested among the students.

Culturally blind educators view students' cultural differences to be indications of disobedience, noncompliance, or other deficiencies. They assume that members of dominated cultures do not meet the cultural expectations of the dominant group because they lack either the cultural traditions of the dominant culture (i.e., they're culturally deficient) or the desire to achieve (i.e., they're morally deficient). In reality, the system works only for the most highly assimilated groups. As a result of many educators' blindness to the differences among students, many students are left feeling discounted or invisible in school.

In our conversations with educators who prize their own cultural blindness, they are always painfully unaware of how their behavior affects their students. It is difficult for well-intentioned people who are committed to fairness to believe that they sometimes hurt their students. It is important not to focus on intentions but to become aware of the effect that one's behavior can have on others.

It is important for educators to recognize that students from dominated groups view their differences as important aspects of their identity. Their differences also affect how they are viewed both within their respective communities and in the larger society. These educators are surprised to learn that black children would not choose to be anything other than black, that Cambodian children are proud of their language, and that the child in the wheelchair does not feel disadvantaged.

Culturally blind educators may teach that Abraham Lincoln is a hero to all African Americans, assume that Cinco de Mayo is a holiday for all Spanish-speaking countries, and believe that girls are predisposed toward the arts rather than the sciences. Other examples of cultural blindness in schools include leadership training that fails to address issues of diversity and failure to articulate the school's cultural expectations to all students, staff, and faculty members.

### ■ Cultural Precompetence

Cultural precompetence is an awareness of limitations in one's intercultural interactions. Culturally precompetent people engage proactively and effectively with cultures other than their own, but they are aware that they don't know enough and often are the victims of their own cultural faux pas. They might, for example, believe that the accomplishment of a single goal or activity fulfills any perceived obligation toward the dominated groups in their district and may point with pride at the hiring of one disabled person or the serving of a soul food meal during Black History Month as proof of a school's cultural proficiency. Other examples include recruiting members of underrepresented groups but not providing support for them or making any adaptation to the differences they bring to the workplace, and dismissing as overly sensitive someone who complains about culturally inappropriate comments.

■ Cultural Competence

At the point of cultural competence, schools and educators accept and respect differences, carefully attend to the dynamics of difference, continually assess their own cultural knowledge and beliefs, continuously expand their cultural knowledge and resources, and make various adaptations of their own belief systems, policies, and practices. This is the first point on the continuum that fully addresses the needs of diverse environments. Culturally competent educators incorporate culturally appropriate behavior in performance appraisals; advocate for changes in policies, practices, and procedures throughout the school and community; and speak on issues about handicapped persons, Gay Men, Lesbians, and other underrepresented groups when no members of these groups are visibly present. Chapter 4 has an expansive discussion of the essential elements of cultural competence.

■ Cultural Proficiency

Cultural proficiency is more than the esteeming of culture. A culturally competent educator functions effectively in several different cultural contexts. The culturally proficient educator knows how to learn about culture. Confronted with the challenges of a new cultural setting, culturally proficient educators know how to find out what they need to know in an inoffensive manner, and they know what they need to teach about themselves. A culturally proficient educator has a palpable sense of his or her own culture and has the self-awareness to discern what about themselves may be offensive to others. The culturally proficient leader seeks to add to the knowledge base of culturally proficient practices by conducting research, developing new culturally appropriate approaches, and taking advantage of opportunities to increase his or her awareness and knowledge of others. Culturally proficient leaders unabashedly advocate for culturally proficient practices in all arenas.

## Going Further

1. Read the teachers' statements in the vignette at the beginning of this chapter. Where would you plot each remark along the continuum?

2. Reflect on your own life and think of situations or events that emerged because of the diversity—or absence of it—in that particular environment. Plot each event or situation along the cultural proficiency continuum.

3. Look again at the Diversity Lifeline that you drew after reading Chapter 1. Where on your continuum would you plot the various points along the cultural proficiency continuum?

4. Think of a time when you did not respond well to the diversity in your environment. Where would you plot your own behavior in that situation?

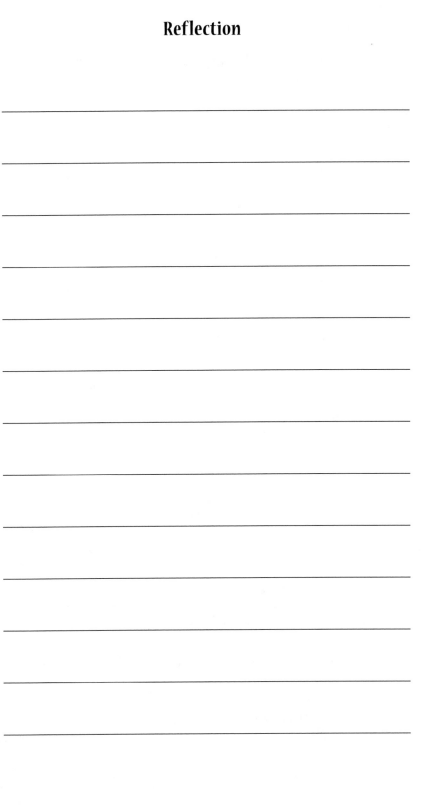

# Reflection

**Activity 3.1:**

# The Cultural Proficiency Continuum

■ Purpose

To identify examples of the points on the continuum

■ Expertise of Facilitator

Moderate

■ Readiness of Group

Intermediate

■ Time Needed

30 minutes

■ Materials

Chart paper
Marking pens
Masking tape
or
Transparencies, pens, and overhead projector

■ Briefing

Let's look at the cultural proficiency continuum presented in this chapter and on Response Sheet 3.1.1 to see what meaning it has in our lives. We are going to develop some examples of the points on the cultural proficiency continuum.

■ Process

1. Divide participants into four groups.
2. Assign one of the first four points on the continuum to each group.

3. Ask the groups to generate examples for the point they were assigned and for cultural competence and cultural proficiency.

4. Have participants categorize their lists of examples as district policies and practices, school policies and practices, or classroom statements and actions.

5. If using chart paper, have participants post their work and then take the time to look at one another's work. If using an overhead projector, have participants present their work in turn.

■ Debriefing

1. What questions of clarification do you have for the other groups?

2. What trends do you see across the data?

3. What do these examples say about the work that must be done in this district or school?

4. How does it feel to look at the district in this way?

■ Variation

Focus the discussion on classroom behavior instead of on district or school behavior.

■ Variation

1. Label six pieces of chart paper with the six points on the continuum. Put one point at the top of each chart. Hang the chart paper on the wall.

2. Distribute a marker and about 10 sheets of 4" x 6" Post-It notes to each participant.

■ Briefing

Think about negative and positive comments about students that you have heard from other educators. Write one comment on each of your Post-It notes.

■ Process

1. Invite participants to work individually, writing examples for any—or all—points on the continuum.

2. After people have written comments on their Post-It notes, invite them to place them on the appropriate chart.

3. As you, the facilitator, read the comments, you may need to move some of the Post-It notes to more appropriate charts. Participants tend to place their comments higher on the continuum than they deserve to be.

4. Encourage participants to mill around, reading all of the comments.

■ Debriefing

1. What did you notice as you wrote the comments?

2. What did you notice as you read the other comments?

3. What did you feel, think, or wonder about the comments or the process?

4. What does this say about you?

5. What does this say about your school or district?

**Response Sheet 3.1.1:**

# The Cultural Proficiency Continuum: Looking at Differences

Cultural proficiency is a way of being represented by the set of values and behaviors in an individual or the set of policies and practices in an organization that create the appropriate mindset and approach to effectively responding to the issues caused by diversity. A culturally proficient organization interacts effectively with its employees, its clients, and its community. Culturally proficient people may not know all there is to know about others who are different from them, but they know how to take advantage of teachable moments, how to ask questions without offending, and how to create an environment that is welcoming to diversity and to change. There are six points along the continuum.

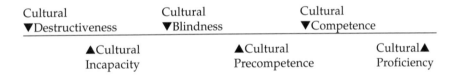

| Cultural ▼Destructiveness | Cultural ▼Blindness | Cultural ▼Competence |
|---|---|---|
| ▲Cultural Incapacity | ▲Cultural Precompetence | Cultural▲ Proficiency |

■ Cultural Destructiveness: *See the Difference, Stomp It Out*

Cultural destructiveness comprises any policy, practice, or behavior that effectively eliminates all vestiges of other people's cultures. It may be manifested through an organization's policies and practices or through an individual's values and behaviors. Sometimes these destructive actions occur intentionally:

- Social reproduction—one group recreates itself, resulting in the exclusion of most other groups

- Discrimination against observable manifestations of ethnicity, such as accent, hair, and adornments

- No institutional support for people whose socioeconomic class affects their work

■ Cultural Incapacity: *See the Difference, Make It Wrong*

This comprises treatment of members of dominated groups based on stereotypes and with the belief that the dominant group is inherently superior. It includes any policy, practice, or behavior that disempowers people who differ from the dominant group. Examples include the disproportionate allocation of resources, discrimination against people on the basis of whether they "know their place," and belief in the supremacy of the dominant culture. Other examples are discriminatory hiring practices, subtle messages to people who are not members of the dominant group that they are not valued or welcome, and generally lower expectations of performance for minority group members. Other examples include the following:

- Questioning the qualifications of people of color
- Assuming that affirmative action appointees are not proficient
- Not perceiving people of color as successful unless they are bicultural
- Establishing committees for compliance, not for commitment, to a goal

■ Cultural Blindness: *See the Difference, Act Like You Don't*

Failure to see or to acknowledge that differences among and between groups often do make a difference to the groups and the individuals who are members of those groups. This is the belief that color and culture make no difference and that all people are the same. Values and behaviors of the dominant culture are presumed to be universally applicable and beneficial. It is also assumed that members of minority cultures do not meet the cultural expectations of the dominant group because of some cultural deficiency or lack of desire to achieve, rather than the fact that the system works only for the most assimilated of the minority groups. Examples are

- Using the behavior of a "model minority" as the criterion for judging all minority groups
- Management training that does not address diversity
- Not articulating cultural expectations of the organization to all of its members

■ Cultural Precompetence:
*See the Difference, Respond to It Inappropriately*

People and organizations that are culturally precompetent recognize that their skills and practices are limited when interacting with other cultural groups. They may have made some changes in their approaches to the issues arising from diversity, but they are aware that they need assistance and more information. They may also

- Recruit people who are not part of the mainstream culture but not provide them with any support or make any adaptation to their differences
- Show discomfort and unwillingness to confront or hold accountable people from dominated groups who are not performing well
- Make rules instead of teaching appropriate behavior, such as rules against hate speech

■ Cultural Competence:
*See the Difference, Understand the Difference That Difference Makes*

Cultural competence involves use of the essential elements as the standards for individual behavior and organizational practice. This includes acceptance and respect for difference; continuing self-assessment regarding culture; careful attention to the dynamics of difference; continuous expansion of cultural knowledge and resources; and a variety of adaptations to belief systems, policies, and practices. Other forms of cultural competence are

- Performance standards for culturally appropriate behavior
- Modeling appropriate behaviors
- Risk taking, such as speaking against injustice, even when doing so may cause tension and conflict

## ■ Cultural Proficiency:
### *See the Differences and Respond Positively and Affirmingly*

Cultural proficiency involves knowing how to learn and teach about different groups; having the capacity to teach and to learn about differences in ways that acknowledge and honor all the people and the groups they represent; holding culture in high esteem; and seeking to add to the knowledge base of culturally proficient practice by conducting research, developing new approaches based on culture, and increasing the knowledge of others about culture and the dynamics of difference.

•

•

•

**Response Sheet 3.1.2:**

## The Cultural Proficiency Continuum Chart

| Continuum | Examples |
|---|---|
| Cultural Proficiency | |
| Cultural Competence | |
| Cultural Precompetence | |
| Cultural Blindness | |
| Cultural Incapacity | |
| Cultural Destruction | |

**Activity 3.2:**

# Circle of History

■ Purpose

To share the collective history of a group or an organization with all of its members. This activity will help participants to understand how far they have come or how certain norms and traditions in the organization were established. During this activity, more mature participants and skilled facilitators will also identify the cultural expectations of the group.

■ Expertise of Facilitator

Moderate

■ Readiness of Group

Beginning

■ Time Needed

1–3 hours, depending on the age of the organization and the number of participants

■ Materials

A room large enough for all participants to sit in one circle or a large horseshoe

Four or five chairs in the middle of the circle or at the open end of the horseshoe

■ Briefing

You are going to share the history of this group by telling your stories. Each person in turn will talk about the organization from the perspective of "when and where I entered."

■ Process

1. Ask participants to sit in the circle according to when each became a member of the group or organization. For most people, this will be the year they were hired. For volunteers or parents, it will be the date they first had an encounter with the school or district.

2. Notice any patterns as you look down the line. In some groups, for example, the people who have been there the longest will be white males. Those who have been in the organization the least amount of time will be women or emerging majorities. Encourage the participants to articulate any other patterns they may observe.

3. Starting with those people who have been in the organization the longest, invite them to take the chairs in the middle of the circle or at the end of the horseshoe.

4. Ask participants to talk about the organization and tell what it was like when they joined, how they learned about it or decided to become a part of it, who was there, what were the rules, and other information. As the story progresses, new participants will take the seats in the center and those who have spoken will sit in the circle.

5. If someone entered the organization, left, and then returned, he or she may take a speaker's seat a second time, when his or her story once again becomes part of the chronology.

6. If necessary, prompt the speakers so that they provide necessary details or redirect the speakers if they get off track or get more engrossed in their personal stories rather than in the organization's story.

■ Debriefing

1. What did you notice?
2. What surprised you?
3. What did you learn? About yourself? About others? About your organization?
4. What do you understand now that was puzzling before?
5. What shall we do now that we all know our collective history?

■ Variation

You may want to videotape this session.

■ Variation

1. Affix chart paper to the walls of a room.
2. Segment the charts into increments of time—years or decades as appropriate.
3. Provide markers, Post-It notes, labels, and other materials and ask the participants to fill in the time line, noting the major events in the life of the organization.

**Activity 3.3:**

# Human Relations Needs Assessment

■ Purpose

The Human Relations Needs Assessment Instrument surveys a respondent's opinion about cultural relations in a school or district.

■ Expertise of Facilitator

Extensive

■ Readiness of Group

Beginning

■ Process

Arrange the items in random sequence for administration. For analysis purposes, organize the items according to the five essential elements of cultural proficiency: assessment of cultural knowledge, value for diversity, ability to manage the dynamics of difference, adaptability to diversity, and ability to institutionalize cultural knowledge.

The instrument can be used at least two ways. First, it can be administered to a group as a preintervention guide. Second, it can be used to contrast the opinions among groups, for example, educators, students, parents, and businesspeople in your community. However you choose to use the instrument, it should never be used as a diagnostic instrument, only as information to guide a school's planning.

We have used this instrument with an entire school district, combining the data from the instrument with other data collected. For example, you could audit district policies through document analyses and selected personnel interviews; we conducted a curriculum and instruction audit by reviewing documents, conducting interviews, and making school visits, and we analyzed newspaper and archival materials for the past 15 years. All data were analyzed using three sets of criteria: the district's core values, the five essential elements of cultural proficiency, and our posing the question, "How are they doing?" These data then became the frame for commendations and recommendations regarding district policies and procedures, curriculum and instruction, school relationships, and community relationships.

■ Variation

Another use for the instrument is in combination with other data collection instruments and techniques to gauge the progress of university students in a teacher training program.

**Response Sheet 3.3.1:**

# Human Relations Needs Assessment Instrument

1 = Rarely, 2 = Occasionally, 3 = Sometimes, 4 = Often, 5 = Usually

**School Districts Should . . .     This District Does . .**

## Assessment of cultural knowledge.

1. Have a policy against racist and sexist jokes, slurs, and language

          1  2  3  4  5  NA       1  2  3  4  5  NA

2. Impose sanctions on those who use racist or sexist jokes, slurs, and language

          1  2  3  4  5  NA       1  2  3  4  5  NA

3. Provide opportunities for people to describe their cultural groups to others

          1  2  3  4  5  NA       1  2  3  4  5  NA

4. Teach people the effect that their ethnicity and gender have on those around them

          1  2  3  4  5  NA       1  2  3  4  5  NA

5. Examine organizational policies for unintentional discrimination

          1  2  3  4  5  NA       1  2  3  4  5  NA

6. Explicate clearly its norms, values, and cultural expectations

          1  2  3  4  5  NA       1  2  3  4  5  NA

## Value for diversity

1. Have a formal selection process for materials that are inclusive

          1  2  3  4  5  NA       1  2  3  4  5  NA

2. Display materials that have culturally diverse images

          1  2  3  4  5  NA       1  2  3  4  5  NA

3. Sponsor activities to encourage making acquaintances with people of different cultural groups

          1  2  3  4  5  NA       1  2  3  4  5  NA

4. Take overt actions to hire people at all levels to represent a diverse workforce

          1  2  3  4  5  NA       1  2  3  4  5  NA

5. Establish policies that support diversity

          1  2  3  4  5  NA       1  2  3  4  5  NA

6. Promote activities that value the commonalities and differences among people

1  2  3  4  5  NA                    1  2  3  4  5  NA

7. Promote activities that recognize that there are differences within ethnic groups

1  2  3  4  5  NA                    1  2  3  4  5  NA

8. Promote activities that recognize that each ethnic group has its own strengths and needs

1  2  3  4  5  NA                    1  2  3  4  5  NA

## Ability to manage the dynamics of difference

1.  Teach people how to ask others appropriately about their cultural practices

1  2  3  4  5  NA                    1  2  3  4  5  NA

2.  Acknowledge that conflict is a normal phenomenon

1  2  3  4  5  NA                    1  2  3  4  5  NA

3.  Use effective strategies for intervening in conflict situations

1  2  3  4  5  NA                    1  2  3  4  5  NA

4.  Teach collaborative problem-solving techniques

1  2  3  4  5  NA                    1  2  3  4  5  NA

5.  Regularly review policies to ensure that there are no subtle discriminatory practices

1  2  3  4  5  NA                    1  2  3  4  5  NA

6.  Hold educators accountable for demonstrating high expectations

1  2  3  4  5  NA                    1  2  3  4  5  NA

7.  Hold all faculty and staff accountable for their performance

1  2  3  4  5  NA                    1  2  3  4  5  NA

## Adaptability to diversity

1. Develop policies that promote inclusive, relational organization culture

1  2  3  4  5  NA                    1  2  3  4  5  NA

2. Have policies that prohibit discrimination

1  2  3  4  5  NA                    1  2  3  4  5  NA

3. Sanction, when appropriate, those whose behaviors conflict with practices that promote diversity

1  2  3  4  5  NA                    1  2  3  4  5  NA

4. Encourage students and school employees to talk about differences without making judgments

1  2  3  4  5  NA                    1  2  3  4  5  NA

5. Encourage cooperative learning strategies as a technique to get students to work and play together

1  2  3  4  5  NA                    1  2  3  4  5  NA

6. Teach students in their native language

       1 2 3 4 5 NA          1 2 3 4 5 NA

7. Employ and promote educators who reflect the ethnic and cultural makeup of the student body

       1 2 3 4 5 NA          1 2 3 4 5 NA

## *Ability to institutionalize cultural knowledge*

1. Provide opportunities for learning about one's own culture

       1 2 3 4 5 NA          1 2 3 4 5 NA

2. Provide opportunities for learning about others' cultures

       1 2 3 4 5 NA          1 2 3 4 5 NA

3. Provide classes on different cultures for all students

       1 2 3 4 5 NA          1 2 3 4 5 NA

4. Provide workshops on different cultures for all employees

       1 2 3 4 5 NA          1 2 3 4 5 NA

5. Have policies that mandate learning about other ethnic groups

       1 2 3 4 5 NA          1 2 3 4 5 NA

6. Teach that ethnic groups often communicate in different ways

       1 2 3 4 5 NA          1 2 3 4 5 NA

7. Teach how to acknowledge the differences among people based on ethnicity

       1 2 3 4 5 NA          1 2 3 4 5 NA

8. Teach how to acknowledge the difference among people based on physical abilities and invisible differences

       1 2 3 4 5 NA          1 2 3 4 5 NA

9. Teach how to acknowledge the differences among people based on gender

       1 2 3 4 5 NA          1 2 3 4 5 NA

10. Provide a process for developing cultural understanding among all groups

       1 2 3 4 5 NA          1 2 3 4 5 NA

11. Ensure that the cultural groups within the community are represented on advisory groups (e.g., PTA)

       1 2 3 4 5 NA          1 2 3 4 5 NA

12. Ensure that the cultural groups within the community are represented in decision-making groups

       1 2 3 4 5 NA          1 2 3 4 5 NA

# 4

# The Second Tool, Behavioral Competencies: The Essential Elements of Cultural Proficiency

*Culture is a problem-solving resource we need to draw on, not a problem to be solved.*

—Terry Cross

At Rolling Meadows High School, the faculty curriculum committee was charged with assessing the extent to which the school's curriculum was aligned with the emerging Social Studies Standards. The committee is composed of new and experienced teachers, an administrator, the school counselor, and parents from the School Site Council. Dina Turner, the principal, is the chair of the task force studying the social science standards.

Also on the task force are teachers, Celeste and Bobby, and a parent, Barbara Latimer. The diversity consultant, James Harris, had introduced the five essential elements early in the planning process and received enthusiastic support for using them to frame this planning.

"I see this as a very important task, one that is going to take considerable time and study," said Dina as they began the work of the task force.

"Boy, I couldn't agree more," said Celeste, "and as a relatively seasoned teacher, I am so pleased to have Bobby on our team. Bobby has been a history teacher here and in his role as counselor, he remains the one most knowledgeable about the breadth and depth of our curriculum."

"It seems to me," said Mrs. Latimer, "that a place to begin is to get from Bobby a sense of how balanced he sees our curriculum. In other words, Bobby, what do you see as our strong points and what are the points of omission?"

After a moment of reflection, Bobby responded, "I'm comfortable with that as a starting point, but I want you to know that I don't know everything. For example, since the terrorists attacked the World Trade Center, I've realized how little I know about the Middle East, the Muslim religion, or our country's policies that affect these issues. One of the things I see coming from this study is that even though our school has no Middle Eastern or Muslim students that I know of, it will be important for our curriculum to be inclusive of them."

"Yes, the new state standards for social studies," offered Dina, "are very explicit on our students being prepared to live and function in an interdependent, global world. I am sure, Bobby, that your concerns are shared by many of us. We need that kind of openness to do this work well."

✿

The cultural proficiency continuum takes a broad look at the range of behaviors and attitudes that address the issues that emerge in a diverse environment. It gives you a common language for describing situations and encounters that you might experience or observe. The essential elements enable you to go deeper to explore the values, behaviors, policies, and practices at the end of the continuum that describe positive and healthy responses to diversity.

With this tool, you have behavioral markers with which you can develop curricular standards for learners and performance standards for teachers, administrators, and staff. Our clients have used the essential elements as the basis for establishing competencies in performance appraisals, for developing objectives in schoolwide plans, and for framing their core values. After making a commitment to become a culturally proficient organization, many of our clients have used the essential elements as the basis for designing training and staff development.

The essential elements of cultural proficiency are behavioral standards that can be applied to both individuals and organizations. Remember that organizations have dynamic cultures that both influence and are influenced by the behaviors and values of the people within the organizations. It is easy to observe the behavior of people to see if they comply with the standards set by the elements. It is also important to observe the culture and the practices of the organization. It is often here that one will find apparently benign policies that unintentionally discriminate. As with the other tools of cultural proficiency, the essential elements can be used effectively with both the organization and the individual.

## The Essential Elements of Cultural Proficiency

### Assess Culture: *Name the Differences*

- Recognize how your culture affects the culture of others.
- Describe your own culture and the cultural norms of your organization.
- Understand how the culture of your organization affects those with different cultures.

### Value Diversity: *Claim Your Differences*

- Celebrate and encourage the presence of a variety of people in all activities.
- Recognize differences as diversity rather than as inappropriate responses to the environment.
- Accept that each culture finds some values and behaviors more important than others.

### Manage the Dynamics of Difference: *Frame the Conflicts Caused by Differences*

- Learn effective strategies for resolving conflict, particularly among people whose cultural backgrounds and values differ.
- Understand the effect that historic distrust has on present-day interactions.
- Realize that you may misjudge others' actions based on learned expectations.

### Adapt to Diversity: *Change to Make a Difference*

- Change the way things are done to acknowledge the differences that are present in the staff, clients, and community.
- Develop skills for intercultural communication.
- Institutionalize cultural interventions for conflicts and confusion caused by the dynamics of difference.

### Institutionalize Cultural Knowledge: *Train About Differences*

- Incorporate cultural knowledge into the mainstream of the organization.
- Teach the origins of stereotypes and prejudices.
- For staff development and education, integrate into your systems information and skills that enable all to interact effectively in a variety of intercultural situations.

ఎ

Cultural proficiency has not always been the approach to diversity that was supported by the Coolidge school board. It took several years of seeing the tools used successfully in individual classrooms and schools before the board members understood that culturally proficiency was applicable to their work as well. Two years ago, after middle school principal Richard Diaz heard that the board of education voted not to embrace cultural proficiency as a district policy, he decided to include the essential elements of cultural proficiency as standards for both his teachers and their students. He encouraged the teachers to meet regularly in cohort groups to offer one another support and encouragement for implementing their goals for cultural proficiency.

To move his school toward cultural proficiency, Richard carefully studied the essential elements, then decided to start with the element *adapting to diversity* because many of his staff members fervently resisted any change and could not see how their behaviors prevented all children from learning. Their practices ranged from cultural incapacity to cultural blindness. At the same time, Richard had a couple of teachers like Derek and DeLois who truly valued diversity and who were willing to chair committees to develop ideas for manifesting a value for diversity throughout the campus.

Initially, many of Richard's staff members resisted change because they didn't think they had done anything wrong. Given that resistance, Richard spent time allowing his teachers to grieve their perceived losses and he gently pushed them toward new ways of doing things. He made a case for change by showing the resisters how some of their behaviors had damaged the students, the school's relationships with the community, and the school's reputation in the district. He then worked to convince his teachers that the proposed change was integral to the school program, not just a supplement to it.

He is pleased to report that despite several false starts, teachers began to recognize language and attitudes that were, at best, pre-competent. To insure long-term success, he has created an environment where the faculty experiences some immediate success with a few "feel good" cultural assemblies. He knew this was superficial, but it created momentum and got the resisters talking. After a discussion with his faculty, facilitated by James, the diversity consultant, the teachers have been seeking ways to address the issues of diversity in their classrooms.

Grace Ishmael, the principal at Coolidge High School, decided to focus on the element *managing the dynamics of difference*. Some of Grace's resisters declared that because they were not directly involved in any of the conflicts raised by the Citizen's Human Relations Council, they should not be punished by having to attend any workshops. Grace surmounted the resistance by reframing the situation. She pointed out that current activities were not punishment; they were simply a response to changes in the school's culture that heretofore had not been acknowledged well. This was an opportunity to show students and parents what good teachers they were and how well they could respond to their students' needs; otherwise, they were disempowering themselves and their students with behaviors that could only be described as cultural incapacity. They all needed to learn how to recognize conflicts caused by cultural differences, and they all needed to find appropriate ways to respond to them.

❧

## ■ Assess Your Culture

Cultural proficiency is an inside-out response to the issues that emerge in a diverse environment. Rather than talking about "them," the culturally proficient leader starts with herself by asking: *What do you bring to the environment that may serve as a barrier to healthy interactions? What do you bring that is manifested in the way you look, the language you speak, and the cultures with which you identify that will assist in creating a culturally proficient school climate?* Understanding culture in its broadest definition, the culturally proficient leader is cognizant of her own culture, the culture of her school and district, and the culture of her students and their families. Assessment of culture results in knowledge that is deeper than the ability to name the various groups represented in the district. Culturally proficient leaders also understand how these groups affect one another and influence the culture of the schools and district.

Culturally proficient leaders analyze themselves and their environments so that they have a palpable sense of their own culture and the culture of their schools. As a culturally proficient educator, you start with yourself and your own school. You do not assume that everyone will share your values, nor do you assume that everyone knows what behaviors are expected and affirmed in a culturally proficient school; in fact, most people are simply unaware. Therefore, you understand how the culture of your school and district affects those whose culture is different. You will state and explain the cultural norms of each classroom, school, or district so that people whose cultural norms differ will know how they must adapt to the new environment. By recognizing how the school's culture affects other people, you will gain the information you need to make adjustments in style or processes so that all people feel comfortable and welcomed.

## ■ Value Diversity

There are many diversity programs that use the word "tolerance" in their titles. Tolerance is a place to start; on the cultural proficiency continuum, behaviors and policies that are tolerant of diverse groups fall around the point of cultural incapacity. Reflect on how you might respond to a baby: You *tolerate* that you have to clean up the baby's messes. You *accept* that the baby makes those messes And you *value* the baby. As a culturally proficient leader, you are delighted that you have such a heterogeneous mix of students, teachers, and staff. You accept that in such an environment, there are many challenges that you must face, and you tolerate the fact that not everyone is as committed as you are to creating a positive learning experience for everyone.

Consequently, you are proactive in involving a wide variety of people from all areas of the school in creating programs, developing appropriate policies, and establishing standards for performance and learning. You demonstrate your value for diversity by openly addressing the need to serve all people effectively. As a culturally proficient school leader, you provide leadership in developing policy statements on diversity and ensuring that the school and district's mission and goal statements address the issues that emerge in diverse environments. You take these statements and act on them by communicating in inclusive ways to marginalized groups and by directing human and financial resources into curriculum, training, and other school endeavors to address their needs proactively.

## ■ Manage the Dynamics of Difference

Human beings, in general, have difficulty with conflict; the humans in the United States are no exception. We are taught to deny, ignore, marginalize, and circumvent problems rather than confront and resolve them. In a diverse environment, the problems caused by conflicts are compounded by the cultural lenses through which the situations are perceived. Consider the conflicts that you have with people you know—people with whom you have long-standing and intimate relationships. A school that values diversity is not without conflict. Imagine the increased level of complexity of the conflicts when you involve people who do not share your history, language, lifestyle, or worldview. Reflect on the difficulty of teachers and site administrators who are required to mediate conflicts daily without the necessary skills. This is where the culturally proficient leader starts: acknowledging the current situation and then providing the information and skills to the people who must survive in these environments.

A culturally proficient leader wants more than survival for his colleagues and students. He wants them to thrive. As a culturally proficient leader, you acknowledge that conflict is a natural state of affairs and you develop effective, culturally proficient strategies for managing the conflict that occurs. Once you have embraced the value for diversity and have begun to articulate the cultural expectations of your school or classroom, the differences among the school's community members will be more apparent. As a leader, you will provide training sessions and facilitate group discussions so that people will understand the effect of historical distrust on present-day interactions. You realize that the actions of others may be misjudged based on learned expectations, and you implement programs and processes that create new cultural expectations for the culturally proficient community.

## ■ Adapt to Diversity

To move toward culturally proficiency is to honor relationships. The best dancers always adjust their style to the movements of their partners. The dance of diversity requires the same kind of adjustment. When engaging in a long-term committed relationship, the partners implicitly promise to change. They both know that the success of the relationship is tied to their ability to adjust and adapt to one another. Each partner retains what is most important and also releases habits and rituals that are no longer necessary or that are not productive in this relationship. In the best of relationships, the partners do not compromise—they are transformed. That is the goal of cultural proficiency. The organization examines its

core culture and acknowledges what it will seek to retain and then artic-
ulates the values and the cultural expectations to all who are in the organization. At the same time, when new people are invited into the organization, they are not invited to be guests but rather to become members of
the community. This means that the community makes space for them
and makes changes to adapt to the unique needs of the new community
members.

To adapt to diversity is first to recognize that everyone changes. With
some approaches to diversity, the groups that are not a part of the dominant culture are expected to change and to adapt to the culture of the
dominant group. The culturally proficient approach to diversity invites
and encourages everyone to change. Once you make the commitment to
cultural proficiency, you help all aspects of the school community to
adapt. You help the host groups change by becoming more conscious of
cultural norms that deny the value of diversity and the goal of cultural
proficiency. You encourage the newer or less dominant groups to change
because they know clearly the cultural expectations of the school. You
enable the school or district to change by using culturally proficient
behaviors as the standards for performance appraisal and as the basis for
analyzing and revising school and district policies.

## ■ Institutionalize Cultural Knowledge

When a school or district takes on a diversity initiative, it is marked by
focus groups, interviews, and training. As the program—or, in this case,
the tools—for responding to the issues that are found in diverse environments becomes integrated into the culture of the school or the district, it
is no longer seen as something external or supplemental to the "real"
work of the school. The processes for teaching, learning, and growing are
institutionalized. The classrooms, the schools, and the district have all
become learning communities.

As a culturally proficient school leader, you prize ongoing staff
development that promotes a commitment to lifelong learning. You understand that the exponential growth of information and technology dic-
tates the need for continuous upgrading of knowledge and skills. You
readily integrate into systems learning the information and skills that
enable educators and students to interact effectively in a variety of
intercultural situations. You affirm the importance of cultural knowledge not only for the climate of the school or district but also as a knowledge base on which all students will continue to build throughout their
lives.

Table 4.1 summarizes the roles and responsibilities of all leaders in
the school community as they work to become culturally proficient. As a

culturally proficient leader, you also realize that students need knowledge about both the cultural practices of different people and groups and the experiences that many of these people and groups have had with stereotyping and prejudice. With this awareness, you provide your school communities with an understanding of how prejudices and stereotypes are developed and maintained in the society. You also help students and colleagues develop skills for eliminating prejudices through various human interactions, curricula, and instructional programs in schools.

## Roles of School Leaders

As a culturally proficient school leader, you need to understand what currently exists before you can begin to understand what *should* exist (Giroux, 1992b). Table 4.1 provides a matrix by which to examine schools. The first column lists the most typical roles of school leaders (school district administrators, site administrators, teachers, parents and other community members, and school board members) and identifies the function of each role in creating a culturally proficient school or district. The other columns represent the five essential elements of cultural proficiency and describe behaviors related to each of the elements. In constructing this table and the discussion that follows, we have drawn on the works of Argyris (1990), Banks (1994), Senge et al. (1994), and Wheatley (1992). Their combined works affirm this inside-out approach to culturally proficient leadership. Together, they provide two frameworks: (a) an *inwardly oriented framework* for examining assumptions about those who differ from one another, for understanding how schools function, and for seeing how each school's culture facilitates learning for some students and impedes others from learning; and (b) an *outwardly directed framework* for discovering how and why educators learn about others, engage in team learning, and examine data for the purpose of making informed changes in school practices.

In culturally proficient schools, each participant has a definite role to play. The roles overlap in some instances, but they retain distinctive characteristics. Some people will be more proficient at executing their distinctive roles than will others. Barriers to culturally proficient leadership arise from myriad sources. For example, in school districts that have traditionally failed to involve parents and community members in school decision-making processes, part of the movement toward cultural proficiency will be to help parents and community members learn their roles. Some of them will be reticent to be involved, whereas others may

**TABLE 4.1** Responsibilities of Culturally Proficient School Leaders

| Roles | Essential Elements of Cultural Proficiency | | | | |
|---|---|---|---|---|---|
| | Assess Culture | Value Diversity | Manage the Dynamics of Difference | Adapt to Diversity | Institutionalize Cultural Knowledge |
| Teachers *Observe and Instruct* | Assess own culture and its effect on students, assess the culture of the classroom, support students in discovering their own cultural identities | Teach all subjects from a culturally inclusive perspective, insist on classroom language and behaviors that values differences | Use conflict as object lessons, teach students a variety of ways to resolve conflict | Learn own instructional and interpersonal styles, develop processes to enhance them so that they meet the needs of all students, help students to understand why things are done in a particular way | Teach students appropriate language for asking questions about other people's cultures and telling other people about theirs |
| Site Administrators *Lead and Supervise* | Assess the culture of the site and articulate the cultural expectations to all who interact there | Articulate a culturally proficient vision for the site, establish standards for holding teachers and staff accountable for the vision | Provide training and support systems for conflict management, help faculty and staff learn to distinguish between behavioral problems and cultural differences | Examine policies and practices for overt and intentional discrimination and change current practices when appropriate | Model and monitor schoolwide and classroom practices |

(Continued)

**TABLE 4.1** (Continued)

*Essential Elements of Cultural Proficiency*

| Roles | Assess Culture | Value Diversity | Manage the Dynamics of Difference | Adapt to Diversity | Institutionalize Cultural Knowledge |
|---|---|---|---|---|---|
| District Administrators *Implement Policy* | Assess culture of the district and the administrator's role in maintaining or changing it | Provide guidelines for culturally proficient practices and establish standards for appraisal | Provide resources for developing and establishing new conflict management strategies including culturally specific mediation techniques | Assess policy and propose changes when appropriate | Propose and implement culturally proficient policies |
| Parents and Community *Articulate Expectations* | Share with school personnel their perceptions of the school's culture and practices | Elect board members who represent cultures in the community | Discern and point out to school personnel the nature and source of conflict when it occurs | Identify policies and practices that need changing | Serve as resources to the formal school leaders |
| School Board Members *Set Policy* | Assess the cultures of the district and the board and the effect of those cultures on the community | Establish standards for culturally proficient practices | Articulate the need and value for culturally specific conflict management and mediation | Review and change policies as the student population changes to maintain culturally proficient environment | Establish all policies from a culturally proficient perspective |

manifest anger at being excluded for so long. Still other parents and community members will clearly articulate their expectations of what they want the school to do for their children.

As a culturally proficient leader, you recognize that silence does not mean a lack of interest or concern, just as anger does not signify parents' irreverence for their children's educators. You will have to develop processes to involve these diverse people in school matters. In addition to responding to these differences, you must remain committed to listening for the messages of wanting to be involved and then providing support for involvement.

In other school districts, role conflicts may pose barriers to cultural proficiency. For example, the recent history between teachers and district administrators may have been so acrimonious that civility is rare. In this situation, too, the culturally proficient leader must listen for messages of wanting to be involved, remembering that the form of the message may not be what is expected from the dominant culture in the community. Leaders in various roles implement cultural proficiency in divergent ways:

- Community leaders and parents communicate to educators what they want their children to gain from their education.
- School board members set school policy that represents the wishes of the community in serving the diverse needs of their children. They work with school leaders to determine policies that ensure the application of the essential elements of cultural proficiency.
- District-level administrators implement the policies of the board of education by acting as a conduit between the school board and the local schools. Not only do they interpret policy for those at the local schools, but they also carry data about local schools back to the district office to inform decision-making about future changes in policies or procedures.
- Site administrators have the responsibility to provide formal leadership at the local school and to supervise for the purpose of providing support to classroom teachers.

Classrooms are where the action is, and classroom teachers have the responsibility to carry out curricular and instructional programs consistent with the district's cultural proficiency policies. They also have the responsibility to observe their students, to raise questions about student needs, and to work with site administrators in gathering data about student achievement and social interactions for the purpose of continuing to improve the educational climate at the school.

The cultural proficiency tools that you will use most often are the essential elements. In order to learn what they are and how they relate to everything you do as an educational leader, you will need to practice applying them to different aspects of your work. In our book, *Culturally Proficient Instruction*, we devote an entire chapter to each one of the elements. In the context of expanding your skills as a culturally proficient leader, we suggest that you spend time with the activities in this chapter.

## Going Further

1. Develop your own descriptions of the essential elements.
2. Review each of the elements; for each one, suggest three activities that would help to reinforce the concepts of that elements.

## Reflection

_____

_____

_____

_____

_____

_____

_____

_____

_____

_____

**Activity 4.1:**

## Exploring Behaviors Along the Continuum

■ Purpose

To reinforce the essential elements of cultural competence and their relationship to the cultural proficiency continuum.

■ Expertise of Facilitator

Moderate

■ Readiness of Group

Intermediate

■ Time Needed

30–60 minutes

■ Materials

Response Sheet 4.1.1: Essential Elements of Cultural Proficiency
Response Sheet 4.1.2: Behaviors Along the Continuum

■ Briefing

Now that you have been introduced to the continuum and the essential elements of cultural competence, let's see how you would describe the behaviors at other points along the continuum

■ Process

1. Introduce or review the essential elements of cultural proficiency.
2. Divide the participants into at least four groups of 3–5 people.
3. Assign each group one point on the continuum to work on.
4. Ask each group to create a short statement that parallels the essential elements and that describes the behavior for their point on the continuum. Each point has one example given.

5. After each small group has finished, ask it to share its responses with the entire group and have the other participants refine their contributions.

## ■ Debriefing

1. How difficult was it to describe each element for the other points on the continuum?
2. How does this add to your understanding of the continuum or the elements?

## ■ Variation

Assign small groups to one empty cell on Response Sheet 4.1.2. This will save time and reduce frustration as they do their work.

**Response Sheet 4.1.1:**

# The Essential Elements of Cultural Proficiency

Cultural proficiency is the set of values and behaviors in an individual or the set of policies and practices in an organization that creates the appropriate mindset and approach to effectively responding to the issues caused by diversity. A culturally proficient organization interacts effectively with its employees, its clients, and its community. Culturally proficient people may not know all there is to know about others who are different from them, but they know how to take advantage of teachable moments, how to ask questions without offending, and how to create an environment that is welcoming to diversity and to change. There are five behavioral elements of cultural proficiency:

■ Assess Culture: Name the Differences

- Recognize how your culture affects others'.
- Describe your own culture and the cultural norms of your organization.
- Understand how the culture of your organization affects those with different cultures.

■ Value Diversity: Claim Your Differences

- Celebrate and encourage the presence of a variety of people in all activities.
- Recognize differences as diversity rather than as inappropriate responses to the environment.
- Accept that each culture finds some values and behaviors more important than others.

■ Manage the Dynamics of Difference: Reframe the Conflicts Caused by Differences

- Learn effective strategies for resolving conflict among people whose cultural backgrounds and values differ.
- Understand the effect that historic distrust has on present-day interactions.

- Realize that you may misjudge others' actions based on learned expectations.

## ■ Adapt to Diversity: Change to Make a Difference

- Change the way things are done to acknowledge the differences that are present in the staff, clients, and community.
- Develop skills for intercultural communication.
- Institutionalize cultural interventions for conflicts and confusion caused by the dynamics of difference.

## ■ Institutionalize Cultural Knowledge: Train About Differences

- Incorporate cultural knowledge into the mainstream of the organization.
- Teach origins of stereotypes and prejudices.
- Integrate into your staff development and education systems information and skills that enable all to interact effectively in a variety of intercultural situations.

**Response Sheet 4.1.2:**

## Behaviors Along the Continuum

| Cultural Destruction | Cultural Incapacity | Cultural Blindness | Cultural Precompetence | Cultural Competence | Cultural Proficiency |
|---|---|---|---|---|---|
| | | Deny culture | | Assess culture | |
| Seek homogeneous uniformity | | | | Value diversity | |
| | Blame others for their problems | | | Manage the dynamics of difference | |
| | | | Make exceptions for those who are different | Adapt to Diversity | |
| | | | | Institutionalize cultural knowledge | Be a learning community |

**Activity 4.2:**

# Understanding the Essential Elements

■ Purpose

To reinforce the essential elements of cultural competence and to begin the process of translating the concepts into individual behaviors and organizational practices.

■ Expertise of Facilitator

Moderate

■ Readiness of Group

Beginning

■ Time Needed

40 minutes

■ Materials

Response Sheet 4.1.1: Essential Elements
Response Sheet 4.2.1: Culturally Proficient Practices
Response Sheet 4.2.2: Activities to Reinforce the Essential Elements

■ Briefing

Now that you have been introduced to the essential elements, let's see what cultural proficiency would look like at this school.

■ Process

1. Introduce or review the essential elements of cultural proficiency on Response Sheet 4.2.1.
2. Divide the participants into groups of 3–5 people.
3. Assign each group one element to work on.

4. Ask each group to describe the behaviors of an individual or the practices of the school by completing one row of Response Sheet 4.2.1. Encourage groups to be as specific as possible.

5. After each group has finished, ask it to share its responses with the entire group and have the other participants add to the list of behaviors and practices.

## ■ Debriefing

1. How difficult was it to describe what each element would look like in our school?

2. Was it easier to describe individual behavior or organizational practices?

3. Did you notice whether people set standards for others or for themselves?

4. How does your list compare to Response Sheet 4.2.2?

5. How would you like to use these lists?

## ■ Variations

1. Focus on a work group, a department, or a classroom.

2. Save the lists for use during schoolwide planning.

3. As you increase your understanding of the elements, add to the lists.

**Response Sheet 4.2.1:**

# Culturally Proficient Practices

| Essential Element | Current Practices | Proposed Practices |
|---|---|---|
| **Assessing Culture**<br>*Naming the Differences*<br><br>Guiding Questions:<br>• What are the unwritten rules in your school?<br>• How do you describe your own culture?<br>• How does your school provide for a variety of learning styles? | | |
| **Valuing Diversity**<br>*Claiming Your Differences*<br><br>Guiding Questions:<br>• How would you describe the diversity in your current professional setting?<br>• How do you react to the term *valuing diversity*?<br>• How do you and your colleagues frame conversations about the learners? | | |
| **Managing the Dynamics of Difference**<br>*Reframing the Differences*<br><br>Guiding Questions:<br>• How do you handle conflict in the classroom?<br>• What skills do you possess to handle conflict?<br>• Describe situations of cross-cultural conflict that may be based on historic distrust. | | |

| Essential Element | Current Practices | Proposed Practices |
|---|---|---|
| **Adapting to Diversity**<br>*Changing for the Differences*<br><br>Guiding Questions:<br>• How have you recently adapted to the needs of a new member?<br>• How has your organization recently adapted to the needs of new members?<br>• Describe examples of inclusive language and of inclusive materials.<br>• How do you teach your clients about the organization's need to adapt to cultures? | | |
| **Institutionalizing Cultural Knowledge**<br>*Training About Differences*<br><br>Guiding Questions:<br>• What do you currently know about the cultural groups in your organization and among your clients?<br>• What more would you like to know about those cultures?<br>• How do you and your colleagues learn about these cultural groups? | | |

**Response Sheet 4.2.2:**

# Activities to Reinforce
# the Essential Elements of Cultural Proficiency

■ Assess Culture

1. Have a real sense of your individual culture.

2. Use films, videos, and other resources to show different cultures.

3. Role-play and use drama, songs, and books.

4. Have students share their feelings about their classroom.

5. Hold focus groups to discuss cultural issues.

6. Exercise: "What I hold near and dear."

7. Exercise: "My Cultural Identity Circle."

8. Exercise: "My Family Cultural Values."

9. Identify staff who speak other languages.

10. Have parents, teachers, and students share their values and cultures.

11. Understand how your culture or the culture of your school affects those whose culture is different.

12. Give students a caretaker "buddy" of the same subculture or gender.

13. Have the buddy provide an orientation tour of restrooms, the bus, the lunchroom, and the playground.

14. Give responsibilities that include them as part of the group.

15. Inform staff of corporate culture to integrate with their own.

16. Establish a task force to assess culture.

17. Give the new member a seat, a place to be. Make him or her feel included by giving the person a name tag, a cubbyhole for storage, or whatever are Table Text individual properties.

18. Have students decide what is important to tell new students; institutionalize the orientation information.

19. Conduct a systems review—identify the practices and assumptions derived from practices and the beliefs or values based on those practices and assumptions.

20. Present case studies, resolve the situation, and examine values of the group that led them to the decision.

## ▪ Value Diversity

1. Recognize difference as diversity rather than as inappropriate responses to the environment.
2. Respect personal space.
3. Accept cultures of students and explain the school's culture.
4. Celebrate the native languages of students.
5. Stay open-minded to various experiences.
6. Create an opportunity for managers and participants to express their fears, concerns, and anxieties and address them.
7. Work with managers to develop job descriptions with clearly defined tasks and performance expectations.
8. Send a profile sheet introducing new faculty or staff. Highlight some of his or her accomplishments. Identify what he or she hopes to contribute.
9. Accept that each culture finds some values and behaviors more important than others.
10. Collectively define *value*.
11. Share individual values.
12. Share reasons for the importance of the values.
13. Note and discuss similarities.
14. Acknowledge differences in work performance attitudes.
15. Develop the necessary training programs to develop skills and abilities.
16. Develop a screening process to identify individuals with appropriate skills and backgrounds to match the organization's needs.

## ▪ Manage the Dynamics of Difference

1. Understand the effect that historic distrust has on present-day interactions.
2. Issues of power and dominance affect all cultures. To illustrate this, use time lines, role-plays, role reversals, murals illustrating reactions to the distrust (e.g., migrations and insurrection), Venn diagrams and tables, narratives, poetry, essays (analysis), and plays.

3. Establish liaisons with cultural groups (e.g., schools and community centers).

4. Realize that you may misjudge others' actions based on learned expectations.

5. Acknowledge that it is okay not to be perfect.

6. Ascertain people's motives for their actions before reacting to them.

7. Use literatures from diverse cultures.

8. Analyze significant historical events and discuss why people today may be resentful of these past situations.

9. Drawing from students' cultural backgrounds, have them role-play situations that could be misunderstood.

## ■ Adapt to Diversity

1. Teach origins of stereotypes and prejudices.
   a. List
   b. Discuss
   c. Expose outcomes and ramifications
   d. Solve problems

2. Institutionalize cultural interventions for conflicts and confusion caused by the dynamics of difference.

3. Teach cultural truths and facts that will cause understanding rather than encourage the perpetuation of negative stereotypes.

4. Teach cultural holidays and why they are important.

5. Establish cross-cultural mentoring.

6. Provide formal training to share the organizational culture.

7. Accept that there will be times during which everyone will be uncomfortable and realize that it is a first step to growth.

8. Review policies, guidelines, and procedures for items of cultural incompetence.

9. Develop a system of conflict management recognizing that change creates stress or conflict and that this is okay.

10. Seek out unusual opportunities to create diversity through brainstorming techniques and going outside of boundaries of comfort.

11. Begin the behavior, knowing that the attitude will follow.

■ Institutionalize Cultural Knowledge

1. Incorporate cultural knowledge into the mainstream of the organization.
2. Conduct inservice training.
3. Compile school lists of community role models and speakers who can be invited to the classroom.
4. Use parents.
5. Provide seminars or workshops so that administrators and the board understand the importance of diversity.
6. Include cultural diversity in the mission and values of the district.
7. Teach about differences within cultures.
8. Reflect the mission and vision in personnel policies and practices.
9. Increase the number of mentors from emerging majorities.
10. Provide diversity training for all staff and volunteers.
11. Develop skills for cross-cultural communication.
12. Make it okay to ask questions to clarify cultural conundrums.
13. Learn the language of clients and community.
14. Learn cultural mores of other groups represented in the organization.
15. Provide a written procedure manual that includes goals and objectives specifically regarding diversity.
16. Include diverse images in art and the environment.

**Activity 4.3:**

# Essential Elements of Cultural Proficiency

■ Purpose

To identify leadership behaviors associated with each of the elements of cultural proficiency

■ Skill of Facilitator

Moderate

■ Readiness of Group

Intermediate

■ Time Needed

30 minutes

■ Materials

A copy of Response Sheet 4.1.1: The Five Essential Elements of
    Cultural Proficiency
Table 4.1: Responsibilities of Culturally Proficient Leaders
Chart paper
Markers

■ Briefing

Now that we know what the five essential elements are, let's discuss what they look like as specific behaviors for leaders and classroom teachers.

■ Process

1. Distribute or post a copy of Response Sheet 4.1.1: The Essential Elements of Cultural Proficiency.
2. Divide the participants into at least five small groups.

3. Assign one element to each group.

4. Ask the participants to brainstorm specific leader actions.

5. When the lists are completed, have each group share its work and invite the other participants to respond to the lists with additions and critical comments.

6. Reinforce the different elements by asking participants to indicate whether they agree that an activity is related to the specific element being discussed.

## ■ Debriefing

1. Ask participants to discuss their level of comfort with the process of brainstorming activities.

2. Then ask them to discuss what it would take to implement the activities.

3. Decide as a group what you will do with the lists of activities.

## ■ Variations

1. Reproduce and distribute the lists. Ask the group to refine them.

2. Assign committees to implement particular activities.

3. Repeat the activity focusing on the school or district culture.

4. Repeat the activity with different audiences (e.g., students, parents, teachers, and staff).

5. Compare the lists to the self-assessment in Response Sheet 4.8.1.

6. Ask participants to create their own self-assessments.

**Activity 4.4:**

# Planning with the Five Essential Elements

■ Purpose

To use the essential elements of cultural proficiency for planning. This activity is particularly effective when made an integral part of long-range or strategic planning.

■ Skill of Facilitator

Moderate

■ Readiness of Group

Intermediate

■ Time Needed

90 minutes–2 hours

■ Materials

Response Sheet 4.1.1: The Essential Elements
Response Sheet 4.2.2: Activities to Reinforce the Essential Elements
Response Sheet 3.3.1: The Human Relations Needs
    Assessment
Chart paper and markers *or* blank transparencies, markers, and
    an overhead projector

■ Briefing

We are going to plan activities related to the essential elements of cultural proficiency for our school.

■ Process

1. Review the essential elements in Response Sheet 4.1.1. Refer to Response Sheet 3.3.1: Human Relations Needs Assessment and Response Sheet 4.2.2 for examples of activities.

2. Divide the participants into small groups of about 5 people.

3. Ask the groups to identify activities at the classroom and school level that would reinforce each element.

4. Have each group share its list.

5. Invite critical examination and revision of each list by the entire group.

6. What must be done to implement these activities?

7. How do these plans fit into the larger plans for the school or district?

## ■ Debriefing

1. How difficult was it to identify activities?

2. Were some elements more difficult than others?

3. What must happen to ensure that these activities take place?

4. If we do everything on these lists, will we be culturally proficient?

5. What else must happen?

6. How should we use the lists that we have generated? What will be our next step?

7. What is the relationship of these activities to the other things we have planned for this school?

## ■ Variations

1. Ask each group to specialize in one element.

2. Examine the school's current strategic plan and identify places where the activities generated could be incorporated.

3. Conduct this activity for specific units at the district level.

**Activity 4.5:**

# Performance Competencies
# and the Essential Elements

■ Purpose

To identify minimal competencies for each of the essential elements. This activity is very useful for translating the concept of cultural proficiency into competency-based behavior.

■ Skill of Facilitator

Extensive

■ Readiness of Group

Advanced

■ Time Needed

90 minutes–2 hours initially, plus follow-up time

■ Materials

1. Definition of competency as used in your school or district
2. Examples of the competencies used at your school or district
3. Copies of Response Sheet 4.5.2: Words Used to Describe Oppressed and Entitled Groups
4. Copies of Response Sheet 4.5.1 on paper or transparencies
5. Chart paper and marking pens *or* transparencies and markers
6. An overhead projector

■ Briefing

Let's see if we can write competencies that we can use to assess performance at our school and relate them to the essential elements of cultural proficiency.

■ Process

1. Distribute the Response Sheets and competencies currently used to assess performance.

2. If you have to establish competencies, engage in a conversation to define what is meant by competencies for faculty, staff, and administrators. Discuss why competencies are necessary and how they are used. In some schools, competencies are implied rather than explicit.

3. Ask each person to spend 15 minutes taking notes on a Response Sheet, noting his or her individual ideas and thoughts about competencies for each of the five elements.

4. Encourage participants to stay conscious of the language they use by referring to Response Sheet 4.5.2.

5. Organize participants into groups of 4–6 members. Be sure to have each group represent the diversity of the total group as much as possible.

6. Give participants 30–60 minutes to discuss each essential element and the related competencies for faculty, staff, and administrators.

7. Ask each group to present the results of its work on chart paper or transparencies.

8. Encourage critical discussion, clarification, and revision of the competencies.

■ Debriefing

1. What did you think, feel, or wonder when you first received the Response Sheets?

2. What did you think, feel, or wonder about the discussion in your small group?

3. To what extent do you think the ideas generated from all subgroups will be helpful in this school?

4. What did you learn about yourself? Your colleagues? Your school?

5. What is the implication of this activity for you in your role at school?

6. What information or skills do you believe you need to do an even better job?

7. How shall we use these competencies?

■ Variation

1. Have each small group specialize in just one set of competencies—for example, for faculty, staff, or administrators.
2. Write teaching standards for each element.
3. Write behavioral standards for each element for your elementary or middle school grade level.
4. Write curriculum standards for each element for your secondary subject area.

**Response Sheet 4.5.1:**

## Performance Competencies and the Essential Elements

| Essential Elements | Performance Competencies *(with examples)* |
|---|---|
| Assesses Culture | *Provides orientation to unit that includes description of the culture and the unwritten rules.* |
| Values Diversity | *Insists on competent staff from underrepresented groups.* |
| Manages Dynamics of Difference | *Coaches staff and colleagues in effective language that will reduce conflict.* |
| Adapts to Diversity | *Holds everyone to the same standards for quality work.* |
| Institutionalizes Cultural Knowledge | *Provides examples of problem situations that can be used as cases during training.* |

**Response Sheet 4.5.2:**

# Words Used to Describe
# Oppressed and Entitled Groups

■ Oppressed                    ■ Entitled

    Inferior                      Superior

    Culturally deprived           Privileged

    Culturally disadvantaged      Advantaged

    Deficient                     Table Text

    Different                     Regular

    Diverse                       Uniform

    Third world                   First world

    Minority                      Majority

    Underclass                    Upper class

    Poor                          Middle class

    Unskilled workers             Leaders

**Activity 4.6:**

# Intercultural Communication

■ **Purpose**

To articulate differences between and among group when communicating across cultures. This activity provides participants with the opportunity to define how their cultural groups prefer to receive communication and to learn the same about other groups' communications preferences and styles.

■ **Expertise of Facilitator**

Moderate

■ **Readiness of Group**

Intermediate

■ **Time Needed**

2 hours

■ **Materials**

Chart paper
Markers

■ **Briefing**

This activity will give you an opportunity to share information with the other participants that they need for talking effectively with members of your cultural group. It will give you a chance to shatter some stereotypes on one hand, but on the other hand it will allow you to share some useful generalizations.

■ **Process**

1. Have the group members sit with other members of their ethnic groups. If they want to divide into subgroups, allow them to do that. For example, if the African Americans want to divide into a

middle-class, college-educated group and a working class, grass-roots group, this may be useful.

2. Ask each group to list some rules, suggestions, and tips for interacting with that particular group. They may want to use some of these categories:

   Initial approach

   Presenting oneself to the group (credentials, background, and other helpful information)

   Attitude toward time

   Introducing change

   Giving feedback

   Disagreeing

   Pointing out errors

   Things that help communication

   Things that impede communication

3. Encourage each group to discuss among itself the paradigms members might use for judging newcomers. What are the rules of discourse that they use when interacting with outsiders? What should a newcomer do if he or she wants to be accepted and listened to?

4. Allow each group to present its list.

## ■ Debriefing

Make sure you ask questions that clarify and underscore the subtle but important differences in the expectations of each group when communicating. Seek to determine whether one group has different expectations for different ethnic groups. Talk about clothing and appearance if you perceive this to be an important issue as well.

## ■ Variations

1. This exercise could be used to explore differences in cross-gender or intergenerational communication.

2. With a mature group and an experienced trainer, a similar activity could start by identifying "things that are annoying or frustrating about talking with. . . . [xxx group]."

**Activity 4.7:**

# Managing Conflict with Our Core Values

■ Purpose

To discuss the relationship of your school's core values, the elements of cultural proficiency, and managing conflict.

■ Skill of Facilitator

Extensive

■ Readiness of Group

Advanced

■ Time Needed

60–90 minutes

■ Materials

Copies of Response Sheet 4.7.1: Managing Conflict With Our Core Values

A grid that has the same three-column headings but is otherwise blank (Response Sheet 4.7.2). This can be on paper or on transparencies.

Chart paper and marking pens *or* an overhead projector and markers

A list of the school's core values or shared values, Activity 1.2

■ Briefing

We are going to talk about the relationship of our core values to managing conflict.

■ Process

1. Distribute a list of the school's shared or core values.
2. Distribute Response Sheets 4.7.1 and 4.7.2.

3. Complete one row of the blank chart as a large group

4. Ask each person to spend 15 minutes making notes that reflect his or her individual views and perspectives regarding the organizational responses to its stated core values on Response Sheet 4.7.1.

5. Organize participants into diverse groups of 4–6 members.

6. Give participants 30–60 minutes to discuss each core value as it relates to managing conflict and to complete the blank Response Sheet 4.7.2.

7. Ask participants to post their work on chart paper or on the transparencies.

8. Invite critical review of each group's contribution.

9. Note the similarities and differences in the groups' products.

## ■ Debriefing

1. What did you think, feel, or wonder when you first received the Response Sheet?

2. What did you think, feel, or wonder during the discussion in your group?

3. How can your incorporate your new understanding of conflict into your daily practice?

4. What did you learn about yourself? Your colleagues? Your school?

5. What is the implication of this activity for you in your role at school?

6. What information or skills do you believe you need to do an even better job?

7. How can we use this information?

## ■ Variations

1. Step 5 in the process can be done within culturally defined groups, and the information can be shared among cultural groups.

2. Use this activity at the classroom or district level.

**Response Sheet 4.7.1:**

# Managing Conflict
## With Our Core Values—*Example*

| Core Values | Relationship of Core Values to Managing Conflict | What I Can Say or Do to Reduce Tension and Conflict |
|---|---|---|
| **Quality** | Unresolved conflict reduces the quality of your products. | "I am concerned about the quality of the work we are doing here. Can we talk about how it can be improved?" |
| **People** | Without the people, we would have no business. | Involve the people who are having the conflicts in resolving them: "I think we need to clear the air. Let's sit down and talk about what the real issues are." |
| **Integrity** | Acknowledge your contribution to the conflicts that arise around you. | "It was not my intention to offend you. I was trying to say. . . ." |
| **Caring** | Demonstrate that you care about your colleagues by taking the time to reduce tension and solve the problem together. | "I am on my way to a meeting, but I do want to address these issues. Let's plan to talk at. . . ." |

**Response Sheet 4.7.2:**

## Examining Your Core Values

| Core Value | Relationship of Core Value to Managing Conflict | What I Can Say or Do to Reduce Tension and Conflict |
| --- | --- | --- |
| | | |
| | | |
| | | |
| | | |
| | | |
| | | |

**Activity 4.8:**

# Cultural Competence Self Assessment

■ Purpose

To provide a baseline of information and a starting point for conversation about becoming culturally proficient. This checklist will *not* certify anyone. It simply provides some key questions for exploration.

■ Materials Needed

Response Sheet 4.8.1

■ Time

20 minutes to complete the assessment, and an additional 20–40 minutes to discuss the results

■ Briefing

This instrument will ask you questions that will help you to determine where to start as you develop your cultural competence.

■ Process

1. Distribute Response Sheet 4.8.1.
2. Encourage participants to be candid about their responses.

■ Debriefing

1. How do you think you did?
2. Was there any pattern to your responses?
3. What would you like to know, do, and learn as a result of your answers?
4. What additional questions would you add to this self-assessment?
5. Where shall we go as a group?

■ Variations

1. Organize the participants into cohort groups. Have them share their responses with one another and decide as a group what they would like to do next.

2. Organize the participants into five groups, one for each element. Have the group brainstorm ideas for developing skills and knowledge that will increase their competence for that particular element.

**Response Sheet 4.8.1:**

# Cultural Competence Self-Assessment

Circle the numbers that best reflect your responses to the questions:

Rarely = 1    Seldom = 2    Sometimes = 3    Often = 4    Usually = 5

| Assesses Culture | | | | | |
|---|---|---|---|---|---|
| 1. I am aware of my own culture and ethnicity. | 1 | 2 | 3 | 4 | 5 |
| 2. I am comfortable talking about my culture and ethnicity. | 1 | 2 | 3 | 4 | 5 |
| 3. I know the effect that my culture and ethnicity may have on the people in my work setting. | 1 | 2 | 3 | 4 | 5 |
| 4. I seek to learn about the culture of this organization. | 1 | 2 | 3 | 4 | 5 |
| 5. I seek to learn about the cultures of this organization's employees. | 1 | 2 | 3 | 4 | 5 |
| 6. I seek to learn about the cultures of this organization's clients. | 1 | 2 | 3 | 4 | 5 |
| 7. I anticipate how this organization's clients and employees will interact with, conflict with, and enhance one another. | 1 | 2 | 3 | 4 | 5 |
| **Values Diversity** | | | | | |
| 8. I welcome a diverse group of clients and colleagues into the work setting. | 1 | 2 | 3 | 4 | 5 |
| 9. I create opportunities at work for us to be more inclusive and more diverse. | 1 | 2 | 3 | 4 | 5 |
| 10. I appreciate both the challenges and opportunities that diversity brings. | 1 | 2 | 3 | 4 | 5 |
| 11. I share my appreciation of diversity with my coworkers. | 1 | 2 | 3 | 4 | 5 |

12. I share my appreciation of diversity with other clients.     1   2   3   4   5

13. I work to develop a learning community with the clients (internal or external) I serve.     1   2   3   4   5

14. I make a conscious effort to teach the cultural expectations of my organization or department to those who are new or who may be unfamiliar with the organization's culture.     1   2   3   4   5

15. I proactively seek to interact with people from diverse backgrounds in my personal and professional life.     1   2   3   4   5

## Manages the Dynamics of Difference

16. I recognize that conflict is a part of life.     1   2   3   4   5

17. I work to develop skills to manage conflict in a positive way.     1   2   3   4   5

18. I help my colleagues to understand that what appear to be clashes in personalities may in fact be conflicts in culture.     1   2   3   4   5

19. I help the clients I serve to understand that what appear to be clashes in personalities may in fact be conflicts in personal or organizational culture.     1   2   3   4   5

20. I check myself to see if an assumption I am making about a person is based on facts or upon stereotypes about a group.     1   2   3   4   5

21. I accept that the more diverse our group becomes, the more we will change and grow.     1   2   3   4   5

## Adapts to Diversity

22. I realize that once I embrace the principles of cultural proficiency, I, too, must change.     1   2   3   4   5

23. I am committed to the continuous learning that is necessary to deal with the issues caused by differences.     1   2   3   4   5

24. I seek to enhance the substance and structure of the work I do so that it is informed by the guiding principles of cultural proficiency.      1   2   3   4   5

25. I recognize the unsolicited privileges I might enjoy because of my title, gender, age, sexual orientation, physical ability, or ethnicity.      1   2   3   4   5

26. I know how to learn about people and cultures unfamiliar to me without giving offense.

## Institutionalizes Cultural Knowledge

27. I work to influence the culture of this organization so that its policies and practices are informed by the guiding principles of cultural proficiency.      1   2   3   4   5

28. I speak up if I notice that a policy or practice unintentionally discriminates against or causes an unnecessary hardship for a particular group in this organization's community.      1   2   3   4   5

29. I take advantage of teachable moments to share cultural knowledge or to learn from my colleagues.      1   2   3   4   5

30. I take advantage of teachable moments to share cultural knowledge with this organization's clients.      1   2   3   4   5

31. I seek to create opportunities for my colleagues, managers, clients, and the communities we serve to learn about one another.      1   2   3   4   5

 5

# The Third Tool,
# Underlying Values:
# The Guiding Principles
# of Cultural Proficiency

*Culture is not an exotic notion studied by
a select group of anthropologists in the
South Seas. It is a mold in which we are
all cast, and it controls our daily lives in
many unsuspected ways. . . . [C]ulture
hides much more than it reveals, and
strangely enough what it hides, it hides
most effectively from its own participants.*

—Edward T. Hall

೭৬

Bill Fayette, the superintendent of the Coolidge district, has hired a diversity consultant, James Harris, to provide training for faculty on cultural proficiency. At the first staff development session, James explains the underlying principles that inform his approach to dealing with the issues

**Figure 5.1.**   Approaches to Diversity

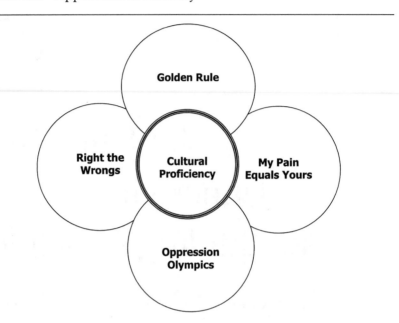

that emerge in a diverse environment. He also explains that the response to these issues usually falls within one of four categories:[1]

*Right the Wrongs:* Some people are angry or have a strong sense of justice. If something is wrong, they think it should be fixed immediately, and if necessary the wrongdoers should be punished.

*The Golden Rule:* These people want everyone to get along. If we all just treated everyone equally, with courtesy and kindness, there wouldn't be a problem," they say.

*My Pain Equals Yours:* Then there are those who say, "Everyone has been discriminated about something. I got over it; so should they. We need to forget the past and move forward."

*Oppression Olympics:* These people recognize that every group has suffered some form of discrimination; they are, however, certain that the group they are in has suffered the most and should not be minimized by discussing anyone else's alleged experiences of oppression.

"Each of these perspectives has some serious drawbacks," says James, "and each one also is useful. If we diagrammed these positions as adjacent circles, we would place cultural proficiency in the center, slightly

---

[1]Thanks to our colleague, Stephanie Graham, for sharing this model with us.

overlapping each of the others. With cultural proficiency, we draw from the best of each of these positions, adding to it our understanding of the cultural proficiency tools so that we can make a difference for our students, our colleagues, and our community." He presents the group with a list of comments he has collected from teachers and administrators in a number of districts:

"Doesn't focusing on differences just make it harder for us to get along?"

"I don't have a culture. I'm just a generic person. Heinz 57."

"He sure didn't sound black on the phone when we talked."

"I didn't know there were Chinese people over six feet tall."

"You are different, but we're comfortable with you."

"We would have more of your kind around if they were just like you."

"Why do they have to have a special program?"

"I think everyone should be given the same attention and information. That's fair."

James uses these comments to illustrate the Guiding Principles of Cultural Proficiency.

ᴕ

# The Guiding Principles of Cultural Proficiency

**Culture is a predominant force.**

**People are served in varying degrees by the dominant culture.**

**Group identity is as
important as individual identities.**

**Diversity within cultures is vast and significant.**

**Each group has unique cultural needs.**

Prominently placed in most of the organizations we have worked in, usually in a beautiful frame, is the organization's mission and values. In some organizations, the employees wear identification badges, and, often, laminated on the back of the ID is a list of the organization's core values. In every public place and in the staff lounge are statements that say what the organization believes in and how it intends to treat people. As part of a cultural audit, we will examine personnel polices, look at memos sent to all of the employees, and listen to the people as they tell us what it is like to work at that particular school or in that particular

district office. Invariably, there is a disconnection between what the organization says it is and how the employees, the clients, or the community
experience the organization. In simple things like the personnel policy,
we see major conflicts. The values statements speak of trust, honesty,
harmony, and co-creation. The personnel polices are written in legalistic
terms from the underlying assumption that employees cannot be trusted
and must fear punishment so they won't do anything wrong.

Clients—in this case, students and their families—tell us how they
are treated as unwelcome interlopers in the school community. Office
staffs complain that if it weren't for the students, they would be able to
get their work done. Students tell of teachers who are rude, insulting,
and vindictive while demanding unquestioning obedience and extreme
deference from the same students whom they oppress through their
abuse of power and position. Now you may be thinking, *This doesn't happen where I work*, or *You must be citing extreme cases*, or *There is a reason that
these things happen, after all we can't. . . .* In many cases, you will have significant and valid points to make. The point that we seek to make here
with you is that if you say that you represent an open, inclusive, learning
community that values all people and their contributions, then everything that you do and say must reflect that. There cannot be a disconnection between what you say you are or want to be and how you behave on
a daily basis. Your character is who you are under stress, not how you are
when everything is peaceful and going your way.

It is easy to articulate good values. It is much harder to incorporate
those values into all of the systems and structures of your organization. It
is even harder as a leader to hold the people in the organization accountable for policies, practices, and procedures that are consistent with the
mission and the values of the organization. If you can do this, then you
not only have learned the importance of a strong core culture, but you
also have learned how to create an environment where all members of
the community understand their role in maintaining it. The tool to help
you do this is the Guiding Principles of Cultural Proficiency.

### ■ Culture Is Ever Present

You cannot *not* have a culture. Nor can there be an environment that
is culture-free or without cultural bias. Culture is like the air; it is everywhere and you don't notice it until it changes. People in dominant
groups often say that they don't notice culture. And that is the main
point. If you are in the dominant group, you don't have to pay attention
to cultural norms and cultural expectations. You just know what they
are. Just as you know the rules for riding in a public elevator or the rules
for entering a concert that is in progress, if you are part of the group that

makes the rules, you know them intuitively. That is part of your privilege and it is a source of your power. You know what to do. Culturally proficient educators recognize that what they experience as normal or regular is part of their culture. This may create a sense of entitlement, but by recognizing these feelings, they can then acknowledge and appreciate the subtle cultural differences among members of the dominant culture.

Your culture is a defining aspect of your humanity. It is the predominant force in shaping values and behaviors. Occasionally, you may be inclined to take offense at behaviors that differ from yours, but as a culturally proficient leader, remind yourself that offensive behavior may not be personal; it may be cultural. Recognize that members of emerging majority populations have to be at least bicultural, and this creates its own set of issues, problems, and possible conflicts. All people who are not a part of the dominant group have already gained competence in one culture before they began to learn standard English or dominant U.S. cultural norms. Therefore, when members of dominated cultures resist or hesitate in using the language or cultural norms of the dominant culture, they are not necessarily ignorant or incompetent; rather, they simply may be using language or cultural behaviors with which they are more familiar or more comfortable. The culturally proficient leader remembers that culture—the culture of the individuals and the culture of the organization—is always a factor.

## ■ People Are Served in Varying Degrees by the Dominant Culture

Common knowledge is not common, and things are only self-evident to those who share your worldview and culture perspective. Just because a person is working in the school district or a child has made it to the fifth grade doesn't mean that they have learned all of the rules—the cultural expectations—that the dominant group uses as criteria for success. Think about the last time someone new joined your staff. Although most people made gestures of welcome and courtesy, there was also a bit of standing back to watch and wait. You wanted to see who this person was and whether they would fit in. After three or four days, you could hear people saying *Boy, she is really great*, or, *Well, he's not going to last long around here*. These comments reflect the unconscious evaluation of the person by using the cultural expectations of the group as the criteria for determining the person's *fit* or success.

Imagine what it would be like to welcome someone into the organization by saying, *Here's the personnel policy manual, and here are the employee procedures, and here are our cultural expectations—our practices. Read these practices first, and when they contradict something in the other two documents, go with the cultural expectations. That is how we really do things around here.* It's hard to imagine, but that is what would happen in a culturally proficient organization. Moreover, before inviting new people into the community, there would be a conscious effort to align the policies and procedures with the practices. Additionally, as the group became diverse, the policies, procedures, and practices would be examined to eliminate unintentionally discriminating policies and practices.

Culturally proficient educators adjust their behaviors and values to accommodate the full range of diversity represented by their school populations. They recognize that some individuals from minority cultures find success in varying degrees in schools where only the dominant culture is acknowledged and valued. Although educators and students in the dominant culture may profit from such a setting, and members of some dominated groups may do well despite such a setting, many other students and educators will find such an atmosphere stifling and limiting. Such an imbalance of power puts the total burden for change on one person or group. Culturally proficient leaders see the need to ensure that members of dominant groups, dominated groups, and emerging groups share the responsibility for change.

## ■ People Have Group Identities and Personal Identities

A common experience among people of historically oppressed groups is the model minority syndrome. This occurs when one member of the dominated group learns and uses the cultural norms of the dominant group. Because model minorities are bicultural, they can assimilate into the dominant culture without causing discomfort to those in the power group and without calling attention to their differentness. The guest, not the host, does all of the accommodation. The only acknowledgement of this syndrome is when one of the members of the dominant group says, *You know, you aren't like the other _____, you're different. You seem to fit right in,* or, *Your English is so good. I can understand everything you say,* or, *You read speech so well that I totally forget that you are deaf.* Although these comments are meant to be compliments, they are not. They are insulting because they deny that the person has any connection or identification with the group being denigrated. In essence, these statements say, *Thanks for selling out. I can tolerate you because you act just like me.*

It is important to treat all people as individuals as well as to acknowledge each group's identity. It demeans and insults individuals and their cultures to single out particular assimilated members of ethnic groups and to tell them that they differ from members of their own group, implying that their differentness somehow makes them better— or more acceptable—to the dominant group. Culturally proficient leaders know that to guarantee the dignity of each person, they must also preserve the dignity of each person's culture.

Often, so-called personality problems are actually problems of cultural differences. Culturally proficient leaders address these problems. They recognize that cultural differences in thought patterns (e.g., those of non-Western, non-European people versus those of Westerners) reflect differing but equally valid ways of viewing and solving problems. No cultural group appears exclusively to use just one particular approach for processing information and solving problems. Although some cultures are traditionally associated with one approach more than others, there is no evidence that one approach is superior to others across all situations. Culturally proficient leaders recognize these and other cultural differences, and they use this knowledge to promote effective communication among diverse people.

■ Diversity Within Cultures Is Important

A prospective client who was responsible for "minority recruitment" to an exclusive college said to us that she was not going to be successful because the bus lines didn't run past the school. She had assumed that all people of color were poor and would be riding the bus if they attended the school. She did not realize that within any group there are vast differences in wealth, income, education, and lifestyle. Because diversity within cultures is as important as diversity between cultures, it is important to learn about ethnic groups not as monoliths (e.g., Asians, Latinos, or whites) but as the complex and diverse groups that they are. Within each major ethnic group are many distinctive subgroups. Although a significant portion of a dominated group may occupy the lower rungs of the socioeconomic ladder, within each group there is great diversity. Often, because of the class differences in the United States, there is greater commonality across ethnic lines, between groups that share the same socioeconomic status (SES), than there is within an ethnic group between the upper and lower SES of that group.

For example, upper-middle-class U.S. citizens of European, African, and Japanese descent will be more likely to share values and a similar worldview than will members of any one ethnic group who come from socioeconomic backgrounds varying from working class to upper class. For the client to be successful in her recruitment, she would need to know this and know how to access people of color who fit the socioeconomic profile of those who attended the school. Culturally proficient leaders recognize these intracultural differences and provide their faculty, staff, students, and parents with access to information about people who are not like themselves in various ways. Culturally proficient schools create an environment that fosters trust, safety, and the inclusion of all people who work and learn in them.

### ■ Each Group Has Unique Cultural Needs

There was a time in the history of educational practices when all children were expected to dress, talk, and respond to their teachers in the same way. Adults who are creative, intuitive, extremely bright, or dyslexic often talk about the horrible experiences they had in school because they didn't conform to the one-size-fits-all mode of education that was offered to them. They grew up thinking they were defective in some way because they could not learn the way they were being taught. In the past 50 years, educators have learned to acknowledge in their curriculum and in their teaching different learning styles, different cognitive styles, and the different ways people process information. Still, there are schools that refuse to change their policies to adapt to differences in grooming needs, dietary restrictions, or physical accommodations.

European Americans can assume that a public school in this country will have information about the history and culture of their people in the United States as well as about their countries of origin. Other U.S. citizens and U.S. immigrants cannot make such assumptions. The desire to learn about oneself and one's people is unique only in that each group wants different information. Additionally, schools may be invited to accommodate students in large and small ways—all of which will be significant to the people who are not in the dominant group. These changes in how things are done will also be teachable moments for members of the dominant groups to learn about others. The culturally proficient educator will teach and encourage colleagues who are members of the dominant culture to make the necessary adaptations in how schools provide educational service so that all people have access to the same benefits and privileges as members of the dominant group in society.

## Make It Count

The tools of cultural proficiency assist you in shifting the culture of the organization. This is not something that can take place after a few staff development sessions; it requires commitment at the top, accountability systems at the bottom, and an ongoing intention of everyone to pay attention to the things that count. According to a popular legend, Albert Einstein had a sign in his office that said, "People spend too much time counting things that don't count, and not counting the things that do. " Nicely framed values statements don't count. Teachers who consistently model courtesy and respect to one another and to all of their students do count. A beautifully articulated mission statement doesn't count if there is no relationship of the mission to the programs that operate on a daily basis or if the front office staff does not see its work as one of the ways in which the mission is fulfilled.

By deliberately and systematically implementing the behavior outlined in the essential elements of cultural proficiency, you can become a culturally proficient school or district. To carry out this ambitious task, you need strong core organizational values (Collins and Porras, 1997; Deal and Peterson, 1998). In addition to the values you currently hold, you can use the values of culturally proficiency—the guiding principles—as the foundation on which you re-create your classroom, your school, or your district.

## Going Further

1. Take the statements made in the case by the teachers and decide to which of the guiding principles they apply.
2. As you reflect on how your school or district responds to the issues of diversity, can you cite examples of counting what doesn't count? Can you identify some things that should be counted?

# Reflection

_____

_____

_____

_____

_____

_____

_____

_____

_____

_____

_____

**Activity 5.1:**

# Guiding Principles Discussion Starters

■ Purpose

To reinforce the guiding principles of cultural proficiency
To identify how the principles of cultural proficiency can be translated into school behavior

■ Skill of Facilitator

Extensive

■ Readiness of Group

Intermediate

■ Time Needed

60 minutes

■ Materials

Response Sheet 5.1.1: Guiding Principles
Response Sheet 5.1.2: Cultural Proficiency Discussion Starters

■ Briefing

Let's look at the principles of cultural proficiency to make sure we
know what they mean in relationship to how we do things at this school.

■ Process

1. Distribute Response Sheets 5.1.1 and 5.1.2.
2. Divide the group into small groups, assigning one question to
   each group.
3. Ask the small groups to respond to their question. Note that each
   question relates to a corresponding principle.

4. Reconvene the large group and share the responses, encouraging critical reflection and review.

■ Debriefing

1. What happened in your small groups? How easy or difficult was it to answer the questions?
2. How do you feel about your responses?
3. Have you ever thought of parents, community, students, or one another as customers?
4. How does thinking in terms of customer or client relations alter the way you respond to these groups?
5. What are the implications for your responses?
6. How will you use this information?

■ Variations

1. Examine the principles from the perspective of a classroom or the district.
2. Conduct this activity with one large group, inviting discussion and responses of everyone to all the questions.
3. Use Response Sheet 5.1.3 instead of 5.1.2
4. Use one of the following headings on Response Sheet 5.1.3.

| Guiding Principles of Cultural Proficiency | What would your classroom look like if this principle were acknowledged? | Strategies for responding to this principle in your classroom |
| --- | --- | --- |

| Guiding Principles of Cultural Proficiency | Issues That May Arise When This Principle Is Not Acknowledged | Examples and Types of Conflicts |
| --- | --- | --- |

**Response Sheet 5.1.1:**

# The Guiding Principles
# of Cultural Proficiency

■ **Culture Is a Predominant Force**

Acknowledge culture as a predominant force in shaping behaviors, values, and institutions. Although you may be inclined to take offense at the behaviors that differ from yours, remind yourself that it may not be personal; it may be cultural.

■ **People Are Served in Varying Degrees by the Dominant Culture**

What works well in organizations and in the community for you and others who are like you may work against members of other cultural groups. Failure to make such an acknowledgment puts the burden for change on one group.

■ **Group Identity Is as Important as Their Individual Identities Are**

Although it is important to treat all people as individuals, it is also important to acknowledge the group identity of individuals. Actions must be taken with the awareness that the dignity of a person is not guaranteed unless the dignity of his or her people is also preserved.

■ **Diversity Within Cultures Is Vast and Significant**

Since diversity within cultures is as important as diversity between cultures, it is important to learn about cultural groups not as monoliths, for example Asians, Hispanics, Gay Men, and Women, but as the complex and diverse groups that they are. Often, because of the class differences in the United States, there will be more in common across cultural lines than within them.

■ **Each Group Has Unique Cultural Needs**

Each cultural group has unique needs that cannot be met within the boundaries of the dominant culture. Expressions of one group's cultural identity do not imply disrespect for yours. Make room in your organization for several paths that lead to the same goal.

---

**Response Sheet 5.1.2:**

# Cultural Proficiency Discussion Starters

Use these questions and statements to further your discussion about the guiding principles of cultural proficiency.

1. **Culture is ever present.**
   List aspects of culture—yours and your customers'—that affect how your message is received.

2. **People are served in varying degrees by the dominant culture.**
   What works for the dominant culture may not work for dominated cultures. What alternatives might you consider?

3. **People have group identities and personal identities.**
   List some words and phrases that might insult or discount members of cultural groups in your school or district.

4. **Diversity within cultures is important.**
   List specific names for members of these major U.S. cultural groups:

   > Asian
   > Black
   > Homosexual
   > Hispanic
   > People of the First Nations (Native American)
   > White

5. **Each group has unique cultural needs.**
   What are some of the unique cultural needs of your clients and colleagues?

**Response Sheet 5.1.3:**

## Discussion of the Guiding Principles

| Guiding Principles of Cultural Proficiency | Cultural Proficiency Discussion Starters | Things that I can do in my work setting: |
|---|---|---|
| **Culture is a predominant force.** Acknowledge culture as a predominant force in shaping behaviors, values, and institutions. Although you may be inclined to take offense at the behaviors that differ from yours, remind yourself that it may not be personal; it may be cultural. | *List aspects of culture—yours and your customers'—that affect how your message is received.* | |
| **People are served in varying degrees by the dominant culture.** What works well in organizations and in the community for you and others who are like you may work against members of other cultural groups. Failure to make such an acknowledgment puts the burden for change on one group. | *What works for the dominant culture of your organization that may not work for all of its clients or employees?* | |
| **Acknowledge the group identity of individuals.** Although it is important to treat all people as individuals, it is also important to acknowledge the group identity of individuals. Actions must be taken with the awareness that the dignity of a person is not guaranteed unless the dignity of his or her people is also preserved. | *List some words and phrases that might insult or discount members of cultural groups in your organization.* | |

| Guiding Principles of Cultural Proficiency | Cultural Proficiency Discussion Starters | Things that I can do in my work setting: |
|---|---|---|
| **Diversity within cultures is important.** Since diversity within cultures is as important as diversity between cultures, it is important to learn about cultural groups not as monoliths, for example Asians, Hispanics, Gay Men, and Women, but as the complex and diverse groups that they are. Often, because of the class differences in the United States, there will be more in common across cultural lines than within them. | *What are some of the subgroups of the major cultures represented in your organization? How might the differences within groups affect the nature of the conflict you may experience or the way you deliver your services?* | |
| **Respect unique cultural needs.** Each cultural group has unique needs that cannot be met within the boundaries of the dominant culture. Expressions of one group's cultural identity do not imply disrespect for yours. Make room in your organization for several paths that lead to the same goal. | *What are some of the unique cultural needs of your clients and colleagues?* | |

**Activity 5.2.1:**

# My Work Values

■ Purpose

> To identify individual values that affect the workplace
>
> To increase awareness of how apparently positive values may cause
> conflict in the workplace

■ Expertise of Facilitator

> Intermediate

■ Readiness of Group ·

> Beginning

■ Time Needed

> 60-90 minutes

■ Materials

> Chart paper
> Markers
> Masking tape

■ Briefing

Think about lessons you learned in your parents' home. What were
the values on which those lessons were based? Identify three values that
you learned at home that you now bring to the workplace. Share how
these values affect your perceptions and relationships at work.

■ Process

1. Organize the participants into small groups of 3-5 people. Encourage the participants to diversify their groups.

2. Model for the group three values that you learned from your parents or the family in which you grew up and still use in the workplace. For example: *My father always told me to get an education, be nice to your siblings, and don't get pregnant. This translates today into my expectation that everyone will want to learn and be glad to go to training; that people will be especially courteous to the people they work with; and that they will be responsible for the consequences of their actions.*

3. Clarify for the participants that in the small groups they do not need to agree with all the values shared.

4. After participants have shared in the small groups, ask them to chart their values. Hang the charts around the room.

■ Debriefing

1. Each group shares the values and the some of the stories that explain them to the large group.

2. Discuss the apparent and subtle similarities and differences of the values.

3. Identify how values that in isolation are perceived as positive may clash and cause conflicts with the values of other people. For example: *Get an education* and *Education is a privilege* are two positive and potentially conflicting values. Both of these are positive but will result in very different expectations and attitudes about learning.

**Activity 5.3:**

# Demographics

■ Purpose

To identify the demographic makeup in a community

■ Skill of Facilitator

Moderate

■ Readiness of Group

Intermediate

■ Time Needed

2 weeks; this activity will take place outside of a formal training room.

■ Materials

A list of appropriate websites, for example, those of your city and county and those of your local and county school district offices
A description of the process for gaining access to
    Newspaper files and resources
    Census bureau data
    District demographic data

■ Briefing

This process will familiarize you with the demographic makeup of your school's community.

■ Process

1. Divide the group into teams of 3-4 people.

2. As a large group, identify the major and minor ethnic groups represented in the district.

3. Brainstorm on how to gather information about a particular group of people: churches, cultural centers, libraries, newspaper libraries, and specific social and civic organizations. Encourage the group to also consider non-formal techniques used by anthropologists, such as observation, participant-observation, and use of a cultural informant

4. Let each team select a group about which it will gather demographic information.

5. Provide a list of minimally acceptable data: total population in city, total population in district, area of the city that is most densely populated with this group, socioeconomic status, languages spoken, and resources for teachers about this group of people.

6. Challenge each team to find the most useful and interesting information about its group.

7. Discuss ethnically appropriate protocol and etiquette so that team members are not viewed as culturally incompetent intruders by other ethnic groups.

8. Describe the format in which the information should be presented.

## ■ Debriefing

Ask each team to present its information to the group in a way that is interesting and entertaining. Remind them to be nonjudgmental and to be aware of unintentional stereotyping. As part of or after the presentation, ask each team to respond to these questions as well as others from members of the large group:

1. What did you learn about yourself in the process?
2. Did you have any serendipitous adventures?
3. What was the greatest challenge of this activity?
4. What was the greatest surprise?
5. How will you use what you have learned?

**Activity 5.4:**

# Assessing Your School's Culture

■ Purpose

To identify the cultural expectations and the underlying values of a
school

■ Expertise of Facilitator

Extensive

■ Readiness of Group

Intermediate

■ Time Needed

3 hours or more

■ Materials

Chart paper
Response Sheet 5.4.1: Assessing the Culture of Your School

■ Briefing

This activity will give us the opportunity to take a close look at the
kind of school we are. We are going to articulate the unstated rules and
values of this school in an attempt to see if who we say we are is who we
really are.

■ Process

1. Review the definitions of culture, cultural expectations, overt values, and covert values as described in Chapter 2.
2. Organize participants into workgroups of 4-6 people. They may
want to organize according to the grade levels or departments in
which they work, or they may want to organize so that there is a

representative of each grade level or department in each group. The former strategy will reveal aspects of the subcultures in the school. The latter strategy will enable people to hear and explore different perceptions and experiences of the same school.

3. Provide each group with two sheets of chart paper, markers, and Response Sheet 5.4.1.

4. Allow 30 minutes initially, checking to see how much additional time the groups need. It will take about one hour for the groups to explicate in detail the many aspects of the school's culture.

5. While the groups are working, make sure that they are writing the real values, that is, the rules of behavior that reflect the way things are rather than the way they would like things to be.

## ■ Debriefing

When articulating the unspoken rules of a culture, participants are often disturbed by the negative descriptions of the school, and consequently themselves. To debrief this activity effectively, it is important to acknowledge the discomfort some of the participants may have. It is equally important to provide adequate time for the debriefing of the information gathered. Before starting the process, review the following typical approaches that people take when discussing their culture and indicate that you will remind participants gently when their presentations begin to reflect on these nonproductive approaches.

1. *Make nice.* Speakers will use words to obfuscate, mute, or invalidate their description of their values.

2. *Deny.* In response to the speaker's truth, participants will deny that the rule exists or that such activities take place in this school.

3. *Make excuses.* Participants will justify the existence of a rule to rationalize its existence.

4. *Defend.* Similarly, participants may want to defend the existence of a rule because it has filled a need personally, for the school, or for a group within the school.

**Response Sheet 5.4.1:**

# Assessing the Culture of Your School*

The culture of a school can be examined by using a number of different models. This model easily adapts to most schools and groups. Use it to assess the culture and identify the cultural expectations of your school.

**Heroes, sheroes, and their legends:** The stars of the school and the stories that are told about them that underscore the organizational value the stars exemplify.

**Rituals:** Routine activities that reinforce the values because they establish predictable patterns of behavior.

**Ceremonies:** Special rituals that celebrate the rites of passage of the members of the school, reinforce the values of the school, and acknowledge the heroes and sheroes.

**Play:** Activities that provide an outlet for anger and a release from day-to-day tensions and frustrations. What is considered funny? How do group members joke around? What is laughed at?

**Communication and language:** The process of interacting and sharing information. Special vocabularies used by the members of the group.

**Signs, symbols, and sacred spaces:** The tangible indicators of the school's norms and values. These also include the special places set aside for the heroes and sheroes within the school, for example teacher of the year awards, senior quad, and spelling bee plaques. Signs are sometimes used to mark or identify group members.

**Values—overt and covert:** Overt rules are the things that we say we are. Covert rules are the "hidden curriculum "—the rules that we actually abide by. How does the school treat its students, its parents, and its teachers and aides in regard to:

*Relationships:* What are the roles played by members of the group?

*Economics:* Psychic pay, perquisites (perks), resource distribution and allocation. What is the currency of exchange within the group? What is wealth and how is it acquired and used?

*Education:* Which is valued most—formal schooling, experience in the field, or length of service within the school? How is information acquired? What kind of information is valued?

*Politics:* Who has the power? How is it acquired and shared?

*Ethics:* Morals. How are right and wrong and good and bad defined? What is the ethos of the school?

*Aesthetics:* What is considered to be beauty and how is it displayed in the physical environment?

*Health:* How are safety and hygiene issues addressed?

*This response sheet is adapted from materials in Kennedy and Deal and from conversations with Thelma Kannas Johnson of Sacramento, California.

**Activity 5.5:**

# Examining Your Organizational Values

■ Purpose

To identify the barriers to cultural proficiency that are evidenced in the covert values of your school or district.

■ Skill of Facilitator

Extensive

■ Readiness of Group

Advanced

■ Time Needed

90 minutes—2 hours

■ Materials

Copies of Response Sheet 5.5.1: Examining Your Organizational Values on paper or transparencies

Copies of the school's core values or shared values for diversity Activity 1.1

Chart paper and marking pens or overhead projector and transparency markers

■ Briefing

This activity will provide you with the opportunity to apply your understanding of (a) the sense of entitlement and (b) unawareness of the need to adapt. You will also examine the relationship between our stated and unarticulated values and the implication that this has for creating change in our school. The activity will be a mix of personal and group viewpoints and experiences.

## ■ Process

1. Distribute the school's shared values, or core values, for diversity.

2. Review the meaning of *covert value* or *unarticulated value*. Remind participants that it is the hidden curriculum.

3. Add your school's core values in the first column. You may do this ahead of time.

4. Ask each person to spend 15 minutes making notes on the response sheet that reflect his or her individual views and perspectives.

5. Have participants form into diverse groups of 4-6 people.

6. Give participants 30-60 minutes to discuss each core value and complete the response sheet.

7. Request that participants post their work on a chart or onto transparencies.

8. Encourage critical review of and reflection on the responses.

## ■ Debriefing

1. What were your feelings when you first received the response sheet?

2. What did you think, feel, or wonder about the discussion in your small group?

3. How do you feel about the levels of congruence between the stated and unarticulated values?

4. What observations do you have about the columns "Consequences " and "Implications for Change "?

5. What did you learn about your school? Your colleagues? Yourself?

6. What is the implication of this activity for you in your role at school?

7. What information or skills do you believe you need to do an even better job?

8  How will you use this information?

## ■ Variations

1. Divide the participants into culturally specific small groups.

2. Use the data you gathered about your school or district culture from the assessment you did after completing Activity 3.3 or Activity 5.4.

# Response Sheet 5.5.1:

## Examining Our Organizational Values

■ Example

| Value | Overt or Covert? | Unarticulated Information | Implications for Change | Organizational Value |
|-------|------------------|---------------------------|-------------------------|----------------------|
| *Organizational value* | *Is this an overt or covert value?* | *Is there an unarticulated contradiction or addendum to this value?* | *What behaviors or practices do you see as a result of this value?* | *Given this value, what are the implications for culturally proficient behavior or practices?* |
| **Example:** Excellence in all things | Overt | If it goes to the director, it is perfect; otherwise, just make it good. | The work is inconsistent in quality. Some people get praised for good work; others are chastised for "perfectionism." | We need to publicly state that there are two sets of standards and teach people how to use them. |
| **Example:** Caring | Overt | We care about people as long as they meet our expectations. | Everyone does not receive fair and equitable treatment. | I need to examine my own personal prejudices before I take an action. |

■ Examining Our Organizational Values

| Value | Overt or Covert | Unarticulated Information | Consequences | Implications for Change |
|---|---|---|---|---|
| *Organizational value* | *Is this an overt or covert value?* | *Is there an unarticulated contradiction or addendum to this value?* | *What behaviors or practices do you see as a result of this value?* | *Given this value, what are the implications for culturally proficient behavior or practices?* |
| | | | | |
| | | | | |
| | | | | |

# Part III

# Overcoming the Barriers to Cultural Proficiency

# Culturally Proficient Leadership: Formal and Nonformal Leaders

*The transforming leader looks for potential motives in followers, seeks to satisfy higher needs and engages the full person of the follower. The result of transforming leadership is a relationship of mutual stimulation and elevation that converts followers into leaders and may convert leaders into moral agents.*

—James MacGregor Burns

❧

Rolling Meadows Superintendent Watson recognizes that during his tenure, the demographics of the district have shifted from being almost totally white to increasingly multiethnic. He has gathered data on student achievement, noted the interracial fights at the high schools, and heard parents' complaints about the curriculum.

The request for proposal (RFP) that his staff prepares seeks consultants to conduct a year-long cultural audit and needs assessment that taps into the views and beliefs of all sectors of the district—the educators, the staff, the students, and members of the community. Although he has not yet been introduced to the concept of cultural proficiency, he knows intuitively to move in this comprehensive direction and to involve many layers of the district administration for them to understand his vision for all students in the district. He uses his formal position to lead the district into this process.

ᕙ

## School Leadership

When asked about school leadership, most people in the school community focus on various specific behaviors they observe in formal leaders, then judge how those behaviors measure up against what they believe to be appropriate behaviors. Some people prefer leaders who leave them alone, whereas others prefer leaders who are deeply involved with them in their classrooms. Everyone has a different list of specific items. We prefer to broaden our vision to look at the overall qualities of leadership, particularly qualities that facilitate movement toward cultural proficiency. In this chapter, we provide a context for understanding the leadership at your school, a necessary step for developing culturally proficient leadership skills in yourself and in those with whom you work.

Leaders can motivate others to excel and to move in desirable directions, or diffuse or otherwise block plans for change. In either case, contemporary researchers have found that effective leaders consistently show several key characteristics (Argyris, 1990; Banks, 1994; Senge et al., 1994; Wheatley, 1992) whether the leaders are in private businesses, corporate enterprises, or local school districts. These characteristics include taking responsibility for one's own learning, having a vision for what the school can be, effectively sharing the vision with others, assessing one's own assumptions and beliefs, and understanding the structural and organic nature of schools. We have observed that culturally proficient leaders show these characteristics whether they do so intuitively or as a result of carefully studying how to lead effectively. Furthermore, culturally proficient leaders learn and use what they learn about themselves, those with whom they work, and the school within which they work.

The formal leadership of schools has historically been the domain of white men. Although the trend is changing, the demographic profile of formal school leaders remains predominantly white and male. Educational data (National Center for Educational Statistics, 1994) show that 84% of district administrators and 77% of principals and assistant principals are white, and 59% of district administrators and 60% of assistant principals and principals are male. Perhaps because white men are mainly in charge of the development of school systems, many of the educational policies and practices have tended to benefit members of the dominant culture more than other people. For example, in their attempts to apply rules of science to school leadership, educators have developed top-down organization structures, systems for tracking students of differing abilities, and standardized tests to ensure that students are learning.

Whereas management, or school administration, is the process of getting work done through others, *leadership* is the process of inspiring others to work together to achieve a specific goal. Virtually any book you read on school leadership emphasizes the importance of leaders having and communicating a vision, guiding the creation of a shared mission, and building strong school cultures (Argryis, 1990; Fullan, 1991; Gilligan, 1983; Oakes & Lipton, 1990; Ogbu, 1978; Owens, 1991; Sizer, 1985; Wheatley, 1992).

❧

Coolidge Middle School Principal Richard Diaz is also ready to conduct a needs assessment. This urban school's student demographics have changed from virtually all African American to about one-fourth Latino in fewer than five years. Among the many changes he has initiated at the middle school is to provide instruction in Spanish to all students. This not only provides those whose primary language is Spanish the opportunity to develop bilingual skills in both their native tongue and English, but it also offers native English speakers the chance to learn Spanish, which will prepare them to function in multilingual settings as teenagers and adults. His vision helps African American students learn about the lifestyles of the Spanish-speaking students, and it mitigates any tensions that could result from having two language-based cultural groups in the school.

❧

## Effective Leaders

Effective Leaders Have

**A vision of what the group can be that is greater than what it is**

**The ability to communicate that vision in language
that is understood by the prospective followers**

**The skills to assess and respond appropriately to the needs
of the people and the environment in which they are working**

**The values and personality needed to build a strong school culture**

Usually, when people speak of leaders, they are thinking of formal leaders: those who have titles and official positions according them a certain degree of authority and coercive power. Although nonformal leaders have no official role assigning them the authority to direct a group, they have personal attributes—such as charisma, vision, and eloquence—that cause people to listen and to take action. A nonformal leader can be more powerful than a formal leader because the attributes of leadership are internally driven rather than externally conferred.

Massey (1979a) asserts that people are products of the decades during which they turned 10 years old and that the values inherent in those time periods do as much to shape their perspectives as anything else does. This assertion seems to hold true for many educational practices. Educators often accept roles as teachers, administrators, counselors, or other school-related professionals without assessing many of the practices in the school, let alone understanding how these practices came into use. Whether by design or default, the education system that prevailed the U.S. through the 1960s was a two-tiered system of policies and practices that did not serve the educational needs of most females or students from the marginalized caste cultures, for example people of color and poor people. Educators who began their careers after that time often inherit the worldview or the organizational culture that perpetuates this two-tiered system.

In analyzing current practices, leaders must be able to identify issues of class, caste, culture, and gender. Ogbu's (1978) notion of a caste system in the U.S. yields a crucial observation about poverty and racism: It is no accident that low-achieving students in the United States are over-represented by African American, Latino, and First Nation students who are from families of lower socioeconomic status. In the U.S., the apparent permanence of these socioeconomic groups gives rise to the reality of caste systems not unlike those many people assume exist in other countries.

Similarly, Freire's (1970) view of the inadequate teaching offered to the lowest economic groups of the United States provides a stark view of the role of schools. His work with people around the world, most notably in Central and South America, has illustrated time and again that students and their families are capable of high levels of achievement if they are taught how to learn, provided with the resources to learn, and given a reason to believe that they can control their own destinies. Gilligan's (1983) work on gender issues illustrates how the male-centered perspective in this country has too often denied women the educational and other advantages afforded to half of the population.

The teachings of Ogbu (1978), Freire (1970), and Gilligan (1983) correlate with culturally proficient practices. Culturally proficient leaders first develop a vision and then a mission that serves the needs of all students. In addition, they recognize and use both the formal and nonformal systems in the school, they know about the cultural issues that affect learning, and they have access to the resources necessary for an appropriate learning environment within the school. Culturally proficient school leaders know and appreciate how different school systems have evolved and are equipped to work with people and to guide others in challenging their assumptions and translating their perspectives, perceptions, values, and goals into agendas for school change. Having this knowledge of systems enables them to access the formal and nonformal leadership structures of their schools. They are able to support and lead school personnel as they formulate their plan for school change.

# Beyond Formal Leadership

Although the trends are changing, the demographic profile of formal school leaders remains predominantly white and male. Schools and districts in which members of emerging majorities have assumed formal leadership positions are often no more culturally responsive than those run by members of the dominant group. When looking at the national profile of school leaders and the universities that educate and train them, one sees primarily a fraternity of European Americans. It is therefore important to remember that even if the faces of leaders change, but the policies and practices that influence student achievement do not, the students will not fare any better. Perhaps because white men are mainly in charge of the development of school systems, many of the educational policies and practices have tended to benefit members of the dominant culture more than other people.

## ■ Collegial Leadership

Successful superintendents and principals are adept at amplifying their efforts by working with teachers, staff members, students, parents, and other community members who are respected by their constituents. In this chapter, we focus mainly on formal leaders, secondarily addressing the key role of nonformal leaders in school. We do so because although we can attest to the tremendous influence of nonformal leaders, we believe that formal leaders should bear the primary responsibility for creating the changes described in this book. The formal leaders of schools—namely, the superintendents, district office administrators, site-level administrators, and teachers—are employed to educate all children. How well they use the skills of the nonformal leaders, including students, parents, community members, and key staff members is a measure of their success.

ᔬ

Leatha Harp, director of credentialing and certification in Coolidge Unified School District, has gathered a small team of teachers and administrators who have agreed to serve on employment interview panels this school year to hire administrators for the district. They are reviewing anonymous comments written by other teachers and administrators when asked to discuss the type of leaders desired at Coolidge schools. The team has pulled out the comment sheets that reflect patterns or themes in the responses. About the formal leaders in the district, they read:

- What that school needs is a strict disciplinarian so the kids will know who is in charge.
- The Latino kids need a Latino administrator so they can have a positive role model.
- Principals come and go, but I will always be here.
- This school is entirely too tough for a woman administrator!
- I may not agree with her, but I know where she stands.
- One thing I will have to give the principal, he sure does relate well to the parents.
- She may be an expert in instruction and supervision, but how can she evaluate my physics lesson?

"I had no idea the comments would be so personal," exclaims Brittney. She is one of the middle school teachers, with a provisional credential. "Some of them sound so jaded."

"Oh, they are not all bad," says Leatha. "They tell us a lot about what people want in their leaders. Look at this pile of comments," Leatha continues. "They tell us a lot about where the nonformal leadership is in this district."

"What do you mean by nonformal?" asks Brittney.

"Nonformal leaders are not officially appointed or chosen, but rather emerge from the group, based on the needs and aspirations of those who work in the environment," explains Leatha.

"Nonformal leaders are usually people like teachers, aides, students, or parents. People whose positions don't give them a lot of power, but who have a lot of influence nonetheless. Barbara Latimer, who is on the board of the Citizens Human Relations Council, is a nonformal leader. She doesn't have a formal position of leadership, with a title, but everyone respects her and listens when she speaks. She is always at the district office and the board meetings, even though her daughter attends school in Rolling Meadows.

"Look at these comments; they acknowledge the nonformal leadership we have in this district."

- That secretary has trained seven principals!
- If you want to reach out to the parents, just tell Mrs. Latimer, Kim's mother—that woman is well respected in this community.
- To include more bilingual parents in school governance, you may want to use the services of the aide in Room 7; she knows all of the parents and they respect her highly.
- The union representative is a very important member of the leadership council, but DeLois Winters is the teacher to whom the others look for guidance.

⤞

Leaders come from all sectors of the school and the community it serves, and student leadership is vital to culturally proficient schools. Schools exist for students to gain knowledge and skills for adult life. In the 21st century, these skills and knowledge must include the ability to work in multicultural environments. Although, students should not have to lead change, effective leaders will find ways for them to contribute to it. Effective leaders acknowledge and support student leaders while assuming their own primary responsibility for making the school work for all students. Ideally, they do so proactively with foresight and vision, rather than reactively by responding to student or community pressures.

## ■ Changing Styles of Leadership

Increasingly, contemporary school leaders are expected to recognize and value the skills of both formal and nonformal leaders. This expectation represents a paradigm shift for those trained in traditional ways and those who work in traditionally organized schools, who are being pressured to change by union advocacy, community members' dissatisfaction with low student attendance and performance, and teachers' demands to be involved in decision making. In addition to student leadership, school leadership involves teachers through union activities as well as parents and community members. The roles and responsibilities of school administrators, particularly site-level administrators, are undergoing rapid transformation to more participative practices. These participative practices are consistent with the observations that (a) relationships are fundamental to school success (Wheatley, 1992), and (b) shared vision and team learning are fundamental to developing schools for learning (Senge et al., 1994). Culturally proficient leaders prize these participative practices and they organize their work in the school around them. Culturally proficient leaders see their schools as learning organizations where all are devoted to learning about the school, the community, and its children. Owens (1991) summarizes the emerging role of educational leaders:

> This has heightened our awareness that the power of educational leaders emanates not so much from their legal clout as from their ability to elicit the enthusiastic voluntary involvement of others—including students, teachers, community residents, and those in the official hierarchy—in the never-ending processes of creating and perfecting the educational institution (ix).

Culturally proficient principals exercise leadership by using the talents of other leaders in the school community. They fully appreciate and know how to involve widely diverse constituencies in making their school work for children.

# Choosing Effective Leaders

In most areas of the country, any impetus for placing people of color and women into formal leadership positions has been preceded by actual or pending legislation or by precedent-setting court cases. Nonetheless, gender and ethnicity still correlate very highly with who ascends to formal leadership roles in schools. Culturally proficient school leaders recognize that schools profit from having multiple perspectives, including those based on differences in gender, ethnicity, social class, sexual orientation, or physical or sensory ability. To this end, culturally proficient leaders actively solicit people who represent the widest spectrum of views for both formal and nonformal leadership roles.

Usually when people discuss leadership, they focus on the formal leader, the person who has the role and title such as *principal* or *director*. What is important to remember for the health and life of the organization is that leadership can be both formal and nonformal. A person does not have to be on the board or the head of a department to exert leadership. Culturally proficient leaders have a vision for the open, inclusive and relational school climate they seek to create, they communicate that vision in language that others can understand, and . they inspire and mobilize people to turn their vision into a reality.

# Leadership Styles

Traditionally, leadership styles have been categorized as autocratic, democratic, and laissez faire. Descriptions of leadership styles have also been based on the personality of the leader: driver, promoter, relater, or analyzer. Other literature describes the situational leader, one whose style changes to meet the needs of changing situations. Another way to categorize leadership is related to the way people respond to the life cycle of the organization. They may contribute by creating, developing, sustaining, deconstructing, or reconstructing.

Organizations, like people, go through phases of change and development. At one point, the organization's culture is formed by the energy of creating new programs or establishing and opening a new site. At another time, the programs are being nurtured as they mature and develop. Sometimes, an organization has the right people and programs in place and they just need to be maintained; at other times, old ideas, outdated programs, and ineffective people must be thanked, discarded, or encouraged to move on to environments where they can be most effective. Most leaders are good at responding to some of these tasks; few can respond to them all effectively. Consequently, it is important as a leader to know what you can contribute to the organization and to recognize what the organization needs. You can avoid unnecessary failure if your leadership style corresponds with the organization's developmental needs.

Creators are entrepreneurial in their approach to leadership. They rely more heavily on their creativity and willingness to take risks rather than on rules and traditional roles. Creators might develop some of the many ideas they have, but they usually don't. They are too frenetic and too filled with ideas to take the time to develop one into a completed project. They can't sit still long enough. There is too much noise and not enough space in their head to focus on one thing at a time. They generate ideas and give them away or just enjoy the fact that they had a good idea. Sometimes, the creator/developer style is found in the same person.

Developers might have their own ideas, but most of the time they are inspired by the ideas of others and are comfortable building on the ideas of the creators. Unlike many creators, developers will take the group's vision and help to make it real. They grow ideas into things. Usually, however, by the time they have gotten the idea to the point at which others can also see that it is a good thing, they are bored and ready to move on to something else. That is when the organization must find a leader who is a sustainer. These are the people who keep the lights on and the water running.

Sustainers are most effective when the organization is neither growing nor declining. Sustainers may not start new programs, but long after the developers or creators have burned out, the sustainers will see that the programs that have been initiated are monitored and sustained. Sustainers pay the bills on time and take out all the garbage, not just the wastebasket nearest the door. They are responsible and dependable. Sustainers make sure that whatever developers build continues working and stays in good condition. Sustainers work well with reconstructors because sustainers notice when things need to be fixed, whereas the reconstructors mend and repair things.

Reconstructors take things that look dead and bring them back to life. They research the initial ideas and figure out how something has been altered. They return things to their original condition or re-create them to fit into current situations. They seldom have original ideas, but they often make the ideas of others look far better than the original developer had imagined. Deconstructors simply take things apart. They challenge current processes, dismantle systems, and end relationships. Their motives and what they take apart define the three types of deconstructors. Malicious deconstructors damage and disrupt healthy relationships, beautiful projects, and productive organizations. They need to be identified and isolated. Benign deconstructors ignore what is going on and allow both healthy and unhealthy things to fall apart. They need to be identified and supported in attending to the health of the organization. Benevolent deconstructors safely disassemble defective or decaying structures and provide the catalyst for rebuilding.

Rarely do you find the creator and sustainer qualities in the same person, or a developer/deconstructor combination. The skills and perceptions of each are anathema to the other. Good leaders know what gifts and skills they contribute to the organization. It is important to know what you do best, and what the organization needs at a particular time, even though over time, you may have to play all five roles. You will come up with the idea and develop the project. On occasion, you will have to restore something you have damaged or terminate a relationship that is irreparable. You may greatly dislike destroying things, but sometimes, the only way for you to proceed toward your goal is to go backwards and then go forward again. Sometimes, to get what you want, things have to be taken apart completely and you have to start all over. Introducing cultural proficiency as the approach your school or district will take as it responds to the invitations and challenges of a diverse environment will require the cooperative efforts of more than one leader. Knowing what you do well will help you to determine what skills to seek and nurture among your team members.

Once a diverse group of leaders is in formal leadership roles, the leaders must be coached and supported in their new roles. They need support systems to be able to further develop successful leadership behaviors. In the past, the support system for white males was often referred to as the "good old boys' club." Although that infrastructure still exists in many school districts, in culturally proficient school districts, it is being replaced by formal systems of mentoring in which all new administrators are formally inducted into their leadership positions. States such as California have gone so far as to formalize approaches to mentoring through the state administrator certification process (California Commission on Teacher Credentialing, 1995). Likewise, organizations of professional administrators have embraced notions of mentoring and coaching as part of their responsibility for seeing to the success of new administrators.

## Leadership in Action

A school cannot become culturally proficient without effective leadership. Someone or some group has to have a vision of a culturally proficient school or district. Someone has to communicate that vision to the administrators, teachers, and community members and inspire them to transform themselves.

∾

Although Rolling Meadows Superintendent Watson, the formal leader, has not been formally introduced to cultural proficiency, his values and many of his current practices are definitely precompetent. He has vision for maintaining the school district's excellence during a time of changing student population. Instead of accepting declining test scores, initiating repressive disciplinary measures at the high schools, or turning a deaf ear to parents, he gathers data so that the district can examine its practices and make necessary changes based on the data and consistent with the district's values. Argyris (1990) refers to this process as double-loop learning, in which school leaders gather data to determine leverage points where changes in the school system are needed. In this case, the leverage points are student achievement, teachers' perceptions of a need for higher expectations, interracial clashes among students, and parental complaints about curriculum. Rather than blaming the teachers, the students, the students' families, or their cultural experiences for these areas of weakness, Watson gathers information to improve the school's processes. In the case of student achievement, he seeks alternative ways to teach and test students.

∾

Typically, leaders either reinforce the existing structures or promote change through dialogue and collaboration. Effective leaders evaluate the needs of the group. As those needs change, these leaders provide appropriate support for making adjustments to those changes. Culturally proficient leaders help the school's faculty and staff assess its culture and determine how the school affects the students and its community. They develop strategies for resolving conflict effectively and for addressing the dynamics of difference within the school. In shaping the school's formal and nonformal curriculum, they include information about the heritage, lifestyles, and values of all people in society.

Such exemplary leadership is rare; when schools become increasingly African American or Latino, district administrators often fail to provide adequate support for leaders to make systemic interventions in the schools. If these leaders then fail to reverse or to stop a downward trend, the district administrators blame the students, their families, or their cultures—or perhaps the principals—for the continuing problems.

Valverde and Brown (1988) describe the problems faced by school administrators of color. They must

> demonstrate loyalty to superiors, fellow administrators, and teachers; explain dysfunctional practices of school districts in the education of minorities; and help district personnel to understand what is important to minority groups. All the while they serve as agents of change on behalf of policies and practices considered appropriate to the enhancement of minority children and youth (p. 152).

Teachers, administrators, and educational consultants have seen that culturally proficient leadership can be exercised well by anyone independent of gender, ethnicity, social class, sexual orientation, or physical or sensory ability. Those who are effective are most often formal leaders who know how to use the talents of nonformal leaders. They have a vision of what education at the school can be for all students, they can communicate that vision to others, and they have the knowledge and skills to work with others to assess the school's needs and to devise ways of providing for student needs in achieving their shared vision.

## Historical Changes in School Leadership

Another key attribute of culturally proficient leaders is their awareness of the history of their schools in particular and education in the U.S. in general. The political, economic, and cultural context of education in the United States has influenced many of the changes in schools, such as the change from exclusively educating wealthy white boys to providing education for children of all socioeconomic strata, girls, and children of color. Many educational policies and practices have similarly affected the institutions and events of the wider society.

Table 6.1 summarizes modern management theory and its influence on schools. We have included historical practices that can be found in most schools today. The first column identifies the management theory predominant during a specific time period. The second column lists

**TABLE 6.1** Management Theory and Its Influence on Today's Schools

| Management Periods | Traditional Practices | Approach to Diversity |
|---|---|---|
| Classical period of scientific management 1890s–1930s | Organizational charts, tracking, testing | Schools teach basic subjects to most students; high schools allocate students to socioeconomic classes based largely on racially based castes. |
| Human relations period 1930s–1950s | Site-level processes, role of principal | More students from diverse socioeconomic groups attend school; class and caste still affect the quality of the education offered. |
| Organizational behavior period 1950s–1970s | Schools as social systems | School desegregation further mixes students of various castes and classes; students are expected to improve academic performance because of with whom they attend school. |
| Modern period 1980s–2000s | Diversity as a dynamic | Schools attempt to develop programs and use approaches that address the educational needs of all students. |

some of the educational practices associated with the corresponding periods. The third column illustrates the corresponding effect on women, emerging majorities, Gay Men and Lesbians, and the differently abled.

## ■ Classical Scientific Management and the Melting Pot

In judging the contributions to education from the classical scientific period to the present, note who attended schools at the turn of the century and for what purpose. Compulsory attendance laws, when they existed, usually required attendance only through the sixth or eighth grade. Also at this time, schools were deeply involved in helping to Americanize immigrants, the vast majority of whom were from eastern and southern Europe. Chiefly, schools' function in society was to provide labor for U.S. factories and farms. Within two or three generations, these immigrants were fluent in English, in many cases had Anglicized their names, and were considered full-fledged U.S. citizens.

For these people, this process of cultural assimilation is often called the *melting pot*. Within two to three generations, they blended into the increasingly diverse United States. Thus "melted" they were allowed to move into professions and other jobs for which high school and college education were needed. The flaw in the melting pot theory is that people from African, Latin American, First Nation, and Asian and Pacific Island cultures would not melt into this emerging new United States. Through personal initiative, many individuals were to become economically successful in this country, but more often than not, most were blocked from progress in schools and places of employment.

Most school districts today require compulsory attendance through high school. Schools in urban centers and schools in many isolated rural settings are largely populated by African American and Latino students. These students simply will not assimilate into U.S. society the way that European American students did. African American and Latino students continue to populate lower-tracked classes disproportionately, drop out early from high school, and perform below norms on standardized tests (Hodgkinson, 1991; Kozol, 1991; Oakes, 1985).

Educators are now grappling with how to provide at least a high school education for all students, and those attempts have succeeded and failed. During the past 20 years, society has explained the failures of students from dominated groups in terms of their disadvantaged or deprived nature—factors internal to them or to all cultures. Educators must accept that the disadvantage these students have is being deprived of educational practices that are successful with them, and then they must examine their assumptions about the factors external to them, what these students bring to school, and what educators need to do differently to be successful in teaching all students (Freire, 1970; Sleeter & Grant, 1991).

Another artifact from the classical scientific management period is standardized testing. Wiggins (1989) notes that "tests grew out of the 'school efficiency' movement in the years between 1911 and 1916" (pp. 704-705). Furthermore, "the reformers then, as now, were far too anxious to satisfy external critics and to reduce complex intellectual standards and teacher behaviors to simple numbers and traits" (p. 705).

> Implicitly there were signs of hereditarian and social-class based views of intelligence; the tests were used as sorting mechanisms at least partly in response to the increased heterogeneity of the school population as a result of the influx of immigrants. (p. 705).

Standardized testing and its consequent system of student tracking for instruction is an artifact of the classical scientific management period. Testing and tracking were designed to lead students straight to the careers for which their socioeconomic classes predestined them.

As Ogbu (1978; Ogbu & Matute-Bianchi, 1990) and others point out, First Nation people, Latinos, African Americans, and Asians are not likely to melt into a uniformly European American society. Such an occurrence is not only improbable but also undesirable. In the early 1900s, issues of culture, social class, gender, and ability were different for school policymakers and practitioners than they are for their counterparts today. Today, the challenge is to define a system that provides opportunities for people of diverse cultural, social class, gender, and physical and sensory ability backgrounds to receive an education enabling them to take their rightful positions in a world that now values mental agility more than physical strength. In such a setting, all forms of school testing should be examined in terms of their ability to measure student achievement authentically as well as to facilitate development of effective instructional strategies.

## Business Is Changing

The human relations, organizational behavior, and modern organizational periods have spawned major changes in the way private companies do business. Corporations search for more effective ways to use their workers due to both the pressures from labor unions and the realization that increasingly complex companies need more highly skilled workers. Schools have been affected by the same evolutionary trends that businesses have.

In the human relations period, managers viewed workers as people who could be motivated through intrinsic systems because they had the inner desire to do well (McGregor, 1960). During the organizational behavior period, managers started examining companies not only in terms of organizational charts but also in terms of the organic culture of the workplace (Deming, 1986; Drucker, 1954). During the modern period, managers have acknowledged that the labor force and consumer populations are becoming increasingly diverse, and that having a well-educated and diverse workforce is in the best interests of U.S. businesses (Boaz & Crane, 1985; Hodgkinson, 1991). Schools have adopted these new organizational practices in very uneven ways throughout the country. In fact, one could find in most schools vestiges of the classical scientific management period alongside more modern practices.

Whatever term is used to define the period of the 1980s, 1990s, and 2000s, this epoch will probably be distinguished by great and growing disparities between white children and children of color and between children from middle-income families and those from lower-income ones. It will be defined by whether educational reform programs are implemented systemically to ensure the social and educational successes of children without regard to their culture, different ability, gender, or family income. These systemic reforms will have to include an examination of your own assumptions about these groups, which are embedded in your curriculum and instructional practices, as well as in how you use data to inform your decision-making processes.

If you are to confront this moral dilemma successfully, you must collaborate with other culturally proficient school leaders. Today's uneducated and undereducated citizens have fewer opportunities to enjoy the bounties of this country as compared with their predecessors. Education is central to economic success in modern society. Educators must commit themselves to educating all children, regardless of their ethnicity, social class, gender, sexual orientation or different physical or sensory abilities. Their work must be predicated on the belief that all children can learn. The task is to determine how to provide the relevant, needed education. One way this can be done is to recognize the importance of the theories of leadership and organization that underlie your behavior. Understanding your role as a culturally proficient leader in this context provides you with a clearer sense of how organizations work and why they sometimes do not work.

# Going Further

1. What kinds of changes are needed at your school?
2. What type of leader is needed at this time?
3. Which management periods do you see reflected in your school's practices, or in its approach to diversity?
4. In what environments are you a formal leader? In what environments do you rely on your nonformal leadership?

# Reflection

_____

_____

_____

_____

_____

_____

_____

_____

_____

_____

## Activity 6.1:

# The Great Egg Drop*

■ Purpose

To build team spirit and commitment to a particular team goal. This activity will generate a lot of conversation and laughter.

■ Skill of Facilitator

Moderate

■ Readiness of Group

Beginning

■ Time Needed

90 minutes

■ Materials

Chart paper and markers for recording the scores
For each team of 3-5 people:
      1 raw egg (plus a few extra eggs, just in case)
      23 plastic straws
      23 inches of masking tape
      2 large garbage bags (for cleaning up the mess)
A hard surface, such as concrete, onto which the eggs can be dropped
A means for dropping the eggs from 8 feet above the ground

■ Briefing

Your task is to design an environment that will protect one raw egg dropped from a height of approximately 8 feet.

Your challenge is to achieve this goal using only 23 straws, 23 inches of masking tape, and your imagination. Boiling the egg, removing its contents, or catching it in your hands or before it falls the eight feet are not allowed.

In addition to constructing your product, it must have a name, and you will be expected to deliver a creative presentation highlighting the features and the benefits of your design.

All groups have been given the same task.

Remember this is not just a fun-and-games activity. The egg symbolizes our commitment to becoming culturally proficient, and the straws and tape symbolize our human and material resources.

■ Process

1. Divide the group into teams of 3-5 people.

2. Distribute the materials to the teams.

3. Give the directions orally and then pass out the direction sheets.

4. Tell the groups again what the eggs, straws, and tape symbolize. (Most of them will forget this part, so remember to bring it up again in the debriefing. People tend to get so focused on the goal that they forget the mission.)

5. Although it is perfectly all right for the groups to collaborate with each other, create an environment of secrecy. If they should ask (most don't) whether they could work together, avoid a direct response. If, on the other hand, they ask if they can work in another room so others won't see, let them.

6. Allow 10-15 minutes for briefing, distributing the materials, and getting started. Even with oral and written directions, some people will choose to be confused.

7. Allow 20-30 minutes for designing the protective environment and developing the marketing strategy. Remind them about creating their "pitch."

8. Take the group outdoors or to a floor that is not carpeted for dropping the eggs. Drop the eggs onto one of the plastic bags.

9. Assign one person to be the dropper and another to keep the scores. You may take either of these roles. You will also be functioning as the "ringmaster" because the participants will be quite excited by this time.

10. Ask the teams to present their products one at a time. They should give the product's name and make the marketing pitch. Let the other teams determine how many points they earn for marketing.

11. Count the remaining straws and measure the remaining tape. Add to the score.

12. Drop the product. For this, they will either get 44 points or 0.

■ Scoring Criteria

*Resources:* 1 point for each remaining straw or inch of tape
*Marketing:* The other teams collectively award your team's
    marketing pitch from 0-10 points, 10 being best.
*Product:*

| Resources | + Marketing | + Product | = Total |
|-----------|-------------|-----------|---------|
| (23 + 23) | + 10 | + 44 | = 100 |

1. When all of the teams have presented, clean up the mess, depositing it all in the second plastic bag.
2. Return to the training room and debrief. The debriefing will take at least 45 minutes. Remember that the debriefing is the most important part of this activity. Be sure to create an environment that underscores the importance of debriefing.
3. Distribute the debriefing sheets and ask each team to answer the questions for themselves. Allow 15 minutes.

■ Debriefing

Allow each team a few minutes to make a brief statement that summarizes its discussion.

1. Ask the group to share what it noticed about:
   a. Giving and receiving directions to get started
   b. The way people worked as a team
   c. The assumptions that were made about what they could and couldn't do
   d. How what happened reflects how they work
2. Share any observations you have made about the process.
3. What surprised you?
4. What did you learn?
5. What do you suppose was the purpose of this activity?
6. How can we use this experience?

**Response Sheet 6.1.1:**

# The Great Egg Drop

## ■ Directions

Your challenge is to achieve this goal using only 23 straws, 23 inches of masking tape, and your imagination. Boiling the egg, removing its contents, or catching it in your hands or before it falls the eight feet are not allowed.

In addition to constructing your product, it must have a name, and you will be expected to deliver a creative presentation highlighting the features and the benefits of your design.

For this activity, the egg symbolizes _____

The straws and tape symbolize _____

## ■ Scoring Criteria

*Resources:*   1 point for each remaining straw or inch of tape
            44 points if your design protects the egg from breaking
           0 points if the egg breaks
           0-10 points for the way you market your product

*Product:*

| Resources | + Marketing | + Product | = Total |
|-----------|-------------|-----------|---------|
| (23 + 23) | + 10 | + 44 | = 100 |

*Thanks to Sally Jue of Los Angeles, California, for this activity.

---

**Response Sheet 6.1.2:**

# Analyzing the Great Egg Drop

Now that you have developed your product and had the chance to observe another's group product, work with your team to answer these questions.

1. What was your process for getting started?
2. What criteria did you use for subdividing your team?
3. Did you consider collaborating or consulting with any other group?
4. Why or why not?
5. What were your success criteria?
6. Did your group win?
7. To what degree did you focus on what the egg, straw, and tape symbolized?
8. How was your work together here like your day-to-day interaction?
9. Is that a good thing?
10. What will you do differently when you go back to work?
11. What recommendations do you have for follow-up?

## Activity 6.2:

# Seven-Minute Day

■ Purpose

To use role-playing to practice mediating the conflict that arises from cultural misunderstandings. This activity invites participants to use their problem-solving and decision-making skills when working with parents and other community members in stressful situations. *Although it can be used with only educators, this activity is designed for use with mixed groups of teachers, administrators, and parents.*

■ Skill of Facilitator

Extensive

■ Readiness of Group

Intermediate

■ Time Needed

2 hours

■ Materials

Chart paper
Marking pens
Copies of Response Sheet 6.2.1: Role Descriptions for each of the three role groups
Copies of Response Sheet 6.2.2: General Instructions for all participants
Copies of Response Sheet 6.2.3: Seven-Minute Day Data Sheet for all participants
One room to serve as a communications center
Three break-out rooms

■ Briefing

You will be engaged in a simulated role-playing situation in which you will have the opportunity to play roles other than your current school-related roles. This activity will give you the opportunity to experience how it feels to be a member of another group. You will also practice decision-making, conflict resolution, and problem-solving skills.

■ Process

1. To the extent possible, have teachers role-play administrators, board members, or parents of this school. Likewise, have parents play roles other than parents and board members; have administrators do the same.

2. Distribute and read aloud Response Sheet 6.2.2: General Instructions. Respond to questions of clarification.

3. Distribute and read aloud Response Sheet 6.2.3: Seven-Minute Day Data Sheet.

4. Divide the group into the three role groups and situate them in separate rooms—parents, teachers, and administrators/board members. Distribute their Response Sheet 6.2.1: Role Descriptions and respond to questions of clarification.

5. Provide the groups 20 minutes to do their initial planning.

6. At the end of the 20 minutes, announce, "This is the beginning of Day 1" (You may want to designate it as a specific date or day of the week, such as Monday, October 14).

7. Have one room serve as the communications center, and receive and distribute messages as appropriate. You may just have to step aside and let the process unfold.

8. Announce every seven minutes, "It is now Day two," or, "It is now Tuesday, October 15," and so on. Repeat this process until you have enough information to have a productive discussion. Usually, it takes only 4-6 "days" to provide enough information for a very informed discussion.

■ Debriefing

You can begin the debriefing process in either of two ways:

1. You can ask each group in turn to respond to the questions that follow.

2. You can have each group return to its break-out room and spend a few minutes charting answers to the questions, and then return in 15-20 minutes and post responses.

Then, ask the following questions:

1. What did you think, feel, or wonder when I first described this activity?
2. What did you notice as a member of your role group during the planning phase of the activity?
3. What did you think, feel, or wonder about being a member of your role group during the conduct of the seven-minute days?
4. What did you think, feel, or wonder about the other two role groups? During the planning phase? During the seven-minute day phase?
5. What insights does this provide for the way we do business in schools?
6. What did you learn about your role group? What did you learn about the other role groups?
7. In what ways will you be able to use the information learned in this session?
8. In looking at the outcomes of your meeting, where do you judge them to be on the cultural proficiency continuum? What evidence do you have for your judgment?
9. How could you improve the process of your meeting as well as the outcome of the meeting?

■ Variations

1. Add role groups, such as students, business leaders, activist groups, and other interest groups.
2. Select other issues that have more immediate relevance to your school.

**Response Sheet 6.2.1:**

# Seven-Minute Day Roles

*Administrators and board members:* From your group, select participants to serve as board members, the superintendent, the business manager, the public information officer, the principal of the high school where the fight took place, a middle school principal, and an elementary school principal.

*Teachers:* Select officers for your local association. Designate your group members to be 70% European American, 10% Latino, 15% African American, and 5% Asian and Pacific Islander.

*Parents:* Designate your group members to be 40% Latino, 33% European American, 20% Asian and Pacific Islander, 5% African American, and 2% other.

**Response Sheet 6.2.2:**

# General Instructions

1. Use the initial 20-minute strategy session to develop your course of action. Record it on chart paper.
2. Select a message carrier. All communications are to be delivered to the communications center.
3. Develop responses to the other groups' messages and record them on newsprint during each seven-minute day.
4. Any group may move time ahead and skip a day by informing the other groups in writing.
5. Plan your strategies well.

**Response Sheet 6.2.3:**

# Seven-Minute Day Data Sheet

1. Your district has had a diversity plan in effect for three years. The plan had broad community support when it was first implemented.
2. Parents have recently expressed a concern that there is increasing violence and vandalism in the schools.
3. Teachers have filed grievances over the administration's lack of effective action in handling three recent assaults on teachers.
4. African American and Latino parents have charged the board of education and administration with unfair treatment of their children predicated on the high rate of suspensions and expulsions and their underrepresentation in honors classes.
5. Current student population is 40% Latino, 33% European American, 20% African American, and 5% Asian and Pacific Islander.
6. Current faculty population is 70% European American, 15% African American, 10% Latino, and 5% Asian and Pacific Islander.
7. A fight that occurred two days ago resulted in the suspension of three African American students, two European American students, and two Latino students. They may be recommended for expulsion.
8. A small group of parents went to the school to protest the suspensions, and a heated interchange led to some pushing and shoving. This action led to the arrest of one European American and one African American parent.
9. A group of angry parents is demanding that
   a. The board of education and the administration eliminate the racist practices in the school.
   b. The suspended students be readmitted and their records be cleared.
   c. All charges be dropped against the parents who were arrested.
10. If the demands are not met, the parents will withdraw their students from the school, causing the district to lose finances because of the reduced average daily attendance allotment.

---

# The First Barrier: Unawareness of the Need to Adapt

*There is nothing more difficult to take in hand, more perilous to conduct, or more uncertain in its success than to take the lead in the introduction of the new order of things.*

—Niccolò Machiavelli (1940)

At their staff development meeting with the diversity consultant, Richard Diaz, Coolidge Middle School principal, writes on the board, "That [women and] men do not learn very much from the lessons of history is the most important of all the lessons that history has to teach. Aldous Huxley, 1959."

"There he goes again," Harvey whispers to Lane. Richard has developed a mantra of change and a rallying cry for the new order of things he is trying to establish at Coolidge Middle School. He knows that one speech, one memo, or one staff meeting will not do it. Every time the faculty and staff see him, Richard talks about change and what it will mean for whomever he is addressing, as well as how it will affect the students and the school's community. He consults regularly with the district's consultant, James Harris, so that each one reinforces the work of the other when making presentations.

"These diversity staff development meetings are a waste of time," Harvey continues. "No one's going to change. I've been here for 17 years, and I've seen it all. I have tenure, so I'll just sit tight. These administrators are only here until they get a promotion. Each one brings his or her own program, and each program leaves with the administrator. If I wait long enough, I won't have to do a thing."

Across the room, DeLois and Derek are eagerly taking notes. "I wish I had taken more history courses when I was in college," DeLois sighs. "I'm sure that I could be more effective if I had a stronger historical foundation for what we are doing."

"We're not here to teach history, we're here to teach kids," Derek retorts. "I wish he would just tell us more about this cultural proficiency model so I can figure out what I need to change in my classroom."

"You're right," DeLois sighs. "Richard just needs to mandate what he wants done. Understanding history is not going to change some of the bigots in this room."

➶

## The Barriers to Cultural Proficiency

The primary barriers to cultural proficiency are the presumption of entitlement and unawareness of the need to adapt (Cross, 1989).

### Systemic Privilege: The Presumption of Entitlement

People with a *presumption of entitlement* believe that they have acquired all the personal achievements and societal benefits they have solely on their own merit and character, and therefore, they don't feel a need to release or reorder any societal or organizational perquisites they may have.

### Resistance to Change: Unawareness of the Need to Adapt

*Unawareness of the need to adapt* means failing to recognize the need to make personal and school changes in response to the diversity of the people with whom one interacts, perhaps because it never occurred to anyone in the dominant group that there was a problem. People who are unaware of the need to adapt often believe that if the others—the newcomers—change or adapt to the environment, there will be no problems. They do not yet understand that once the commitment to cultural proficiency is made, everyone changes to create a new school culture.

# Paradigm Shifters

Do you remember when polyester was considered a miracle fabric and "made in Japan" meant cheap and tacky? If you made lists called "working mother" or "father's jobs" in 1965, how would they differ from the same list written in 2000? These are examples of paradigms that have changed. A *paradigm* is the set of rules or criteria you use to judge whether something is correct or appropriate. A paradigm is a filter of perception; it is a frame you put around a concept to understand it and make it fit with your understanding of the world. The cultural expectations of your school or district are paradigms.

Everyone uses paradigms to order his or her world. When you do a double-take because you have observed or experienced something odd, when you argue intensely against a new idea, it is because your paradigms have been challenged. Joel Barker (1989, 1996) is a futurist who has taken the concept of paradigm, used initially and solely by scientists, and reframed it for the world at large. He uses the concept of paradigms to help explain the process of change.

Most people resist change because they feel threatened. They fear that they may lose something that they value. The new idea or process does not fit within the boundaries of their current paradigms, so they resist or actively seek to prove that the new idea is wrong, inappropriate, or unnecessary. *Paradigm shifters* are perceived as misfits or outcasts who move along the margins of the group. They may be older and venerated and therefore have no fear of losing their power or prestige, or they may be new and unseasoned, seeking to prove themselves to veterans in the field. *Paradigm resisters* are people who are vested in a system or who are among the system's elite. They have the most to lose and will be among those who denounce a proposed change most vociferously. They suffer from "hardening of the categories." The culturally proficient leader will be a paradigm shifter and will have to prepare for various types of resistance to change while building a team of paradigm shifters who will help as formal and nonformal leaders to take the school or district through the transition.

# Clearing Up the Myths About Change

One of the ways to start is by addressing directly the myths about change. Myths are too damaging to ignore; they disempower individuals and cripple organizations. These are some of the myths about change. Price Pritchett and Ron Pound (1990) have written a short and useful booklet on change. Table 7.1 summarizes some of the myths about change that they discuss.

With some groups, it may be helpful to address these myths. With others, it will be important for the leaders to remember that these are the myths by which many people order their lives. You will find some people very eager to try out the cultural proficiency tools, but others will neither want to change nor understand why you want them to.

You will also find that even when people want to change, they show some resistance to the change process. That's natural. For most people, change means loss: You must give up some aspect of your current self-perception in order to become something different. When asked to make the changes necessary to address the diversity issues in your schools, your colleagues may feel threatened, both psychically and politically. As you lead your colleagues toward cultural proficiency, you will have to find ways to help them get past these feelings and overcome their resistance to change.

## ■ The Change Process

William Bridges wrote two books on change that you may want to read: *Transitions: Making Sense of Life's Changes* (1980) and *Managing Transitions: Making the Most of Change* (1991). Of these two books, *Transitions* will probably be the most valuable to you because it focuses on personal change and how it affects your relationships and your work. The key to understanding change, says Bridges, is recognizing the stages: endings, transition, and beginnings.

Most people fail to acknowledge that starting something new begins by ending something else. Even the most joyous occasions—birth, marriage, promotion, retirement—involve huge losses. During the ending times, you may mourn your losses, or just need time to say goodbye to old friends, familiar places, comfortable ways of doing things, and a changing sense of yourself. If you end well, your beginnings will be easier to manage. Between your endings and beginnings, however, is a period of transition that also must be managed.

Imagine the process that children go through to learn new things. Take walking, for example. They don't just stand up and walk. They practice a lot. They go through a period of practicing, having small successes, making adjustments in their approach, practicing some more, and experiencing greater success. They also fall down a lot. You can use this image when you are learning or adjusting to new things, because this process is not just what children do. It is how all people learn. Transition periods mark the times that you are changing from one way of doing things to another. You have accepted that the old way is no longer

**TABLE 7.1** Myths About Change

| Myth | Reality |
|------|---------|
| This will go away. *Oh, brother, here we go again. Somebody in top management must have gotten bored and decided to stir things up. It will blow over. It's just a matter of time.* | Change is here to stay. |
| It will help if I get upset about this. *How am I supposed to get my work done with all of these stupid changes? I give up.* | Controlling your emotions increases your control over the situation. |
| This is a bad thing for my career. *Why didn't they put me on a task force to do something I know about?* | Progress often masquerades as trouble. |
| I can just keep doing my job like I have been. *We've been doing it this way for years; I don't see why I have to change because someone else has complained.* | If the company is changing, you probably need to be changing, too. |
| I'm not in a position to make a difference. *All these changes weren't my idea. There's nothing I can do anyway.* | You're either part of the solution or part of the problem. |
| Top management is supposed to make these changes work. *They created this mess; let's see how they fix it.* | If you work here, this is your plan. |
| They don't know what they're doing. *Top management is making life miserable for the average employee.* | Top managers have a pretty good idea what they're doing, but can't do it without running into problems or making some mistakes. |
| The changes weren't really necessary. *Why can't they just leave well enough alone?* | What's necessary now is to make the changes work. |

SOURCE: Adapted from Pritchett and Pound (1990).

available to you or acceptable in your new environment, yet you have not quite mastered the new way of doing things.

The change process is both simple and difficult. Culturally proficient leaders implement the steps in the appropriate order: ending by releasing the old paradigms, transitioning between the old and the new, and beginning to use new behaviors and processes in a consistent way. Most leaders add to people's resistance to change because they don't acknowledge the true order in which change takes place. Table 7.2 outlines the process.

Culturally proficient leaders understand that change begins by ending something. You end the way you have been doing things, for example, your focus on similarities in the diversity program or your goal of cultural blindness. Even if your faculty have intellectually accepted cultural proficiency as the model for addressing issues of diversity, they will be more willing to move forward toward new goals if you acknowledge their losses and their need to grieve those losses.

During the *endings* phase, culturally proficient leaders facilitate the process by spending time with their staff members to acknowledge their feelings of perceived loss and by guiding the members of the school community through the stages of denial and shock, anger and hostility, and elation and grief. In this phase, the leader is challenging the school to create the need for change and the staff members to accept the reality of change. The culturally proficient leader develops a mantra of change and a rallying cry for the new order of things.

## The Dynamics of Change

The *transition* period is marked by activities in which people are no longer doing what they used to do, but they still aren't doing what they want to do. At this time, the leader introduces the new concepts and strategies and works to create a collective vision for how the school will be different as a result of this change. The leader then has the school dismantle the old systems and initiate most of the changes. Some people will be ready to participate immediately; others will be convinced that it won't work; and most will just sit back, waiting to see what happens. During this time, many people will try out new ideas yet revert back to old and comfortable ways of doing things. It is important during the transition periods to remember the seven dynamics of change.

When changes are made in a relationship or in an organization:

**TABLE 7.2** Phases of the Change Process

| Phase of the Change Process | Characterized by These Emotions | Individual Challenges | Organizational Challenges |
|---|---|---|---|
| *Release the old*<br><br>Endings | • Denial, shock<br>• Anger, hostility<br>• Elation, relief<br>• Disbelief<br>• Confusion<br>• Disappointment<br>• Grief | • Accept the reality of change<br>• Release attachment to people and to the old ways of doing things<br>• Acknowledge losses | • Create the need for change<br>• Connect to the history<br>• Allow people to get used to the idea<br>• Include people in the planning process |
| *Change*<br><br>Transition<br><br>*Change* | • Resistance<br>• Sabotage<br>• Depression<br>• Support<br>• Facilitation<br>• Resignation<br>• Humor<br>• Denial<br>• Excitement<br>• Frustration | • Review what has been learned in the past<br>• Overcome resistance<br>• Commit to the future<br>• Connect with the transition | • Communicate a vision of the future<br>• Dismantle old systems<br>• Mobilize commitment to the new vision<br>• Stabilize transition management<br>• Create effective balance of the old and the new<br>• Establish appropriate time lines or phases<br>• Establish and use feedback systems |
| Beginnings<br><br>*Embrace the new* | • Fear<br>• Exploration<br>• Resolution<br>• Commitment<br>• Excitement<br>• Resistance<br>• Anger<br>• Disillusionment<br>• Anxiety | • Master new routines<br>• Learn new cultural norms<br>• Embrace the new organizational climate | • Institutionalize the change<br>• Reward and reinforce the new systems<br>• Introduce new cultural norms<br>• Affirm old values<br>• Identify and respond to unintended consequences<br>• Realign structure and staffing to accommodate the change |

SOURCE: Adapted from Bridges (1980).

223

1. **People are at different levels of readiness for change.**
2. **People will think first about what they are going to lose.**
3. **People will feel awkward, uncomfortable, and ill at ease.**
4. **People tend to be concerned that they will not have enough resources.**
5. **People will feel alone even though others are going through the same thing.**
6. **People can handle only so much at a time.**
7. **When the pressure is off, people will revert back to old behavior.**

The culturally proficient leader continues to challenge, encourage, and shepherd staff members forward while managing the transition. Many staff members complain and sing their songs of lament, foreboding, and ire. They resist, they sabotage, and they fall into depression. The culturally proficient leader remembers at this time that human beings do not change overnight. Children don't learn to read after one lesson, and adults don't learn new behaviors after one structured activity. Just as proficient teachers coach, support, and praise children for incremental improvements, culturally proficient leaders coach, support, and praise staff members as they try out new attitudes and new behaviors.

The *beginnings* of change follow the transition period, which comes some time after the endings have been acknowledged. It is during the beginnings phase that the changes become institutionalized. It is also during this phase that resisters look for evidence that change is not working. Culturally proficient leaders are ready for the naysayers by explaining the process of making changes and setting realistic expectations for everyone. They are also prepared to point out where progress has been made. They find ways to reward the participants for their commitment to change and to reinforce the changes in the school. This is not, however, the time to stop and rest on one's laurels. Once one set of changes has been put in place and the systems within the school are supporting it, leaders look to see what else can be changed and how.

## Overcoming Resistance

With diversity programs, the first barrier of resistance is the unawareness of the need to change. Expect that people will attempt to assign blame and abdicate responsibility. Be prepared to hear:

✍

"We didn't do anything to those people; why do we have to change?"

"This is America; they should be adapting to us."

"This is reverse discrimination."

"Why are we trying to fix something that's not broken?"

"I don't want to have to apologize for being white."

"It seems like white men are the ones being oppressed now."

✍

You will also hear comments that reflect the four approaches to diversity that do not adequately address all of the issues: Golden Rule, Your Pain Equals Mine, Oppression Olympics, and Right the Wrongs. The first two groups will think you are moving too quickly, and the second two groups will accuse you of focusing on the wrong things while moving much too slowly. Culturally proficient leaders respond to this resistance in two ways: (a) They acknowledge the feelings of the complainers: Change is seldom easy and is often unwanted, especially when a commitment to cultural proficiency means having to do more work; and (b) they explain that the changes are being made to serve the students and their families better. The plan is not to fix something that is broken; it is to grow as a school community for the students' benefit. This is also the time to refer back to the appropriate principle or element so that people can see how the cultural proficiency tools can be applied to each problematic situation.

# Resilience

Remember that some people will appear to be handling all of the changes very well and then, when you introduce some very small change, they will have a strong reaction that is out of proportion to the situation. Look at the words used to describe someone's strong, negative reaction to something: *snap, break, fall apart, blow up, lose it.* The language is violent because at those times, people are *feeling* as if they have been treated violently. So pay attention to your colleagues. Invite them to take care of themselves, and intervene if you know that they have only one good nerve and someone is threatening to get on it.

Resilience is the set of qualities and characteristics that enable some people to adjust to, adapt to, and recover from personal trauma and the dramas of life. Resilience is elasticity of character. Think of a rubber band. It only works when there is some tension. And only when it is stretched can you determine its quality. You can twist it, bend it, and pull it. You can use it to hold things or to propel things. Yet, once you release the tension, it will snap back into its original shape. If it is too stiff, instead of stretching when tension is applied, it breaks. As it ages, it loses its resiliency and it does not return completely to its original form, but it is still clearly a rubber band.

Silly Putty, on the other hand, will take on the shape of anything you put it in, yet on its own it is just an amorphous mass—mass without substance or resilience. Silly Putty is flexible, pliable, and adaptable, but it is not resilient. If you pull on it sharply, it breaks. It starts with no basic shape, so it has nothing to return to, and because it has no shape of its own, it never looks the same. Silly Putty can survive in an environment that is rapidly changing, but you never know in what shape it will end. Rubber bands will keep on adjusting, holding things together, and snapping back to their original shape—unless, of course, there is extreme tension, in which case the rubber band will break.

Resilient people may be a little snappy sometimes, but they will thrive during change. People who are more like Silly Putty may appear to be adjusting, but without any external support will just lie there—a shapeless mass that cannot hold itself together. So in the midst of implementing change, build your team from those who have the character traits that foster resilience:

- Flexibility
- Open-mindedness
- Clarity of values
- The ability to prioritize and re-prioritize when necessary
- Focus on goals
- The willingness to identify and correct mistakes

Your team of paradigm pioneers can then support one another and provide the appropriate kind of support to the paradigm settlers. Paradigm settlers are the ones who wait until the new paradigm is almost in place, then they shout to the pioneers, "Is it safe out there yet?" (Barker, 1989).

Rolling Meadows High School Principal Dina Turner is conducting a meeting with her site council. "We are at the midpoint of our year, and our plan specifies that we are to assess our progress by examining our benchmarks. As you recall, our goals for this year were for schoolwide academic improvement in reading and for learning more about our interaction patterns with students."

Bobby, one of her consistently unhappy teachers, replies, "You know, I am all for academic improvement, but I still don't see how it is related to having a teacher observing me in my classroom."

Another teacher, Celeste, speaks up in Dina's defense. "I am not sure I agree with you. Since we have started the schoolwide focus on reading, it's easier for me to talk with my students about reading for fun."

Barbara Latimer, a very active parent in the district, adds, "That is a good point. Just this weekend, my daughter asked if I didn't think that we watched way too much television. I hated to admit it, but she is right. I was just wondering how parents who are not members of the site council are reacting."

Dina says, "Obviously, I am very supportive of our reading initiative. I am also deeply committed to our continued study of student-teacher interactions. Has anyone tried any of the teacher expectations behaviors in their classrooms?"

"I have," said Celeste. "You know, Bobby, even though I know I am a good teacher, those activities are helping me see some of my blind spots. I am beginning to see how my unintentional behaviors can keep kids from learning!"

"What occurs to me," adds Dina, "is that if these unintentional behaviors occur between teachers and students, they must occur among adults, too. It scares me to think about the damage we do to one another without even realizing it."

Barbara has an idea. "You know, we may want to consider some of that training for parents. From what you are saying, it may be very enlightening, possibly a little uncomfortable, but very worthwhile."

"Most teachers are comfortable with the process," Dina replies. "I believe if people see themselves as students and are willing to commit the energy it takes to walk this path to improvement, we will all grow and our kids will really benefit. And, I agree, it would be good for this group too. It would be an excellent topic for training all our parents."

Across town, neophyte teacher Brittney is looking at a framed list hanging on the wall near the desk of her mentor teacher, DeLois. "What is this?" Brittney asked.

"Oh," DeLois said, "I am a quilter, and once, as I made a quilt of ribbon and lace, sewing one small strip after another, I thought about the life lessons that I was learning through quilt making. I try to remember these

things whenever we are trying to implement some change in the district."
This is what was on DeLois' list:

> There is no rehearsal. It all counts.
> Sometimes, you need the big picture before you can start.
> Don't skimp.
> Be patient with yourself.
> Do one square at a time.
> Try it out.
> Take it apart, start over.
> Nonconformity, although beautiful, is sometimes very disruptive.
> Stop when you are tired. It's better to have only three things to do when you are fresh than to have three things to do over when you are frustrated.
> Sometimes, you won't know the best process to use until after you have finished.
> Good work is not always transferable. What works well in one setting may be totally wrong in another.
> Perfection is perception.

≈

Perhaps you can put DeLois's list near your desk as well.

Because change affects people in such personal ways, we have provided a larger number of reflection activities in the Going Further section of this chapter. They are separated into three categories: Personal Change, Resilience, and Organizational Change.

# Going Further

## ■ Personal Change

1. Think of a personal change in your life or the life of your family. Describe the change process in terms of endings, transitions, and beginnings.

2. How many things in your life are in transition today? Do you need to say goodbye or mourn the loss of anything or anyone? Look at Table 7.2. How well does it reflect the transition periods you have experienced? How would you personalize the chart?

3. If you find yourself stuck at the beginning of an ending process, ask yourself, "What am I holding on to?" Remember some of your aborted transitions. List them. Some of these unfinished transitions might still be completed, and, as a result, you would bring more energy and less anxiety to your present situation. What might you do to complete an aborted transition? Completion may involve no more than a belated farewell, a letter, or a call to someone. It may involve an inner relinquishment of someone that outwardly you left behind years ago, of some old image of yourself, or of some outlived dream or outworn belief that you have kept long past its usefulness.

4. Talk with a few people about their personal rituals for managing the transitions in their lives. Create a personal ritual to mark your transition process.

## ■ Resilience

1. How resilient are you? How do you know? Can you think of an object like a Slinky, a rubber band, or Silly Putty that illustrates your degree of resiliency?

2. Talk with some coworkers about the benefits of resiliency at your organization. What would happen if your school or district were not a resilient organization? What happens to the people at your organization who are not resilient?

## ■ Organizational Change

1. After reading about the dynamics of change, go back to the list and select one that invites you to reflect a little more deeply. How has this dynamic of change affected you? To what does it relate in your life? Is there something you need to ask of your colleagues to help you to adjust to some changes in your district? Is there something you need to say to your staff to help adjust to the changes they are experiencing?

2. What are the changes that have been implemented at your school or in your district in the past three years? How many of the changes were permanent? Do you recall how people responded? How did you respond?

3. Make a list of barriers in your school or district. When do people fail to see the need for change? To what do people feel entitled?

# Reflection

_____

_____

_____

_____

_____

_____

_____

_____

_____

_____

**Activity 7.1:**

# The Process of Personal Change

## ◼ Purpose

To raise awareness of how change takes place

## ◼ Skill of Facilitator

Moderate

## ◼ Readiness of Group

Intermediate

## ◼ Time Needed

20 minutes

## ◼ Materials

Copies of Response Sheet 7.1.1

## ◼ Briefing

We have been talking about making change, and you are probably wondering why other people have not changed yet. Let's look at the process for personal change.

## ◼ Process

1. Distribute Response Sheet 7.1.1.
2. Ask participants what they think of it.
3. Discuss the various points on Response Sheet 7.1.1 and the movement from one to another.
4. Elicit examples from the participants for personal changes they have experienced.
5. Discuss what the process would be for someone moving toward cultural proficiency.
6. Discuss the implications for the school's or district's learning process.

■ Debriefing

1. What did you learn or remember from this process?
2. How does this process differ from how children learn?
3. What are the differences between learning something as an adult
4. How should we adapt our expectations to one another as we grow?and learning something as a child?
5. How should we adapt our expectations for our district/school as we implement the cultural proficiency model?

■ Variation

Have participants write their personal examples on the response sheet as they analyze a specific change process situation they went through.

**Response Sheet 7.1.1:**

## The Process of Personal Change

**Unconscious Competence**

Reinforcement

Practice

Change to Value Set B

**Conscious Competence**

Practice

Reinforcement

Feedback

Behavior Change

**Conscious Incompetence**

Attitudinal Shift

Awareness

**Unconscious Incompetence**

Inappropriate Behavior

Value Set A

**Activity 7.2:**

## Seven Dynamics of Change

■ Purpose

To help participants become aware of the normal responses to change

■ Skill of Facilitator

Low Readiness of Participants: Beginning

■ Materials

Room for participants to stand and to pair off with a partner
Response Sheet 7.2.1: Seven Dynamics of Change

■ Briefing

We're going to see how well you and your partner pay attention to your environment. (This statement is intentionally ambiguous.)

■ Process

1. Have participants face their partners. Invite them to take a long, loving look at their partner and then turn around with their backs to one another.

2. Now ask each person to change five things about themselves. They will have many questions, don't answer them. Simply encourage them to quietly change five things. When both partners are ready, have them turn back around to face each other.

3. Ask the partners to notice what has been changed, sharing their observations with their partners. After they do that, tell the entire group to turn their backs to their partners and to change five more things.

4. They will grumble and complain. Ignore it. Encourage them to move more quickly and ask them to please just cooperate and to trust you.

5. Facing their partners once again, ask them to notice what has been changed. There will be much laughter and noise.

6. Quiet them down. Acknowledge how well they are cooperating. Ask them to now change 10 more things (or 15 or 20, whatever is plausible, but at the same time, a number that will be perceived as outrageous). The group will fall apart. Ask them to sit down.

7. Debrief the activity using the Seven Dynamics of Change.

8. Relate the dynamics of change to the changes the participants are experiencing in their lives, work, or organization.


■ Debrief

*Ask the group:* How did you feel when you first heard the request to change things?

*Reinforce this point:* When changes are made in a relationship or in an organization:

**1. People will feel awkward, uncomfortable, and ill at ease.**

*Ask the group:* What was the first thing that you did?
*Probable response:* Remove something.

*Reinforce this point:* When changes are made in a relationship or in an organization:

**2. People will think first about what they are going to lose.**

*Ask the group:* Did you feel embarrassed?
*Probable response:* Yes.

*Ask the group:* Did you notice what other people were doing?
*Probable response:* Probably not.

*Reinforce this point:* When changes are made in a relationship or in an organization:

**3. People will feel alone even though everyone is going through the same thing.**

What did you think when I asked you to change 10 (or 15 or 20) more things?

*Reinforce this point:* When changes are made in a relationship or in an organization:

### 4. People can only handle so much.

*Ask the group:* How many of you actually changed five things the first time and five more the second time?

*Probable response:* Not everyone. Some people probably did not participate at all.

*Reinforce this point:* When changes are made in a relationship or in an organization:

### 5. People are at different levels of readiness for change.

*Ask the group:* What were you thinking when I suggested you change even more things?

*Reinforce this point:* When changes are made in a relationship or in an organization:

### 6. People tend to be concerned that they will not have enough resources.

*Ask the group:* What was the first thing you did when I invited you to sit down?

*Probably response:* Put my clothes back on.

*Reinforce this point:* When changes are made in a relationship or in an organization:

### 7. When the pressure is off, people will revert back to old behavior.

**Response Sheet 7.2.1:**

# Seven Dynamics of Change

When changes are made in a relationship or in an organization:

1. People will feel awkward, uncomfortable, and ill at ease.

2. People will think first about what they are going to lose.

3. People will feel alone even though everyone is going through the same thing.

4. People can only handle so much.

5. People are at different levels of readiness for change.

6. People tend to be concerned that they will not have enough resources.

7. When the pressure is off, people will revert back to old behavior.

---

**Activity 7.3:**

## Differences That Make a Difference

■ Purpose

To name and describe some of the differences that make a difference in your school. This activity is designed to help participants assess some of the barriers to cultural proficiency in the organization.

■ Skill of Facilitator

Moderate

■ Readiness of Group

Intermediate

■ Time Needed

60 minutes

■ Materials

One sheet of chart paper for every four people
Markers for each person
Masking tape

■ Briefing

Making a commitment to cultural proficiency means examining the school's climate to ascertain what goes on in the culture that may cause people to feel uncomfortable. In this activity, we are going to reflect on the differences that make a difference at our school. Think of a time that you bumped into a difference that caused discomfort for you.

**Figure 7.1**

Person 3 writes in this section
⇓

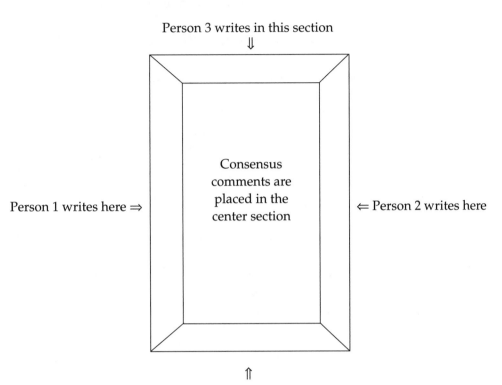

Person 1 writes here ⇒

Consensus comments are placed in the center section

⇐ Person 2 writes here

⇑
Person 4 writes in this section

■ Process

1. Organize the participants into groups of four.

2. Demonstrate for the class how to divide the chart paper. See Figure 7.1.

3. Ask each participant to note in his or her portion of the diagram situations he or she has witnessed or experienced that made him or her uncomfortable.

4. After each person has written in his or her section, the four members of the group discuss what they have written and write a synthesis of their comments in the center of the page.

■ Debriefing

1. What did it feel like to name the differences that make a difference?

2. How would you categorize the differences that create problems in this school?

3. Now that you have named the differences, let's review the essential elements or the guiding principles of cultural proficiency to get some direction for addressing the issues.

■ Variation

This activity can be used to focus on just one group, department, or classroom.

■ Variation

This activity may be used as an awareness process. The group members may be comfortable just naming the issues. Deciding what to do about them can take place later in the group's process.

**Activity 7.4:**

# Paradigms

■ Purpose

To develop common language and a new perspective for viewing the change process

■ Skill of Facilitator

Moderate

■ Readiness of Group

Intermediate

■ Time Needed

60 minutes

■ Materials

Chart paper
Markers
Response Sheet 7.4.1

■ Briefing

A paradigm is a set of rules or criteria that we use to judge the appropriateness or correctness of something. Let's talk about some of the paradigms in your life. (Refer to the discussion of paradigms in Chapter 7.) Now we will discuss the paradigms that affect the work we are doing in our school.

■ Process

Distribute Response Sheet 7.4.1. Assign the questions to small groups. Each group can answer one question, or, if you have more time, each group can answer all seven questions.

1. What paradigms do you want to keep at our school [in our district]?
2. What paradigms do you want to reject?
3. What paradigms are changing or shifting?
4. What paradigms have been challenged unsuccessfully?
5. What new paradigms do you predict will develop in the next few years?
6. What is impossible today but, if it could be done, would fundamentally change the way we address issues of diversity?
7. What are the implications of the answers to these questions for your school?

As the groups present their responses, allow time for discussion, questions, and additions to each group's list by the other members in the class.

## ■ Debrief

Discuss the answers to the questions.

## ■ Variation

Show the video by Joel Barker, "The New Business of Paradigms," available online at: http://www.starthrower.com/barker.html. Discuss the film and then answer the paradigm questions.

We highly recommend this option. The Joel Barker paradigm videos are excellent.

**Response Sheet 7.4.1:**

# Assessing Your Paradigms

Think about the values, habits, processes, and policies that direct your activities at work. These are the paradigms. As you prepare for changes in your life or your organization, ask yourself these questions:

1. What paradigms do you want to keep?
2. What paradigms do you want to reject?
3. What paradigms have been challenged unsuccessfully?
4. What paradigms are changing or shifting?
5. What new paradigms do you predict for the organization?
6. What is impossible today but, if it could be done, would fundamentally change the way you live?
7. What are the implications for the answers to your questions?

# 8 ❦

# The Second Barrier: The Presumption of Entitlement

*If we tell ourselves that the only problem is hate, we avoid facing the reality that it is mostly nice, non-hating people who perpetuate racial inequality.*

—Ellis Cose

൞

The Rolling Meadows consultants are making a presentation to Superintendent Watson's cabinet, and Holly, the assistant superintendent of curriculum and instruction, is not so sure they really understand the situation at Rolling Meadows because she hasn't seen any of these problems. The consultants say, "Throughout U.S. educational history, students have been taught close to nothing about the caste system in this country and very little about U.S. citizens of lower castes. In recent decades, however, most textbooks and school curricula have inserted some materials and lessons mentioning women and people of color, although these insertions have generally been few and segregated from the sweep of U.S. history.

"Acknowledgment of African Americans is generally limited to brief lessons on slavery, the celebration of Dr. King's birthday, and observances of black history month in February. Lessons about People of the First

Nations often range from highlighting their nobility to underscoring their savagery; usually, their only significant role is to attend the first Thanksgiving. Lessons about Latinos are frequently relegated to music, dance, and a lesson about Cesar Chavez or Che Guevara, if they are mentioned at all outside of New York and the southwestern United States. Students learn about Asians as the celebrants of Chinese New Year, the sneaky attackers at Pearl Harbor, and the reluctant recipients of our 'help' during the Korean and Vietnam Wars. Lessons about women often resort to the 'great woman' approach, focusing on a few heroic individuals rather than the historic and continuing role of women in the United States. These discrete lessons lead to the objectification and invisibility of girls and people of color."

☙

In professional development sessions similar to that at Rolling Meadows, we have posed the following question: "As reasonable people, can we agree that systems of oppression like racism, ethnocentrism, sexism, and heterosexism have existed historically in this country, and people have lost rights, benefits, and their lives?" Uniformly, people either nod in assent or verbally agree with the statement. Then we continue by asking, "As reasonable people, then, can we agree that vestiges of these systems persist, and that people are still penalized by these systems?" Again, people nod in agreement or express verbal agreement. Then we ask the important question, "If people have lost, and continue to lose, rights and benefits due to systems of oppression, what happened to those rights and benefits?" One can sense the discomfort as participants begin to have an emerging awareness of the powerful dynamic of entitlement.

# Barriers to Cultural Proficiency

The fourth cultural proficiency tool is the barriers to cultural proficiency. The barriers are the unawareness of the need to adapt and the presumption of entitlement. Entitlement is the systemic privilege that accrues to members of the dominant culture in such a way that (a) they don't realize they have additional privileges, and (b) they become resentful and angry when invited to relinquish them.

Edward Ball (1998), a descendant of slave owners, links historical practices to current realities:

No one among the Balls talked about how slavery helped us, but whether we acknowledged it or not, the powers of our ancestors were still in hand. Although our social franchise had shrunk, it had nevertheless survived. If we did not inherit money, or land, we received a great fund of cultural capital, including prestige, a chance at education, self-esteem, a sense of place, mobility, even (in some cases) a flair for giving orders. And it was not only "us," the families of former slave owners, who carried the baggage of the plantations. By skewing things so violently in the past, we had made sure that our cultural riches would benefit all white Americans. . . .

At the same time, the slave business was a crime that had not fully been acknowledged. It would be a mistake to say that I felt guilt for the past. A person cannot be culpable for the acts of others, long dead, that he or she could not have influenced. Rather than responsible, I felt accountable for what had happened, called on to try to explain it. I also felt shame about the broken society that had washed up when the tide of slavery receded. (pp. 13-14).

For decades, educators and other leaders have recognized that an important step in creating change in schools is to identify barriers to the implementation of new ideas, programs, procedures, or techniques (Freire, 1970; Fullan, 1991; Giroux, 1992b; Owens, 1995). The barriers to cultural proficiency are manifest in the dominant society's view that the issues concerning people of color; women; Gay, Lesbian, Bisexual, and Transgendered people; and other marginalized groups are the problems of those groups and have little relevance to the issues of apparently straight, white males.

To become a culturally proficient school, you must understand entitlement. Entitlement is the converse of the institutionalized forms of oppression—racism, sexism, ethnocentrism, and heterosexism—phenomena that penalize people for their membership in dominated cultural groups. *Entitlement* is the accrual of benefits solely because of membership in a dominant group. Just as dominated people are penalized because of their culture, other people benefit because of their membership in a privileged group within the dominant culture. If examined on a continuum, entitlement is the end at which some people—chiefly, heterosexual white men—have great power and control because of their membership in the dominant cultural group; *institutionalized oppression* is the other end, at which people—chiefly, people of color, women, and homosexuals—have relatively little institutionalized power or control because of their membership in a dominated cultural group.

■ This Chapter Is for Everyone

Within the dominant culture of the United States, the group that has the most power and privilege is straight white men. This does not mean it is the only group with power or the presumption of entitlement. One of the guiding principles of cultural proficiency is that there is diversity within groups as well as between groups. That means that in most groups to which you belong, there will be a hierarchy of power, privilege, and entitlement. These are issues that must be addressed as well. For example, elementary schools used to have a predominantly female faculty and a male principal. The recent trend is to have a school that is predominantly female—administrators, faculty, and staff, which means that the dominant culture often becomes a woman-identified culture, and for a man to thrive in such a school, he must adapt to the female-influenced culture. On the other hand, it does not mean that in most of the environments outside of the school, or in interactions with particular women within the school, the man is not afforded a large proportion of systemic privilege. Moreover, as one of the few men on the campus, he may feel entitled to be chair of important committees or to be the spokesperson for the faculty when dealing with the public. The point here is that even though he is a minority in this particular environment, the man has power and privileges that contribute to his sense of entitlement that come from the larger, dominant culture.

People seeking to shift the balance of power must understand their own distinctive role in ending oppression. Which role they may play depends entirely on whether the cultural group to which they belong is the dominant one. For people in dominant groups, their role requires a moral choice to assume personal responsibility and to take personal initiative. For people in dominated groups, their role is to recognize oppression and to commit themselves to self-determination. In this chapter, we focus on the role of entitled people. As a culturally proficient leader, you will surely need to guide both people who have been historically oppressed and those who are systemically entitled in assuming their distinctive roles. It is our view that the more daunting challenge is to coach entitled people in their roles. This perspective is evidenced by the relatively few resources available for guiding entitled people, compared to the many outstanding resources available for guiding historically oppressed people from marginalized cultural groups (Cheek, 1976; Gilligan, 1983; McIntosh, 1988; Vigil, 1980).

Most members of the dominant U.S. culture do not view themselves as more powerful or privileged than others in society, so they do not see themselves as stakeholders in these issues of power. Therefore, more often than not, entitled people view issues of oppression and entitlement as issues for oppressed people alone to worry about. In fact, the traditional manner of studying issues of equity and diversity (usually prescribed by people from the dominant culture) is to study the power-lessness of people of color, women, and other dominated groups.

Why don't discussions of diversity include white people and men? Entitlement. White people, and more particularly white men, choose—consciously or unconsciously—whether to participate actively in issues of equity and cultural proficiency. They may become angry, guilty, or indifferent to these topics. They may decry their forefathers' actions, they may protest that they never owned slaves, they may become depressed learning of some of the history that was never taught when they were students, or they may shrug it off and quietly declare that it is not their problem. The reality is that once entitled people react, they still can choose whether or not they will address issues of power and to oppose acts that perpetuate oppression. The first step in addressing these issues and opposing these actions is simply to acknowledge that the dynamics of entitlement do not accord people of color or women the same opportunity to choose whether to deal with issues of entitlement and oppression. These issues are part of their daily existence, just as power is an unacknowledged reality for white men.

To understand entitlement, we must understand how the empowered members of society are often oblivious to the ways in which they have benefited from their entitlement. Even as awareness emerges, they may still be reluctant to acknowledge the dynamics of race, gender, and sexual orientation, as well as socioeconomic class, in the expression of power. For example, socioeconomics is clearly a major factor in determining who wields power in this country. The effects of poverty have blinded poor white people to the oppression experienced by other people based on their ethnicity. As a result, impoverished white people often feel a disregard for—and even an antagonism toward—people of color.

## Caste-like Status and Oppression in U.S. History

The terms *racism, ethnocentrism, sexism,* and *heterosexism* are often confusing and frequently misused. Racism has two components: (a) the belief that one racial group is superior to all others and (b) the power to create an environment where that belief is manifested in the subtle or direct subjugation of the subordinate ethnic groups through a society's institutions. Ethnocentrism differs from racism in that it suggests a belief in the superiority of one's own ethnic group, but it says nothing about the group's power to subjugate other groups via societal institutions. Like racism, sexism and heterosexism have two components: (a) a belief that men and heterosexuals are superior to women and homosexuals; and (b) the power to institutionalize that belief, thereby subjugating women and homosexuals both overtly and covertly.

## ■ Caste-Like Status Versus Immigrant Status

U.S. society is stratified by economic classes. These classes are further stratified into castes by the ethnic groups within them. Some claim that the lines between social classes are flexible, and that a person can move from one group to a higher one through hard work and determination. Others know that this movement is difficult, if not impossible, because of the caste status of certain groups. Ogbu and Matute-Bianchi (1990) describe two types of ethnic minority status: immigrant status and caste status. Table 8.1 shows how Ogbu and Matute-Bianchi distinguish between immigrant and caste minorities. In U.S. society, *immigrant status* is a flexible category through which people have moved voluntarily, first choosing to immigrate and then choosing to assimilate, leaving behind their distinctive cultural membership and identification. People with immigrant status reinforce the belief in flexible strata in our society because they frequently cross class boundaries—if not within a generation, then at least over several generations.

In contrast, *caste status* is an inflexible category in which a person's ethnic characteristics, such as physical appearance and language, differ so much from the dominant (white) caste that they prevent—or severely limit—that person's voluntary movement across class boundaries. For the rare individuals of lower castes who are able to cross class boundaries, caste continues to affect their status within their new social class. Thus, a person who has entered the middle class but belongs to a lower caste will be made to feel subordinate to other members of the middle class who are of a higher caste. The existence of a caste system violates the fundamental U.S. belief in the ability to cross class boundaries to improve one's position, at will. Most people reject the notion of a caste system in the United States because it contradicts one of the core overt values of the United States—freedom and justice for all.

## ■ A History of Caste in the United States

The distinction between immigrant and caste minorities has been extremely important in the history of the United States, and much of U.S. society still functions in a caste system (Ogbu & Matute-Bianchi, 1990). Historically, as new generations of Europeans voluntarily migrated to what ultimately became the United States, they moved through

**TABLE 8.1** Types of Minority Status

| | Immigrant Minorities | Caste-like Minorities |
|---|---|---|
| Definition | People who are assimilated into mainstream social and economic classes after one or two generations | People who, as a group, are prevented from moving out of the lowest social and economic classes |
| Reason for immigration | Moved voluntarily to the host society for economic, social, or political reasons | Were brought to host society involuntarily through slavery, conquest, or colonization |
| Characteristics | May be subordinated and exploited politically, economically, and socially | Remain involuntary and permanent minorities |
| | Often successful in school | Believed to be unalterably inferior as a group |
| | May see themselves as "strangers" or "outsiders" | Perception of inferiority perpetuated by myths and stereotypes depicting the group as lazy, sexually primitive, violent, aggressive, and disease ridden |
| | May consider their menial position in this country to be better than what they had back home | Formal and informal barriers to assimilation (e.g., prohibitions of intermarriage, residential segregation) created by host culture |
| | Do not internalize the negative effects of discrimination (as first-generation immigrants) | |
| | Negative effects of discrimination not an ingrained part of their culture | |
| | Affected by U.S. relations with country of origin in two possible ways: (a) worsening political ties between the country of origin and the host country lead to harsh treatment or (b) friendly political ties between the country of origin and the host country improve social and economic opportunities | |
| | Biculturality and bilingualism are perceived as possible and acceptable | |
| Effects | Attitudes toward schooling that enhance strong desire for and pursuit of education | Attitudes and behaviors that internalize host culture's perception of them |
| | Attitudes and behaviors that help them overcome barriers to education and high-status careers | Belief that schooling will not help them advance into the mainstream of society |

SOURCE: Ogbu and Matute-Bianchi (1990).

immigrant status en route to assimilation. Initially, the caste minorities were chiefly enslaved African people and People of the First Nations.

For the most part, the second and subsequent generations of European immigrants were assimilated into the dominant culture of the U.S. In contrast, Africans and First Nation people were prevented from entering the dominant culture by virtue of their caste. By denying their humanity, early European Americans readily justified stealing the land of indigenous people, and the importation and subjugation of African people. Religious zealots often justified this savagery through their ethnocentrism. They neither understood nor appreciated the beliefs and behavior of the Africans and the First Nation people, so they claimed it was their duty to civilize and Christianize these "primitive" people. They rationalized enslavement and brutalization as a means to converting these so-called heathens to the Christian faith. Over time, the colonists institutionalized slavery and the practice of exiling First Nations to small parcels of land often thousands of miles from their homelands.

Following the war against the British, white men looked to British law and tradition to establish the U.S. government, society, and culture. These institutions formalized the political, social, and economic rights of landowning white men. This power, privilege, and entitlement was extended further through court cases, governmental policies, and a capitalist economic system. As new European immigrants arrived, if they were willing to work hard and to suffer many indignities, they—or at least their descendants—were granted entry into the dominant culture.

Meanwhile, racism became institutionalized in the new nation, and First Nations and African Americans were denied both the rights of citizenship and participation in the political and social life of the nation. Africans and African Americans were legally declared to be three-fifths of a white person. First Nations were slaughtered through direct aggression as well as by indirect means, such as exposing them to disease and preventing them from using their land to maintain their existence. Africans were enslaved first as chattel and then in a politically acceptable fashion through Jim Crow laws, which carried the threat of mob violence against African Americans that included tacit legal sanction to lynch with or without cause. First Nations were driven onto reservations and then moved again and again each time European Americans wanted their land or its mineral content.

By the time the U.S. was established as a new nation, slavery was firmly entrenched in the South, and racial prejudices pervaded the country on both sides of the Mason-Dixon line. Thus, the roots of oppression in racial prejudice against lower castes have a long-standing historical basis throughout the white community. In the early 19th century, Alexis de Tocqueville made a seemingly counterintuitive observation about prejudice and oppression in the United States. He said, "The prejudice of race appears to be stronger in the states that have abolished slavery than in those where it still exists; and nowhere is it so intolerant as in those states where servitude has never been known" (quoted in Kovel, 1984, pp. 33-34). This statement becomes understandable only when we consider it in light of entitlement: Northern white abolitionists made Southern slaveholders painfully conscious of their racial prejudices and entitlement, but the Northerners failed to see their own. Folk wisdom among African Americans echoed de Tocqueville 150 years later: *In the south they love the people and hate the race; in the north they love the race and hate the people.*

By the time de Tocqueville made his observation, the differentiation between immigrant and caste minorities had become deeply ingrained in our national psyche. If African Americans, First Nations, or women were to have any rights, those rights would not emerge organically as a natural outgrowth of social progress in a society that fully embraced these people as equal participants. Rather, vocal and often violent struggle was needed to extend the rights of citizenship to members of lower castes. Their strenuous efforts led to the passage of the Thirteenth (1865, abolition of slavery), Fourteenth (1868, equal rights for all people), and Fifteenth (1870, voting rights to all male citizens) Amendments to the U.S. Constitution.

By the beginning of the 20th century, racists were hard-pressed to use their old justifications for their oppressive beliefs and actions. Thus, in place of the rantings of the early Christianizers, the perpetrators of racism pointed to Social Darwinism to rationalize their maintenance of racist institutions. Specifically, European American men perverted the work of Charles Darwin to suggest that they had all the power and all the privileges of society simply because they were the fittest to enjoy such power and privilege. The concept of Social Darwinism legitimized the power and privilege of a higher order of humans (i.e., themselves: white men).

Not everyone blithely accepted Social Darwinism, however. Determined suffragists forced men to pass the Nineteenth Amendment (1920) to the U.S. Constitution, which granted women the right to vote nationwide for the first time. Similarly, outspoken blacks formed the National Association for the Advancement of Colored People (NAACP) and started pressing for social justice through the legal system. Their efforts led to such changes as the *Brown v. Topeka Board of Education* (1954, desegregation of public facilities) decision.

Sadly, it has taken urban violence to prompt many of the changes that ultimately benefited the lower castes. Throughout history and across the country, race riots have shown a consistent theme: People ultimately react violently to being denied human rights considered basic by the dominant classes. After a particularly turbulent summer in the 1960s, President Lyndon Johnson appointed a special panel headed by former Illinois Governor Otto Kerner to determine the causes of urban unrest. Among the many remarkable features of the study, two stand out: (a) that it was written at all and (b) that it was written by black and white moderates, not by radicals and fanatics (Terry, 1970). The Report of the National Advisory Commission on Civil Disorders (known as the Kerner Report; Riot Commission, 1968) identifies the causes of urban unrest as a white problem: "What white U.S. citizens never fully understand but what the Negro can never forget is that the white society is deeply implicated in the ghetto. White institutions created it, white institutions maintain it, and white society condones it" (p. 6).

The Kerner report was not the only outcome of angry and episodically violent reactions to oppression. Much legislation and many judicial decisions resulted that have extended civil rights to specific populations. This rich body of law that speaks to people's inalienable rights includes the Civil Rights Acts from 1866 to 1964, which have continually expanded the guarantees of citizenship to U.S. citizens who are not white, landowning men; the U.S. Supreme Court decision of 1954 (*Brown v. Topeka Board of Education*), which struck down 16 states' antimiscegenation laws; and the Voting Rights Act of 1965, which made it realistic for African Americans to exercise their right to vote throughout the country. These hard-won liberties are still not guaranteed without ongoing efforts to preserve them, however (witness the abdication of affirmative action both nationally and in many localities, and the violation of voter rights in the 2000 presidential election).

Each of these historical and legal events has underlying moral issues. In each case, people identified a wrong and reacted angrily against it, often responding with legislative or judicial action. Perhaps surprisingly, the laws intended to right civil wrongs and inequities highlight the breadth and depth of entitlement: People have had to seek legal remedies to ensure the rights of all cultural groups except wealthy white men. (This is not to deny that most laws, drafted and passed chiefly by middle- and upper-class white men, primarily benefit this empowered group, however.)

By the 1970s and 1980s, the preponderance of U.S. immigrants arrived from Pacific Rim, Latin American, and Asian countries. Now there are large groups of people of color, among which favorable and unfavorable distinguishing characteristics are made. Compounding the problem is the fact that many Latin American immigrants also have African or First Nation backgrounds, and they may speak Spanish, Portuguese, or French as their native language. This multiethnicity blurs the issues of immigrant versus caste status for some groups. For example, the caste and socioeconomic status of wealthy Hispanic (white) Cuban immigrants differs sharply from that of impoverished African (black) Cuban immigrants. Nonetheless, despite some blurring, the caste system is alive and well in contemporary America.

## ■ Caste Status and the Teaching of History

Prior to World War II, white males were the primary recipients of public and private education, and the version of history taught in schools reflected the views, beliefs, and interests of white males. To this day, most U.S. history textbooks fail to address the U.S. caste system or the distinction between caste and immigrant status. They also rarely mention the exclusivity of U.S. government, business, and educational enterprises. Oppressed U.S. citizens appear as single chapters, cursory comments, or footnotes, if they appear at all. The effect of this legacy of omission is an assumption of entitlement by members of dominant U.S. society, particularly white men. This dominant cultural perspective has thus been institutionalized in U.S. public schools. The effect on women has been to ensure their role as subordinate to men. The effect on people of color has been to ensure them of second-class citizenship and to deprive members of most cultural groups of the education and access that would facilitate their success in the U.S. mainstream.

The unfortunate reality of most history textbooks is that they glorify the accomplishments of politicians, barons of industry, and warriors, but they spend comparatively little time on the social issues of each historical period. The accomplishments of white men are the major foci because government, business, and the military have been, and remain, the province of white men. When women and people of color have been recognized for their contributions to the development of our country, history textbooks have recorded their contributions as exceptions. This sends an insidious message to students about who is valued in this country.

The struggle for the rights of oppressed people predates the U.S. Revolutionary War, yet history textbooks have consistently failed to present the role of women and people of color in the development of the United States. For example, though urban violence has historical roots going back to the 18th century, the race riots of the 18th and 19th centuries are rarely recorded in modern U.S. history textbooks (Franklin & Moss, 1988). Hence, most U.S. citizens see urban race riots as an artifact of the modern civil rights movement. The view that urban violence is a recent phenomenon is further enhanced by modern media, which compete to provide the most sensational accounts of contemporary upheavals.

✿

The consultants at Rolling Meadows direct the cabinet's attention to a chart with these quotations from the focus groups they conducted during the cultural audit:

"If we are celebrating diversity, why don't we have celebrations like European American history month?"

"The teacher wrote on my child's paper that she didn't understand the black inner-city experience, and therefore couldn't grade her essay fairly. This child has never lived in the inner city! Her father is a chemist and I am vice president of the Red Cross. Her teacher knows we are a middle-class family."

"These immigrant students don't even have magazines and books in their homes. They are at a tremendous disadvantage when compared to the other students."

After giving the cabinet a chance to reflect on the effect of these statements, the consultant remarks, "Each of these comments assumes that entitled students, the European American students and families of the dominant culture, are the standard of measure for other students. In the first comment, it is not recognized that most traditional school curricula celebrate the dominant culture daily. The second illustration shows the unawareness of the relationship of economic class to ethnic culture. The last quote reflects the assumption that the speaker knows what is in students' homes and that students with books and magazines read them!"

✿

These segregated lessons fail to teach students about how women and people of color have played vital roles throughout all aspects and periods of U.S. history. Lessons about a few isolated events and people cannot help students understand how such people and events relate to all U.S. history. Furthermore, because the history of racism and other forms of oppression is absent from these lessons, most students (particularly white male students) fail to understand how current societal tensions have emerged from historical events and trends.

Although all students are kept ignorant of the history of women and people of color in U.S. life, white male students suffer the least from this omission: They are still able to feel a connection to their past. Their forebears appear on every page and in every lecture. They are clearly a part of the U.S. pageant. In contrast, students of color and female students feel disconnected from U.S. history: none of their forebears appears to have been involved in any significant way, and people of color and women are largely absent from the history being taught. As a result, students of color and female students gain a sense of invisibility in our country's history and literature due to the omissions, distortions, and fallacious assumptions being taught in school.

White boys, never having this experience, have no idea how it feels to be absent from history. Howard (1993) summarizes their experiences well: "The possibility of remaining ignorant of other cultures is a luxury uniquely available to members of any dominant group" (p. 38). This luxury extends to ignorance of the oppression experienced by people of other cultures. This situation places a heavy burden on the culturally proficient educator.

Without an accurate historical perspective, both entitled and oppressed people will continue to be intensely defensive and protective when assessing contemporary and historical social issues. People of color confront racism daily and are often exasperated by white people whose response to their frustrations ranges from hostility to indifference based on profound ignorance. For their part, white U.S. citizens who do not feel personally responsible for racism and men who do not understand their role in perpetuating institutionalized sexism are frustrated by apparently unsympathetic people of color and women. Consequently, discussions of oppression and entitlement often lead to miscommunication and resentment. One side speaks from painful personal experience, whereas the other side perceives only apparently inexplicable anger and personal attack. As a culturally proficient educator, you can guide the teachers of history to be more cognizant of the entitlement of some groups and more proactive in ending oppression.

## Manifestations of Entitlement

The teaching of history is just one way in which entitlement is manifested. In this section, we discuss how entitlement is manifested through the language used for describing oppressed people, the ways in which oppressed people are objectified, and the differing access to power available to entitled people versus oppressed people.

## ▪ The Language of Entitlement

To understand the empowered end of the entitlement continuum, we need to recognize how language dehumanizes people by objectifying them (making them objects). Historically, the dominant white male society has used demeaning terminology to focus social attention on groups with less power, implying that they are the cause of their own status as outsiders. Thus, language reflects the realities of power in this society. Educators are no strangers to uses of terminology that blames the victims for their oppression. Since the mid-1950s, educators have bombarded students, educational literature, and fellow professionals with terms attempting to explain the disparities between oppressed and entitled groups. Table 8.2 presents some of the more common terms.

Each of the terms in the left column in Table 8.2 describes groups that occupy the oppressed end of the entitlement continuum. The ideas represented by these terms are used to explain why students from these groups fail to perform at criterion levels. These terms serve two purposes: (a) Educators can use these terms to view each student, and the student's cultural group, as the source of any educational problem that arises; and (b) they narrow educators' focus so that they disregard the group's environmental context (i.e., the institutionalized oppression to which members are subjected).

By using terms of oppression, we focus on what is wrong with the oppressed, thereby implying that they must be studied (to detect their specific flaws) and then fixed. The unquestioned use of these terms suggests that people of color, who are disproportionately represented on the oppressed end of the continuum, suffer from a pathological condition. At best, they are viewed as others (not us), and at worst, as deviants. This polarity of language and perceptions is reflected in the daily workings of schools. Notice that some labels have no comparable terms for the entitled groups—unless, of course, we wish to use *normal* or some other term signifying that white men are the standard against which other people are measured.

The terms in the right column in Table 8.2 describe the students representing the dominant culture of our country. Pause for a moment to consider this question: How often do you use these terms in your interactions with students and with fellow educators? Most of the people we ask answer not much or never. Most of us rarely utter these words because entitled people do not objectify or name themselves. Entitled people name only others, people they perceive to differ from themselves. Thus, when we use the terms *deficient* and *deprived* in their many

**TABLE 8.2**  Words Used to Describe Oppressed and Entitled Groups

| Oppressed | Entitled |
| --- | --- |
| Inferior | Superior |
| Culturally deprived | Privileged |
| Culturally disadvantaged | Advantaged |
| Deficient | Normal |
| Different | Regular |
| Diverse | Uniform |
| Third world | First world |
| Minority | Majority |
| Underclass | Upper class |
| Poor | Middle class |
| Unskilled workers | Leaders |

permutations, we imply that entitled people are the norm by which we compare other people. We base that norm on white middle-class U.S. values and behaviors and, more specifically, on the values and behaviors of white middle-class men.

Labeling has trapped dominated people in two ways: First, it confirms their status as outsiders to the dominant culture, ensuring that they will be denied access to societally valued privileges of the dominant culture, and then it judges them deficient for failing to demonstrate the behaviors and lifestyles associated with these privileges. The same thing goes for socioeconomic status: Oppressed people are denied access to the middle class, and then they are rebuked for failing to show middle-class values, attitudes, and behavior. In addition, they are denigrated not only as individuals who receive personalized oppressive labels but also as members of cultural groups that are castigated because of their likelihood to be given such labels.

Few entitled people, however, can see the irony of these cultural and economic traps. As educators, we have to work hard to resist these labeling traps so that we can avoid referring to students and their families with multiple oppressive, deficiency-based terms. As a culturally proficient educator, you can guide your colleagues in choosing terminology that affirms the value of each student rather than focusing on how students deviate from the dominant culture.

## ■ Thingification: The Face of the Enemy

Kovel (1984) uses the term *thingification* to describe how members of dominant U.S. society use language to create distance between themselves and others. It gives the dominant group the power to establish, define, and differentiate outsiders as others. When people use such terms as *them* and *you people*, they objectify others. They manipulate people's self-perceptions and perceptions of others while they reinforce a sense of otherness. Similarly, when they continue to use *man* and *he* as inclusive terms for women and men, they *thingify* women, placing women in the category of other (i.e., not men, the acknowledged norm).

Thingification is an extension of the institutionalized oppression never experienced by members of the dominant culture. It is part of a "matrix of culturally derived meanings" (Kovel, 1984, pp. 6-7) that allows the larger and empowered segment of society to communicate that minority groups are never quite as good as the dominant society. Consider a comment a New York teacher made to one of her students: "Shut those thick lips, can't you behave like a human being?" (Rosenfeld, 1976, p. 226). Is it surprising that oppressed people often react in a hostile manner to the use of these expressions of privilege and entitlement?

The dominant culture conveys thingification by more means than just oppressive terminology. Consider the following news headline: "Whites Think Black Kids Can't Learn, Pollster Says," the title of an article reporting the findings of a Louis Harris poll. Among other findings, the article reports that "up to 90% of respondents would support programs to break the cycle of poor, inner-city youngsters ending up on welfare." According to the report, "[T]he view of 7 in 10 [respondents] is that if the U.S. does not properly educate its minorities and poor, then the U.S. will lose its competitive edge." It concludes that "the bottom line is that 37% of white America has written off black America as hopeless" (Association of California School Administrators, 1991). The article implies that the basic reason for educating children is to ensure the economic vitality of the nation.

The article on the poll (Association of California School Administrators, 1991) is an example of thingification. African American children are considered significant only to the extent that they can ensure U.S. economic self-sufficiency. If U.S. citizens could rely on a poorly educated labor force in this information age of the 21st century, as society did in the agricultural and industrial ages, one is led to believe that there would be no concern about the education of these children. The article is written with indifference toward the youths because neither educators nor society have given the education of African American or other nonwhite youths top priority. The reporter shows no moral outrage and makes no ethical comment regarding the observation that white America has written off black America.

Delpit (1988) describes the process of thingification in terms of how insiders (entitled people) are viewed differently from outsiders (oppressed people). Specifically, insiders (i.e., heterosexual white men) are viewed as individuals with personal characteristics, but outsiders (i.e., people of color, women, and homosexuals) are viewed as representing their groups, such that their characteristics are deemed representative of their groups' characteristics. For example, during job interviews, when a white male job applicant exhibits problems, he or she is judged to be a person with individual problems. When a person of color exhibits the same problems in an interview, the problem is assigned to the entire cultural group as a characteristic of that group.

This thingification of outsiders also applies to women and Gay people. Men often discount the anger, annoyance, concerns, and health issues of women as insignificant characteristics of their hormonal cycles. When straight people observe a Gay Man or a Lesbian frequenting a predominantly Gay business, they assume that the person is doing something perverted or unsavory. When a straight man is angry, has a headache, or frequents an all-male business, however, he is considered to be behaving in ways that reflect on him as an individual, not on all men collectively.

Entitlement breeds thingification by making the humanity of thingified people invisible. A person becomes invisible as an individual in many ways: by being viewed as unable to learn, by representing an entire group of people during an interview, or by having value only as a cog in the economic system. When whites perpetuate thingification and invisibility, incessantly view nonwhite groups negatively, and then refuse to acknowledge those realities, nonwhites often feel enraged (Ellison, 1952; Gilligan, 1983; Giroux, 1992a; Kovel, 1984; Wright, 1940). The vast majority of white people, particularly white men, are astonished at this furor, however, because they have never experienced thingification. When confronted with this information, white men often respond by denying their individual participation in the process. They say, *I identify myself as a person, not as a white man*. Only the members of the dominant group are entitled to make such an assertion.

Protestations to deny whiteness eliminate neither the fact nor the problem of white privilege. U.S. culture is color conscious. We sort people by color, to the advantage of some and detriment of others. To dissociate oneself from whiteness by affirming humanness ignores what whiteness has done and how we continue to benefit from it. (Terry, 1970, pp. 18-19)

Granted that straight white men have many pressures to perform, succeed, and survive, these pressures occur in a context absent of the additional and insupportable pressures of institutionalized oppression. Educators must understand these pressures, particularly if they belong to the dominant group in U.S. society. Such understanding is the foundation for creating a school system that addresses the needs of children as members of groups capable of learning, as opposed to being members of groups with deficiencies that limit their full participation in school or society.

## ■ Power

As mentioned in the discussion of U.S. history, the disenfranchised have had to seek legislative and judicial remedies to gain any power in this country, but wealthy, white, landowning men have assumed power from the very beginnings of U.S. history. Jacksonian democracy broadened the participation of U.S. citizens in the political and economic spheres of this country, but it denied such participation to anyone other than white men. U.S. white men have enjoyed power, as manifested in the form of privilege or entitlement, as an integral part of their history, tradition, and economic status.

The power that accrues to the entitled in U.S. society is so pervasive that those who have it do not see the pervasiveness. This makes the goal of cultural proficiency difficult to achieve. In much the same way that people do not appreciate their liberties until they are threatened, most entitled white men do not appreciate the power of their entitlement because they have never experienced the absence of power. Moreover, the milieu of entitlement insulates them from hearing the cries of those who live in fear of sexual assaults, battering, racist acts, and other forms of discrimination or of those who protest against the systematic denial of their access to societal power. Delpit (1988) notes two distinct responses to entitlement: (a) Those with greater power are frequently least aware of, or least willing to acknowledge, its existence; and (b) those with less power are often most aware of power discrepancies.

"What is at stake for white America today is not what [oppressed] people want and do but what white people stand for and do" (Terry, 1970, p. 15). Once all U.S. citizens understand and accept that some people receive entitlements based on gender and race, that other people have impediments placed before them for the same reason, and that all

U.S. citizens have a responsibility to recognize that everyone is an integral part of both the problem and the solution, then true progress toward cultural proficiency can begin.

### ■ Recognizing Entitlement in Education

Since the late 1970s, we have involved thousands of educators, parents, and students in the simulation *Starpower* (see Activity 8.4) (Shirrts, 1969), which helps people notice the effects of entitlement and inequity. In this simulation, participants create a three-tiered society in which power and access are disproportionately distributed, experience interactions within and among the groups in this simulated society, and then debrief by discussing their feelings in their roles as well as the applications of this experience to the real world.

In the simulation, one of the three groups is awarded the right to make the rules. The entitled group consistently makes rules that are to its advantage and that either overtly or covertly disadvantage the remaining two groups. In the debriefing discussion, those in the disadvantaged groups are incredulous that the rule makers do not see that they did not earn their power. The society was organized to favor them.

Delpit's (1988) observation of educators debating issues related to educating children of color supports this notion of unawareness:

> For many who consider themselves members of liberal or radical camps, acknowledging personal power and admitting participation in the culture of power is extremely uncomfortable. On the other hand, those who are less powerful in any situation are most likely to recognize the power variable most acutely. My guess is that white colleagues . . . did not perceive themselves to have power over the non-white(s). . . . However, either by virtue of their position, their numbers, or their access to that particular code of power of calling upon research, the white educators had the authority to establish what was to be considered truth regardless of the opinions of people of color, and the latter were well aware of that fact. (pp. 283-284)

Given that most educational policymakers and decision makers are white men, this absence of information and insight becomes especially crucial to the culturally proficient leader. Many entitled members of society believe that all people in this country have the opportunity to succeed but choose instead to pick the scabs on old wounds so that they do not have to put forth effort in new endeavors. Entitlement creates either unawareness or denial of the reality that not all U.S. citizens have a common base of inalienable rights. These beliefs and denials are supported by curricula that are silent about the pluralistic nature of our country's history and development.

◈

As a young teacher of social studies, James Harris was aware of being ill prepared to provide for the black students in his classroom even before moving to an urban district with a large number of African American students. To remedy that inadequacy, he enrolled in a degree program at a major midwestern university and took coursework on the history of the U.S. Negro. It did not take him long to identify the gaps in his undergraduate education. Moreover, he realized quickly that his European American students would also benefit from this material, while at the same time he continued to puzzle many of his European American professors and colleagues. They did not understand why a bright, young, European American man with a fairly secure future would want to waste his time this way.

James also noticed the degree to which entitlement had affected his own perceptions. First, his prior education provided almost no information on black history, thereby rendering it invisible or discounted entirely. Second, his original motivation to enroll in the courses, which had been to prepare himself to teach black students, changed with his realization that such information is of benefit to all students.

For a time, he lived in California, where he taught students of Mexican and Portuguese descent for the first time. He experienced the same sense of inadequacy he had felt in his midwestern classroom. Then, in discussing curricular content with colleagues, he was shocked to learn that U.S. citizens of Japanese ancestry had been incarcerated in U.S. relocation camps during World War II. His shock and anger were derived from two sources: (a) that his own country could do such a thing to its own citizens, and (b) that he had earned degrees in social studies from two reputable universities yet had no knowledge of this event.

◈

The authors of history textbooks have routinely excluded some cultural groups from their writing; more insidiously, they have also excluded major events. When authors exclude this information from students' textbooks, they romanticize U.S. history, thereby failing to help young people understand many of the social conflicts that occurred.

Both the teaching of U.S. history and the outcomes of the simulation illustrate how entitlement is reinforced by experience.

Another illustration of how white men lack awareness of entitlement and deny its existence comes from the many sessions on cultural proficiency that we have conducted in recent years.

ᢙ

During an inservice session on cultural proficiency at the Coolidge district, James Harris, the consultant, overhears this conversation between European American Principal Steve Petrossian and Puerto Rican Principal Richard Diaz:

Steve says, "You know, this activity in determining how prejudice differs from racism or sexism gives me some new ideas to work with. I had never considered the concept of power; it just never occurred to me. Let me ask you this: One of my African American teachers said that his student is 'a good athlete for a European American boy.' Now isn't that racism?"

"Steve," Richard replies, "let me get this straight: You have been on this planet for decades, and you have never thought about the power that European American people have in this country?"

Steve is defensive. "Hey, why attack me? I'm being honest with you. Power is something I've just never considered. Shoot, just because I'm European American doesn't mean that I have power. Besides, you haven't answered my question. Isn't my story an example of racism?"

James responds to Steve, "No, it isn't. Although your story illustrates an ethnocentric use of a stereotype and is definitely cultural incapacity, the teacher in your story lacks the power to institutionalize his beliefs. The term *racism* implies the power to act on one's bigotry. Or reflects the systems within our institutions that discriminate against people of color without the consent or the conscious participation of the people in the system."

James continues, addressing the whole group, "Steve's story also shows his lack of awareness of—as well as his wish to deny—his own entitlement. The teacher in Steve's story was not reinforcing or perpetuating institutional racism, which affects every single person and has grave social consequences no matter whether it is recognized or acknowledged. More often than not, people who are not directly affected by oppression fail to understand when cultural groups speak out about their experiences. Members of the dominant group, whatever that group tends to be, usually fail to notice their power or entitlement."

Richard interrupts: "Yeah, they say, 'If I didn't experience the oppression, or witness it, then you must be overreacting.' Or they want to start talking about their own pain, like this was the Oppression Olympics."

James goes on, "If we are to create an effectively functioning society—and, by extension, a school system that is culturally proficient—we must find ways to address issues of entitlement. By doing so, we can minimize gaps in the education of our educators that perpetuate their lack of awareness and their denial of their own empowerment."

✒

# Educational Practices of Entitlement and Oppression

Unfortunately, the education system as we know it not only has failed to enlighten students and educators about oppression and entitlement but has further institutionalized the oppression of dominated cultural groups by its very structure and operation. Two particularly egregious examples are systems of tracking and educator expectations.

## ■ Systems of Tracking

Oakes (1985), Oakes and Lipton (1990), and Wheelock (1992) have documented both the biases of entitlement built into the tracking system and its negative effects on students as well as on society at large. Tracking emerged during the late 19th and early 20th centuries when educators were seeking ways to incorporate myriad European immigrants into the U.S. mainstream. The manifest function of tracking was to make the instructional system efficient in accord with the then-current emphasis on the scientific management of schools. Today, educators know that the latent—and perhaps often unintended—function of tracking has been to harm students at the oppressed end of the entitlement continuum. Throughout the country, as schools move toward cultural proficiency, they are beginning to dismantle tracking systems and to focus on grouping systems that provide all students with equal access to information, skills, and values that foster success.

Even without a formal tracking system, however, U.S. students are tracked because of their color and the caste status that color imbues. The power of caste and entitlement is reflected in this playground rhyme:

*If you're white, you're alright.*
*If you're black, get back.*
*If you're brown, stick around.*
*If you're yellow, you're mellow.*
*If you're red, you're already dead.*

## ■ Educator Expectations

Extensive research has shown that educators have differing expectations of students depending on the students' race, ethnicity, and gender. These studies have provided consistent data demonstrating stark disparities of class, caste, and entitlement in educators' interactions with students. Interactions based on poor expectations clearly lead to devastating consequences for students in terms of both academic performance and self-image (Oakes, 1985; Oakes & Lipton, 1990; Rosenthal & Jacobsen, 1966; Wheelock, 1992).

Culturally proficient educators can strive to overcome these obstacles to learning through programs that provide models by which they can learn of verbal and nonverbal behaviors that project the cultural expectation that all students can learn, thus providing them with equal opportunity in the classroom. Such programs can provide alternatives to perpetuating the judgments, expectations, and behaviors of entitled people blindly. Wheelock (1992) details scores of such programs that vary from hands-on approaches to conceptual papers. In this book, the activities selected for the resources introduce concepts basic to understanding the cultural bases for expectations.

❧

At Coolidge Middle School, consultant James Harris overhears this conversation in the parking lot:

Teacher DeLois says, "I am really enjoying these sessions on cultural proficiency. I can see where I can use a lot of this information to prepare the girls and Latinos in my classes to assume a responsible role in society."

Harvey, cynical as always, lashes back, "Are you for real? I would like you and this 'cultural expert' to spend a day in the vice principal's office. All day long, he deals with the scum of this school. If those kids were in your classroom, you would know why those people are so behind in school."

DeLois can't believe what she is hearing. "Let me tell you something," she hisses at him. "First, if you think the girls and the Mexicans are the ones who need help, you are in worse shape than you know. The true scum in this school are the educators who don't see students when they come to their office. All they see is the color of their skin . . . and you judge the kids and their families in the same way."

☙

To deny either the overt or the covert presence of the attitudes reflected in this conversation is to be blind to the kinds of oppression to which unentitled children, particularly children of color, are subjected daily. Cultural proficiency is not color blindness. Rather, culturally proficient educators see what color means in the context of entitlement and oppression. Once educators see how they make judgments based on entitlement and oppression, they will recognize how such judgments influence their expectations and evaluations of students, the tracking of students, and the creation of instructional programs. Consider a discussion that takes place among some teachers at Coolidge High School.

☙

Harvey doesn't limit his discontent to his middle school colleagues. Consider a discussion that takes place among some teachers after a union meeting at Coolidge High School.

"I have been in this district for 17 years, and have I seen some changes!" says Harvey.

"Like what?" his friend Lane asks.

"Well, first of all," Harvey responds, "when I first came here, this was a nice, stable, working-class community where the parents wanted their children to have more than they did. Sure we had problems, but nothing like today. Then, 14 years ago, about the same time the forced busing started, the school became all minority in no time at all!"

"And?" Lane challenges.

"What do you mean, 'And'?" Harvey was getting annoyed. "You know exactly 'and what.' That was when our test scores dropped, drug problems began, and the schools became one more ghetto nightmare. And I'm not a racist; these are just facts!"

☙

## Where to Start

Cultural proficiency begins for white people with the awareness of the dynamics of entitlement. Although white men are particularly needful of gaining awareness, all successful public school educators have been indoctrinated in a system that perpetuates racism, sexism, and other forms of oppression. All educators pass through this system as they prepare to transmit the values and the culture of the dominant society to public school children. This preparation is couched in such terms as *responsible citizenship* and *civics*. In reality, through this system, educators learn to prepare students to sustain the status quo and to maintain and support U.S. democratic society as it exists today. Educators might risk being accused of treason or labeled as anarchists if they were to teach students to challenge societal norms overtly, to accept lifestyles and values considered deviant by middle America, or to advocate for societal change. Public schools were not designed to stimulate controversy, and public school educators are not expected to teach students to question, let alone defy, authority.

Culturally proficient leaders understand this process and are aware of the subtle ways in which entitlement and oppression are fostered. They understand that educators have furthered the programs and practices that have served to enhance opportunities for some people while denying access to those opportunities for others, whether intentionally or unwittingly. They encourage their colleagues to recognize that a student's native culture and values are important for the student's survival in his or her family and community. They encourage teachers to complement their native values with an understanding of the values of dominant U.S. society. At the same time, culturally proficient leaders work with colleagues to challenge some of the assumptions of dominant U.S. values and to raise the dynamics of entitlement to a conscious level.

When culturally proficient educators begin to raise their levels of consciousness about the dynamics of oppression, they usually begin with an aspect of oppression that more directly affects them. For example, Peggy McIntosh (1988) recalls her experiences with this personal growth:

> After I realized, through faculty development work in women's studies, the extent to which men work from a base of unacknowledged privilege, I understood that much of their oppressiveness was unconscious. Then I remembered the frequent charges from women of color that white women whom they encounter are oppressive. I began to understand why we are justly seen as oppressive, even when we don't see ourselves that way. At the very least, obliviousness of one's privileged state can make a person or group irritating to be with. (p. 4)

McIntosh's (1988) experience of learning about the bases of sexism led her to an examination of privilege, then dominance, and then power (see Activity 8.3). When she attained higher levels of awareness, she was able to look around herself and see that issues of power included racism and heterosexism as well as sexism. McIntosh then questioned the desirability of her own privilege gained through this process, noting that it can lead to moral weakness in those who depend on it. It is imperative that white men and other entitled people assume this responsibility for consciousness raising. In addition to raising our own consciousness, investigation of one's own prejudices and entitlements enables us both to serve as role models against prejudice and to implement culturally proficient leadership practices (Pate, 1988).

Culturally proficient educators must interpret their discomfort with these issues as a sign of where they need to begin becoming more aware of their own entitlement. Often, when one discusses, debates, and argues about the manifestations of oppression, deep and intense emotions erupt. On the one hand, people who are targets of oppression often feel angry and frustrated with their day-to-day experiences. On the other hand, people who have never experienced these forms of oppression often feel guilty or defensively angry at being held responsible for things they never intentionally created. That anger, in turn, feeds the frustration of those who are victimized, for they cannot believe the naïveté of the dominant groups, and the spiral of ire winds ever higher.

To develop your own consciousness and to be effective as culturally proficient leaders, you must view your own group membership within a realistic context of entitlement and oppression. In his work with counselor educators, Ponterotto (1988) has developed a model of the stages of racial consciousness that readily applies to most educators. Table 8.3 describes each stage and shows how Ponterotto's model compares with cultural proficiency. Ponterotto is careful to note that not all people reach the fourth stage. When expanding the self-examination to include issues of race, ethnicity, and gender, it seems even less likely that all people will reach the fourth stage. The inability to achieve perfection, however, should not deter attempts to strive for greater proficiency. It is the responsibility of all who are striving to become culturally proficient to keep the issues of cultural proficiency out in the open so everyone in the learning community can make steady progress in serving the needs of all students. Such an approach is more ethical and morally responsible because it shifts the focus from blaming the victim to seeking constructive ways to educate all people.

Various educational practices have been developed and studied; when used by educators who understand the oppression-entitlement

**TABLE 8.3** Stages of Racial Consciousness

| Stage | Comparable Place on the Cultural Proficiency Continuum | Description |
|---|---|---|
| Stage 1: Preexposure | Cultural destructiveness or cultural incapacity | People have given little thought to multicultural issues or to their role in a racist and oppressive society |
| Stage 2: Exposure | Cultural incapacity | People are confronted with the realities of racism and prejudice, examine their own cultural values, and may feel guilt or anger |
| Stage 3: Defensive | Cultural blindness | People retreat from the issues altogether |
| Stage 3: Zealot | Cultural precompetence | People zealously or defensively take on the minority plight |
| Stage 4: Integration | Cultural competence and cultural proficiency | The zealousness of the previous stage becomes more balanced in multicultural interests or endeavors, and the defensiveness lessens because the airing of feelings gives way to interest in, respect for, and appreciation of cultural differences |

SOURCE: Ponterotto (1988).

continuum, they result in positive educational experiences for students regardless of their social status. Many researchers (e.g., Comer, 1988; Levin, 1988; Sadker & Sadker, 1994; Sizer, 1985) have demonstrated that all children are capable of excelling in all areas of schooling. Culturally proficient leaders must value the diversity present in the school setting and then take steps to evaluate the culture of the school and its educators by clarifying values, assumptions, and cultural expectations. They must learn about the cultures of the students and their families and assess the dynamic nature of the differences in values and expectations. Cummins (1988) and Sleeter (1991) have observed that:

> Empowering education programs work with students and their home communities to build on what they bring; disabling programs ignore and attempt to eradicate knowledge and the strengths students bring, and replace them with those of the dominant society. (Sleeter, 1991, p. 5)

Culturally proficient leaders work with their colleagues to adapt the school program so that it addresses the needs of all students, not just the entitled ones.

## Going Further

1. What is your initial response to the notion of entitlement?

2. Do you believe that ending racism is the responsibility of white men?

3. People who are members of the dominant group tend to not see their privilege and not recognize their sense of entitlement. In every group, however homogeneous it may appear to outsiders, there is some type of stratification or hierarchy. Think of your school or some other group to which you belong. What are the subgroups within it? Which group has the most privilege and power? How is that manifested?

# Reflection

_____

_____

_____

_____

_____

_____

_____

_____

_____

_____

## Activity 8.1:

# Stand Up*

■ **Purpose**

To raise awareness of the diverse experiences people in a group may have had

■ **Expertise of Facilitator**

Moderate

■ **Readiness of Group**

Beginning

■ **Time Needed**

20 minutes

■ **Materials**

None

■ **Briefing**

I am going to ask you a series of questions. If your answer is yes to any question, please stand up.

■ **Process**

Participants sit in a circle with space for them to stand and look at one another. Ask each question slowly. After each question, invite participants to look around the room to see who is standing or sitting. Invite them to notice what they think, feel, or wonder as they look around the room.

---

*Thanks to Stephanie Graham of Los Angeles, California, for this activity.

1. If you have ever eaten Chinese food, stand up.
2. If you have ever eaten Greek food, stand up.
3. If you have ever worshipped with people who are not of your faith tradition, stand up.
4. If you have ever traveled out of the country, stand up.
5. If you have ever made food from a different culture, stand up.
6. If you know anyone from a different ethnic or racial group, stand up.
7. If you speak more than one language, stand up.
8. If you have ever been in the home of someone of a different ethnic or racial group as a guest, stand up.
9. If you live in a neighborhood where there are people who are not of your racial or ethnic group, stand up.
10. If you have changed your religion, stand up.

■ Debriefing

1. What did you notice as you were sitting and standing?
2. What surprised you?
3. What conclusions can you draw from the answers of the group?
4. What questions do you have for group members?
5. What other questions might have been asked?
6. What patterns did you notice in the questions?
7. What was the purpose of this activity?

■ Variations

Allow participants to ask the questions to which people will stand or sit.

## Activity 8.2:

# Line of Privilege*

■ **Purpose**

To raise awareness of the entitled and stigmatized groups participants belong to or identify with

■ **Expertise of Facilitator**

Moderate

■ **Readiness of Group**

Intermediate

■ **Time Needed**

30 minutes

■ **Materials**

Room for participants to stand abreast in one line and be able to cross from one side of the room to the other, as if preparing for "Mother, May I?" or "Red Rover."

■ **Briefing**

Everyone line up in the A line. You may not talk with one another during this exercise. I am going to make some statements to you, and you will move to the B line or return to the A line based on your responses.

■ **Process**

Make each statement slowly and without inflection. Insist on silence from the participants. After each statement, invite participants to make eye contact with the people who are in the same line they are in and to

---

*Thanks to Stephanie Graham of Los Angeles, California, for this activity.

look across the room to see who is standing facing them. Invite them to notice what they think, feel, or wonder as they look around the room.

1. If you are a woman, move to line B. If not, stay in the A line.
2. If you are less than 5'2", move to line B. If not, return to or stay in the A line.
3. If you or a family member is Gay or Lesbian, move to line B.
4. If you are a person of color, move to line B.
5. If you have an invisible physical handicap, move to line B.
6. If you consider yourself a klutz, move to line B.
7. If you are not athletic, move to line B.
8. If you are over 50, move to line B,
9. If you are under 25, move to line B.
10. If you or your parents were born in another country, move to line B.
11. If you or your parents were born in Asia, Africa, or Central or South America, move to line B.
12. If you are fat, move to line B.
13. If you are not married, move to line B.
14. If you are a woman, over 50, and not married, or if you are a single parent, move to line B.
15. If you were not born into a Christian home, move to line B.
16. If your ride depends on public transportation, move to line B.
17. If you live with your parents in their home, move to line B.
18. If neither of your parents graduated from college, move to line B.
19. If you do not own your own home, move to line B.
20. If you have a family member or you yourself have ever been incarcerated or held involuntarily in a mental institution, move to line B.
21. If you do not consider yourself to be white, move to line B.

## ■ Debriefing

1. What did you notice as you were crossing the room?
2. What surprised you?
3. What made this activity difficult or easy?
4. What conclusions can you draw from the answers of the group?
5. Did you react to any of the questions?
6. What patterns did you notice in the questions?
7. What was the purpose of this activity?

**Activity 8.3**:

# Entitlement Survey

■ Purpose

To raise awareness of the distribution of societal privilege and power in a group

■ Expertise of Facilitator

Extensive

■ Readiness of Group

Advanced. (This activity is particularly powerful if there are people of color among the participants.)

■ Time Needed

60 minutes

■ Materials

Response Sheet 8.3.1: Entitlement Survey

■ Briefing

We have been talking about barriers to cultural proficiency. This survey will give us some data for examining our own power and privilege. Peggy McIntosh began writing an article to examine the privilege of men and ended up realizing that even though she did not have as much power as men, she had a great deal of societal privilege that she had never recognized because she is European American. This survey is based on the article that she wrote, pointing out where she saw her privilege.

■ Process

1. Give participants about 15 minutes to complete the survey and total their points.

2. Invite participants to line up around the room according to their scores.

3. Ask participants what they notice about the patterns of who is in the line and what their scores are.

4. Allow participants to ask questions of one another.

## ■ Debriefing

1. What did you notice as you answered the questions in the survey?
2. Did you react to any of the questions?
3. What did you notice as you looked at the way people are lined up?
4. What surprises you?
5. What made this activity difficult or easy?
6. What conclusions can you draw from the answers of the group?
7. What patterns did you notice in the questions?
8. What was the purpose of this activity?

## ■ Variation*

Rather than taking the survey, ask the participants to line up across the middle of the room, parking lot, or whatever area you decide to use.

Read the statements in the survey and after each statement ask the participants to take one step forward if the answer is true for them and one step backward if the answer is not true for them.

This activity is particularly powerful if you are in an area with stairs and there are people of color among the participants. At the end of the statements, some people will be at the top of the stairs, some at the bottom of the stairs, and some will be around the stairs in a position that hides them from the people at the top of the stairs. This physical placement of people is a powerful metaphor for the marginalization of groups in the United States.

---

*Thanks to Stephanie Graham of Los Angeles, California, for the variation of this activity.

**Response Sheet 8.3.1:**

# A Survey of Privilege and Entitlement

*Please respond to the following statements as candidly as possible,*
*using the following scale:*
*1 = almost never, 2 = rarely, 3 = sometimes, 4 = usually, 5 = almost always*
*When you are finished, please total your points.*

1. I can, if I wish, arrange to be in the company of people of my ethnic group most of the time.   1   2   3   4   5

2. If I should need to move, I can be pretty sure of renting or purchasing housing in an area that I can afford and in which I would want to live.   1   2   3   4   5

3. I can be pretty sure that my neighbors in such a location will be neutral or pleasant to me.   1   2   3   4   5

4. I can go shopping alone most of the time, pretty well assured that I will not be followed or harassed.   1   2   3   4   5

5. I can turn on the television or open the front page of the paper and see people of my ethnicity widely represented.   1   2   3   4   5

6. When I am told about *our* national heritage or *civilization*, I know the speaker assumes that people of my ethnicity are included.   1   2   3   4   5

7. I can be sure that my children will be given curricular materials that testify to the existence of their ethnic group.   1   2   3   4   5

8. I can go into any music shop and count on finding the music of my ethnic group represented, into any supermarket and find the staple foods that fit with my cultural traditions, and into any hairdresser's shop and find someone who can deal with my hair.   1   2   3   4   5

9. Whether I use checks, credit cards, or cash, I am sure that the sales clerk will not use my skin color as a measure of my financial reliability.   1   2   3   4   5

10. I can arrange to protect my children most of the time from people who may not like them.   1   2   3   4   5

11. I can swear, dress in secondhand clothes, or not answer letters without having people attribute these choices to the bad morals,  the poverty, or the illiteracy of my ethnic group.   1   2   3   4   5

12. I can speak in public to a powerful male group without putting my ethnic group on trial.   1   2   3   4   5

| | | | | | |
|---|---|---|---|---|---|
| 13. I can do well in a challenging situation without being called a credit to my race. | 1 | 2 | 3 | 4 | 5 |
| 14. I am never asked to speak for all the people of my ethnic group. | 1 | 2 | 3 | 4 | 5 |
| 15. I can remain oblivious of the language and customs of people of color, who constitute the world's majority, without feeling any penalty for such oblivion. | 1 | 2 | 3 | 4 | 5 |
| 16. I can criticize our government and talk about how much I fear its policies and behavior without being seen as a cultural outsider. | 1 | 2 | 3 | 4 | 5 |
| 17. I can be pretty sure that if I ask to talk to "the person in charge" I will be facing a person of my ethnic group. | 1 | 2 | 3 | 4 | 5 |
| 18. If a traffic cop pulls me over or if the IRS audits my tax return, I can be sure I haven't been singled out because of my ethnicity. | 1 | 2 | 3 | 4 | 5 |
| 19. I can easily buy posters, postcards, picture books, greeting cards, dolls, toys, and children's magazines featuring people who look like me. | 1 | 2 | 3 | 4 | 5 |
| 20. I can go home from most meetings of organizations I belong to and feel somewhat tied in rather than isolated, out of place, outnumbered, unheard, held at a distance, or feared. | 1 | 2 | 3 | 4 | 5 |
| 21. I can take a job with an affirmative action employer without having coworkers on the job suspect that I got it because of my ethnicity. | 1 | 2 | 3 | 4 | 5 |
| 22. I can choose public accommodations without fearing that people of my ethnicity cannot get in or will be mistreated in the places I have chosen. | 1 | 2 | 3 | 4 | 5 |
| 23. I can be sure that if I need legal or medical help, my ethnicity will not work against me. | 1 | 2 | 3 | 4 | 5 |
| 24. If my day, week, or year is going badly, I need not ask, of each negative episode or situation, whether it has racial overtones. | 1 | 2 | 3 | 4 | 5 |
| 25. I can choose blemish cover or bandages in "flesh" color that more or less match my skin. | 1 | 2 | 3 | 4 | 5 |

**Total Score:** ____

**Activity 8.4**:

# Starpower

■ Purpose

Starpower™ helps participants:

- Understand that power must have a legitimate basis to be effective.
- See and feel the effect of disempowerment.
- Realize that sharing power can increase it, whereas hoarding or abusing power can diminish it.
- Understand the effect that systems can have on power.
- Be aware of how tempting it is for well-intentioned people to abuse power.
- Understand that there are different kinds of power.
- Personally experience and discuss the excitement of power and the despair of powerlessness.

■ Expertise of Facilitator

Moderate

■ Readiness of Group

Beginning

■ Time Needed

At least 2 hours

■ Materials

A copy of the Starpower simulation, which is available from Simulation Training Systems in Del Mar, California. Their phone number is 800-942-2900, and they can be found online at http://www. stsintl.com/business/star_power.html.

■ Process

A simulation is a relatively simple activity that recreates some aspect of society in a safe and controlled setting. During a simulation, participants experience the intense feelings that they might experience over a longer period of time in real life without the fear or vulnerability that might occur in real time or in a real situation. Starpower is a simple game played by exchanging poker chips that result in the creation of a three-tiered "society" and the privileges, misunderstandings, and abuses of power that are found in hierarchical systems.

This is one of our favorite activities. We have used it in every environment in which we have served since 1980 with participants from high school through executive managers. It is a simple and powerful activity. We recommend it highly for helping participants to look at how power is distributed and shared in the United States and how it is distributed, shared, and abused within their own organizations.

**Activity 8.5**

# Barriers to Cultural Proficiency

■ Purpose

To identify aspects of the organization's culture that may be barriers to cultural proficiency.

■ Expertise of Facilitator

Moderate

■ Readiness of Group

Intermediate

■ Time Needed

45 minutes

■ Materials

Response Sheet 8.5.1: Barriers to Cultural Proficiency

■ Briefing

Let's see if we can identify some of the barriers to cultural proficiency in our school (or district).

■ Process

1. Distribute Response Sheet 8.5.1
2. Review the meaning of the terms "a presumption of entitlement," "unawareness of the need to adapt," and "symbols of entitlement."
3. Organize participants into groups of 3-5 people.
4. Ask each group to brainstorm examples for each term.
5. Invite each small group to share with the larger group.

**Debriefing**

1. What did you think, feel or wonder as you completed this exercise?
2. What surprises you?
3. What made this activity difficult or easy?
4. What conclusions can you draw from the answers of the group?
5. What would you like to do with this information?

**Response Sheet 8.5.1**

# Barriers to Cultural Proficiency

In your small groups, list examples, within your organization, of these barriers to cultural proficiency

■ Unawareness of the Need to Adapt

Not recognizing the need to make personal and organizational changes in response to the diversity of the people with whom you and your organization interact. Believing instead, that only the others need to change and adapt to you.

■ The Presumption of Entitlement

Believing that all of the personal achievements and societal benefits that you have, were accrued solely on your merit and the quality of your character.

■ Symbols of Entitlement

What is the currency of power and privilege in your home? What is the currency of power and privilege at this school? In this district? What is the language of entitlement and privilege at this school? In this district?

# Part IV

# Making the Commitment to Cultural Proficiency

# Cultural Proficiency: A Moral Imperative

*First organize the inner, then organize the outer. . . . First organize the great, then organize the small. First organize yourself, then organize others.*

—Zhuge Liang

Superintendents Bill Fayette and Hermon Watson continue to have conversations about cultural proficiency. At one of their meetings, Bill shared this story with Hermon.

"My middle school and elementary school administrators had noticed for several years that large numbers of Mexican and Mexican American students regularly visited their families in Mexico around Christmas and Easter. What made this a problem was that the children were often gone for three or four weeks at a time. Consequently, they missed a lot of classroom work and lagged behind the other students.

"The teachers and the administrators at each school implored the parents to respect the school calendar and have their children back when school resumed, but most did not comply. The teachers even developed homework packets that the children could take with them, but those efforts had only mixed results.

"Finally, it occurred to the leadership team that the school was organized around the living patterns of an agriculturally based community that had long ago become an urban center. They decided rather than demanding that the parents respect an anachronistic practice, they could demonstrate respect for the families at the schools by organizing the school calendar around their lifestyles, in much the same way the school leaders' predecessors had done in generations earlier. So now, the schools are closed for four weeks in late December and early January and for two weeks during the observance of Passion Week and Easter. We make up the days in the summer.

"You see," Bill concluded, "once people understood that the school calendar wasn't etched in stone, it was pretty easy to get our priorities in order and decide how we could best meet the needs of our students and their families."

✸

## The Early Years

As educators and consultants, we have been providing what is now called diversity training since the days of confrontational sensitivity groups. During the conversations that led to writing this book, we concluded that reflecting on our past and what we have learned from our clients could be important to others who wish to contribute to peace, justice, and harmony in their communities. Collectively, we have almost 100 years as consultants, many of which have been filled with great frustration because we know that no matter how hard we try, many in our audiences will remain hostile and will change only as a result of court orders or mandates from the hierarchical leaders in the district. Our early years as diversity trainers were frustrating in that we felt unsuccessful because we could see that many of the children and teachers with whom we worked were unsuccessful. Teachers were not reaching children, children were not reaching minimal standards, and educational leaders were not reaching out to their colleagues or their communities in meaningful ways. When we reviewed the effectiveness of the various types of human relations and diversity training, we found, at best, mixed results ranging from major changes in attitudes and behaviors for some individuals to relatively minor changes for most schools and districts.

Laws have been passed and policies have been established that have lowered many of the societal barriers to access, particularly in the areas of race and gender equity. There are still very broad gaps between the perception of what is needed and the activities taken to achieve those goals, however; two people could have the same experience and have opposing views about what it means based on their previous cultural experiences. These disparate opinions range from welfare for immigrants to basic rights for Gay Men and Lesbians.

In a workshop we gave for California staff analysts, one of the participants mentioned that a less-than-sensitive comment made by one of her colleagues was "not culturally competent." After a few questions and a visit to her office at lunchtime, we had in our hands *Toward a Culturally Competent System of Care* (Cross et al., 1989). It was directed toward mental health workers and had been written in response to a situation in which First Nation families were labeled as pathologically dysfunctional because they did not meet the norms that the middle-class European American clinicians were using to assess the health of a family.

We immediately saw the relevance of cultural competence to every organization with which we had ever worked. We had spent most of our careers working in thousands of organizations—schools, businesses, and not-for-profit agencies—which had values that were not culturally competent. We recognized how easily this concept could be adapted to educational settings as well as to other organizations. We also saw what we had missed in our years as frustrated diversity consultants.

We had approached our work from the perspective of first changing attitudes and then expecting the attitudes to result in behavioral changes. We knew that a values-based approach is doomed to fail in environments where people are forced to make change. We also knew that any approach to diversity that is perceived as "added on" as opposed to something that is "integral to" the core curriculum is doomed as well. Cultural competence is a behaviorally based approach to diversity. It does not depend on "right values" to work. Cultural competence is an approach that is easily integrated into the culture of the organization that adopts it. For that very reason, cultural competence looks different in every organization. It becomes a part of the organization's culture. Even in the field of education, one culturally competent school could look quite different from another culturally competent school.

After our first few workshops, which we called "Moving Toward Cultural Competence," our participants told us that if we really wanted to get their attention, we had to change the title. Most people, especially people of color, feel they are already culturally competent. So we raised the stakes. "Come learn to be culturally proficient," we invited them. And they came. Over the past 15 years, we have introduced cultural proficiency to schools throughout California and to many organizations across the country. A few of our clients have made a total commitment to cultural proficiency. One university developed a code of behavior that describes, in terms meaningful to that community, the essential elements of cultural competence. A hospital we worked with for four years has trained all 3,500 managers, staff, and doctors in the approach. It has incorporated the essential elements into its core competencies used for performance appraisal and related the essential elements to the core values of the hospital, which are printed on the ID badges that staff wear every day.

When we began work at the hospital, the executive managers and the human resources team of the hospital (comparable to the administrators and staff development specialists of a school) demanded in-depth training in cultural proficiency because they knew they had to provide the day-to-day coaching, support, and reinforcement. They told us, "If we are going to walk the talk, we need to know not only what we are supposed to do; we need to know how, and we need to practice together." This hospital also has an in-house team of diversity trainers that we trained. After working with us, these trainers developed a training module that they delivered during the first round of training for all employees. Since then, we have implemented a plan for Phase II Intervention. We are very grateful for the opportunities we have had to provide training and to work with the formal and nonformal leaders of schools and other organizations around the country.

Educators are always trying something new, and the education process changes very slowly. Unfortunately, because of this pattern, the educators we encounter are either profoundly impressed with cultural proficiency or fundamentally weary of all they have to do to get through a school day without one more thing added to their agenda—or they are both. The point we emphasize is that cultural proficiency is not an add-on program. It is an inside-out approach to addressing the issues of diversity in a classroom, school, and district. It is an approach that is to be integrated into the culture of the school.

In reading the case study, you perhaps noticed that both Rolling Meadows and Coolidge started slowly and continued to enlarge and enhance the changes made as they worked toward becoming culturally proficient. Movement toward cultural proficiency usually begins with one or two people. We like to think of our sphere of influence as a pebble dropped in a pond. All of us get at least one pebble. We can choose to hold on to it and put it away in our pockets, or we can use it in some way. You can drop your pebble into a small puddle and make a big splash, you can toss it into a large lake and make almost no perceptible difference, or you can join with a few others and together toss your pebbles into the same place and create a rippling effect that affects everything on the surface and profoundly affects those areas on which the pebbles fall.

How the members of a school or district use their influence is related to the leadership that exists there. Many books on organizational development and leadership tell you how to be a leader. We want you to remember that (a) you don't have to have a title to be a leader; and (b) research on leadership, organizations, and change does not have to be written specifically for schools for it to be useful.

Change takes place because people are open and ready for something new. They are able to look around and see a future that is different and better. They are able to rally their colleagues around this vision and work together to make it a reality. This takes place one step at a time, one classroom at a time, one school at a time, one pebble at a time. The first commitment must be to trust the process. Understand that it will take time, and keep working at it until you begin to see changes in the attitudes and behaviors of your colleagues and coworkers. There is a tendency to stop or change programs when the agreed-on processes meet resistance. This is unfortunate, because resistance is a natural and expected step in the change process.

# Where Do You Start?

Start where you are. Use the Cultural Proficiency Continuum (Response Sheet 3.1.1) to assess situations that have taken place in your school. Use the Human Relations Needs Assessment (Activity 3.3) to get a pulse of your district. Use the Cultural Competence Self-Assessment (Activity 4.3) to begin conversations about what you and your colleagues need to learn and do personally. If you have core values or a mission statement for the district, see which parts you can connect to the Guiding Principles of Cultural Proficiency (Response Sheet 5.1.1). At a staff development meeting, conduct the Shared Values Activity (Activity 1.2) to get a collective commitment to addressing the issues of diversity. Once you have gathered these data, you may want to examine the school or district through different lenses.

The continuum data provide you with a perspective on how you and others view the school. You may find widely different points of view on where the school or district places its activities on the continuum. Some may think an activity is culturally competent, whereas others may see it as culturally blind. Sharing your views and earnestly listening to the views of others is an important step in developing consensus about where you are and in what direction you need to go. The needs assessment data provide even more detailed information on how different groups experience the school or district. When analyzed along with the assessments of where the school activities lie on the cultural proficiency continuum, powerful images begin to emerge. You will come to understand why some groups are pleased with the school's approach to diversity and why other groups are very discontented. When you analyze your school or district's core values or mission statement, you will begin to see how perceptions about the school and its needs are aligned— or not—with the core values, the mission statement, and the essential elements. By the time your group is ready to do the shared values activity, you and your colleagues will be ready to commit to becoming an open, inclusive learning environment by embracing cultural proficiency as the approach that will support all students' access to learning.

What you will have created with these activities is agreement to examine schools through a different lens. The new lens frames assumptions about access, oppression, and entitlement. This new lens moves beyond the angst of guilt and anger to taking responsibility for schools effectively educating all students. It moves school leaders away from explaining why groups of students fail toward determining what school leaders can do to create powerful teaching-learning environments that ensure student success. This new lens allows educators to recognize and respond to both individual and group differences.

## A Moral Imperative

Educators have spent much energy studying African American under-achievement, the needs of non-English-speaking students, why girls do not take mathematics, and the perceived deviance of homosexuals, but have spent little or no energy studying the context within which all students perform. Professionals from all fields have debated the success of school, the failure of school, the deschooling of the society, and the reasons for each. They have used private and public funds to document, study, and recommend. Yet the situation continues and does not appear to improve. In fact, it is regressing for African American and Latino males. The problem in education has been studied from every conceivable angle—except where the problem lies: The problem lies in the United States' failure to make a moral commitment to provide education for all groups of society. By making this moral commitment, this country's last tie with its apartheid-based history can be broken and educators will find the means for creating a culturally proficient future.

Despite the historical and legal data pointing to the need, educators have yet to make a moral commitment to confronting entitlement and eliminating oppression. To do so, they must look at schools in the context of a society governed by class, caste, and entitlement, and they must examine the role schools play in inculcating and endorsing the values of dominant society. To do that, educators must abandon the notion that there is something wrong with people because of their culture. They must examine in depth the barriers placed in people's paths, then recognize their own responsibility for tearing down the barriers constructed by straight white men and other entitled groups.

The development of moral character and strength is an important cornerstone of public and private education. When an examination of privilege and power rests on this foundation, educators can construct a stronger edifice of education. To serve the needs of all learners, educators must clearly recognize that today social privileges are given freely to some students and rationed meagerly to others. This may be more important to understand for those who are most entitled than it is for any other sector of society. In the same way that students from oppressed groups need role models, white and male students need role models to help them learn about unearned, unconscious privilege. Once they begin to acknowledge their entitlement, they will be better prepared to take a responsible role in the cultural proficiency continuum.

# Going Further

This book is more about beginnings than endings. With the concepts presented and the activities and cases provided, you now have the tools to begin the process of creating a culturally proficient school. The activities for this last chapter are all *getting to know you* activities. We made this choice to emphasize that cultural proficiency is an inside-out-approach. It all starts within you. Where will you start?

# Reflection

_____

_____

_____

_____

_____

_____

_____

_____

_____

_____

**Activity 9.1:**

# Introductory Grid

■  Purpose

To help people get acquainted with each other. This is a very good *sponge* activity that orients participants to the differences and similarities of the people in the room. As an opener or closer, a sponge activity soaks up extra people and extra time. People do not have to start at the same time to benefit from the activity.

■  Expertise of Facilitator

Moderate

■  Readiness of Group

Intermediate

■  Time Needed

Because this is a sponge activity to be used at the beginning of a session, 10–20 minutes for the activity and the debriefing is sufficient.

■  Materials

Chart paper on walls of room
Markers for participants
Masking tape

■  Briefing

As participants come in, ask them to fill in the blanks on the chart paper.

■  Process

1.  Place a category at the top of each chart paper:

      a. Name

      b. City of birth

      c. Astrological sign

      d. City of residence

      e. Favorite restaurant or type of food

      f. Hobby or leisure activity

      g. Expectation for the session

      h. Other creative categories that will get people thinking and talking

2. Number the lines of Chart A with the number of participants.

3. Participants select a number on Chart A and then complete each chart using the same number so that their answers can be identified.

## ▪ Debriefing

1. What do we have in common?

2. What are some of the differences we have?

3. What conclusions can you draw from the answers on the charts?

4. What questions do you have for group members?

## ▪ Variation

Have members stand and introduce themselves by adding to the information on the charts such as where they work and why they are in the program.

## ▪ Variation

1. Divide the participants into random groups of four or five people.

2. Have each group list the following:

      a. What everyone in the group has in common

      b. Something unique about each member

      c. What they hope to achieve by the end of the program

      d. A name for the group

3. Each small group makes a brief presentation to the larger group.

## ■ Variation

Add to the last page of the grid the category "Significant Family Value." Discuss the differences and similarities of family values and how, even when all the values appear to be positive and laudatory in a common workplace, those values may conflict with one another or cause conflicts within the individual. For example, the values for honesty and courtesy often conflict because sometimes it is impossible to be honest and not hurt someone's feelings, which is considered discourteous.

**Activity 9.2:**

# Totems or Crests—Getting to Know You

■ Purpose

To help members of the group get to know one another in terms of cultural similarities and differences

■ Expertise of Facilitator

Low

■ Readiness of Group

Beginning

■ Time Needed

30 minutes

■ Materials

Blank paper (8½″ x 11″ or larger)
Masking tape
Colored markers

■ Briefing

We are going to engage in an activity so that you can get to know one another better and understand the diversity of your backgrounds.

■ Process

1. Talk about the use of culturally specific icons like totems or family crests. Indicate that these items are being adapted for this activity.
2. Distribute blank sheets. Allow participants to select the form they wish to use.
3. Ask participants to draw symbols on their papers to represent
   a. The group with which they most strongly identify

     b. How they are like the members of that group

     c. How they do not fit a stereotype of that group

     d. An event when they felt very different

     e. A person who has most influenced them in understanding or accepting diversity

4. Tape the drawing to each person's chest and walk around the room looking at the drawings of the other participants, asking questions as appropriate.

■ Debriefing

1. What did you see that surprised you?

2. What did you learn about your colleagues?

3. What did you learn about yourself?

4. What conclusions can we draw about the members of this group?

■ Variation

Change the theme from getting to know you to diversity or some other topic by changing the symbols you ask participants to draw. For example:

1. Where they were born

2. A strong family value

3. Their present occupation

4. A dream or fantasy

5. A personal goal for this program

### Activity 9.3:

# Name Five Things*

■ **Purpose**

To help participants clarify how they define themselves. This activity will also demonstrate the effects of cultural blindness.

■ **Expertise of Facilitator**

Low

■ **Readiness of Group**

Beginning

■ **Time Needed**

30 minutes

■ **Materials**

Blank paper

■ **Briefing**

Think about who you are and how you describe yourself.

■ **Process**

1. Write five words or short phrases that describe the essence of who you are. These should be things that if they were taken away from you, you would not be the same person (five minutes).
2. With a partner, share your list (15 minutes).
3. Cross one item off of your list so that only the purest essence of who you are will be listed.
4. Now cross one more item off of the list.

---

*Thanks to Angeline McGill-King of San Diego, California, for contributing this activity.

5. Participants may try to cooperate, but they will definitely struggle.

6. The point of this activity is to help you to see that when you seek to engage with only one aspect of someone, you are asking them to erase or deny the essence of who they are. It may be more difficult and take more time in a diverse environment, but if you don't, you won't be experiencing all of who the people are.

■ Debriefing

1. What did you notice as you wrote your list?

2. What did you notice as you shared your list?

3. What did it feel like to have to cross items off of your list?

4. What did you learn about your colleagues?

5. What did you learn about yourself?

6. What conclusions can you draw about the members of this group?

**Activity 9.4:**

# Who Are You?

■ Purpose

To help participants clarify how they define themselves. This activity is an effective follow-up to Activity 9.3.

■ Expertise of Facilitator

Low

■ Readiness of Group

Beginning

■ Time Needed

30 minutes

■ Materials

Blank paper

■ Briefing

I am going to ask you ten questions. Without talking, please write your answers.

■ Process

Read the questions slowly and solemnly. Do not respond to any comments the participants make.

1. Question #1.  Who are you?
2. Question #2.  Who are you?
3. Question #3.  Who are you?
4. Question #4.  Who are you?
5. Question #5.  Who are you?

6. Question #6.   Who are you?

7. Question #7.   Who are you?

8. Question #8.   Who are you—really?

9. Question #9.   Who are you?

10. Question #10. Who are you?

■ Debriefing

1. What did you notice as you wrote your list?

2. What did you learn about yourself?

3. Why do you think we did this exercise?

■ Variation

Ask participants to prioritize the items on their lists and share them.

**Activity 9.5:**

# Who Am I?

■ Purpose

To serve as a get-acquainted activity and to understand how others name themselves

■ Expertise of Facilitator

Low

■ Readiness of Group

Beginning

■ Time Needed

45 minutes

■ Materials

Chart paper
Markers
Paper and pencils for participants

■ Briefing

This activity will give you a chance to hear how others in your group define themselves and understand the relative importance of culture and ethnicity.

■ Process

1. As a group, develop a list of adjectives that describe the roles and groups with which the people in the group identify. Complete the sentence stem: "I am a(n) . . ."

For example, "I am a(n) . . .

 . . . woman"
 . . . educator"
 . . . college graduate"
 . . . teacher"
 . . . administrator"
 . . . European American"
 . . . Hispanic American"
 . . . Asian Pacific Islander"
 . . . African American"
 . . . husband"
 . . . significant other"
 . . . partner"
 . . . Gay Man"
 . . . Lesbian"
 . . . daughter"
 . . . brother"

2. Everyone takes the list of descriptors and ranks them individually according to how they define themselves, omitting words that do not apply.

■ Debriefing

1. What criteria did you use to rank the descriptors?
2. What surprised you about your list?
3. What surprised you about the list of the other members in your small group?
4. What have you learned about the members of this group?
5. What have you learned about labels, descriptors, and naming oneself?
6. How will you use this information?

**Activity 9.6:**

# Cultural Portrait

■ Purpose

To graphically describe one's cultural identity. This activity is a creative way for participants to consider the many cultural groups to which they belong and to see how many cultures are represented in the group.

■ Expertise of Facilitator

Moderate

■ Readiness of Group

Intermediate

■ Time Needed

45–60 minutes

■ Materials

Two or three markers for each person
One piece of chart paper for each person

■ Briefing

Each of us belongs to a number of cultural groups. These groups reflect our ethnicity, occupational and vocational cultures, and social groups that shape or reflect our values. Membership in a group is determined by how you identify with the group members as well as how those group members perceive you. On the paper you have been given, draw intersecting and overlapping circles to represent the cultural groups with which you identify. *If you can*, show the relative importance and influence of each group by the size and placement of the circles you draw.

■ Process

1. Encourage each person to create a diagram that reflects the complexity of his or her cultural identity.
2. Have each person hang his or her drawing on the wall.
3. Let members mill around the room examining and discussing the drawings.
4. Alternate to #3: Have each person explain his or her drawing to the entire group.

■ Debriefing

1. How did it feel to draw a diagram of your culture?
2. How well did you represent yourself?
3. What have you learned about your colleagues?
4. What did you learn about culture?
5. How can you apply this knowledge?
6. Given the diversity represented by the drawings in the room, how can you explain your ability to get along with one another?
7. How can you use this information in the work you are doing?

**Activity 9.7:**

# Exploring Your Cultural Roots

■ Purpose

To explore and share information about participants' individual cultures. This is another way for participants to get to know one another while examining the culture of their families of origin.

■ Expertise of Facilitator

Intermediate

■ Readiness of Group

Moderate

■ Time Needed

60 minutes

■ Materials

None

■ Briefing

This activity will allow you to share elements of your cultural background and to learn from others about their cultural backgrounds by using a specific set of cultural markers. Focus on your family of origin and the place where you grew up. Think about how you were in that family. As far back as you can remember, describe these aspects of your family's heritage:

- Education
- Religion
- Wealth, Income
- Food

## ■ Process

1. Give the group about five minutes to reflect quietly about families. Some participants may choose to take notes.
2. Allow each person five minutes to tell his or her story, beginning with the current generation and tracing as far back in the family as possible. You can control the amount of time for this activity by organizing the participants into small groups.
3. Continue around the group until each person has had the opportunity to share his or her story.
4. Listen and compare and contrast from one generation to the next and from individual to individual within the group.

## ■ Debriefing

1. If you have several small groups, they will not all complete at the same time. Circulate among the groups and engage them in initial debriefing by inviting them to share reactions, insights, and observations about the activity.
2. Once all groups have completed, spend a few minutes having the total group continue the debriefing begun in Step 1.
3. Ask for volunteers to share one insight to their own culture that was confirmed through their involvement in this activity.
4. Similarly, ask for members to share any new insights to their own culture that this activity provided.
5. Ask for volunteer members to share one thing that they learned about a fellow participant whom they have known for some time.
6. Ask for volunteer members to indicate the similarities and differences that they experienced among group members.
7. Finally, ask group members to consider how this activity influences their work with other educators, parents, and students.

## ■ Variation

Ask participants to answer the question, "When did you first become aware of yourself as a cultural entity?"

**Activity 9.8:**

# Observation Activity

■ Purpose

To practice the skill of collecting data by observing. Creating change in any school requires the development of a climate for change. The collection of data is one of the skills central to creating a climate for change. In this activity, you practice one of the first steps for collecting data, which is to hone the skills of observation as a technique for data collection.

■ Expertise of Facilitator

Moderate

■ Readiness of Group

Beginning

■ Time Needed

2 hours

■ Materials

Response Sheet 9.8.1: Observation Questions

■ Briefing

Most of us ask questions when we want to know something. This activity will give you an opportunity to gather information and identify how much you can learn by simply observing.

■ Process

Instruct participants to go somewhere alone where there are people to observe, but where they can be unobtrusive observers. They are to find a place to sit where they will not be obtrusive to the environment and where they will not be engaged in conversation. For example, they could sit in the cafeteria during lunch. Then they are to sit for at least 30 minutes and observe what there is to see from that one spot.

■ Debriefing

When participants return, give them a sheet with the following questions to answer. Do not give the questions before participants go, because that will filter what they see. After they have answered the questions for themselves, have them discuss their answers with a partner and then in a large group.

1. How did you choose the site to observe?
2. What were your initial impressions?
3. What happened after you were sitting for about 10 minutes?
4. What did you see?
5. How did you interpret what you saw?
6. Did your interpretations change after you observed for several minutes?
7. Did you see anything that surprised you?
8. Did your impressions change about anything?
9. What have you learned from this process:
   a. About yourself?
   b. About what you observed?
   c. About the tool of observation?

■ Variations

1. Have participants go to a meeting or to a site for observation in the community in which they will conduct their project.
2. Have participants focus on looking for particular issues based on the concepts this activity is used to reinforce.

**Response Sheet 9.8.1:**

# Observation Questions

1. How did you choose the site to observe?

2. What were your initial impressions?

3. What happened after you were sitting for about 10 minutes?

4. What did you see?

5. How did you interpret what you saw?

6. Did your interpretations change after you observed for several minutes?

7. Did you see anything that surprised you?

8. Did your impressions change about anything?

**Activity 9.9:**

# Strength Bombardment

■ Purpose

To build a sense of team among participants through sharing personal stories and discovering similarities and differences. This is a good activity for team building. We have had success with it as an opening activity with a group whose members know one another well. We also have had success with it as a culminating activity for groups that have been working together on a project. This activity provides for a personal focus, allows for individual expression, and uses positive feedback as a communication tool.

■ Skill of Facilitator

Moderate

■ Readiness of Group

Beginning

■ Time Needed

60–90 minutes, depending on the size of the subgroups

■ Materials

Small adhesive labels, preferably colored circles about the size of a quarter; if large colored dots are not available, get labels that are large enough for writing one word. Each participant should have about 20–50 labels, depending on the size of the small group.

■ Briefing

In your small groups, you will be sharing stories about important aspects of your life.

## ■ Process

1. Distribute a plain sheet of 8½" x 11" paper to each participant.

2. Ask participants to write their names in the middle of the page.

3. Ask participants to turn the paper over. Divide your life into 10- or 15-year increments. For each of these time periods, identify things that you have done that you are proud of. This does not necessarily mean achievements from the perspective of society, but accomplishments as you define them. Participants can make notes on the page.

4. Organize participants into groups of 3-6 participants. A group of three people will need about 30 minutes. Add 10 additional minutes of processing time for each additional member of the group.

5. In the small group, each person will take five minutes to share his or her accomplishments. The person is not to be interrupted during the telling of the story.

6. While the first person is telling his or her story, other group members are writing one-word adjectives on the labels that describe their assessment of his or her character in light of the accomplishments. In five minutes, each group member will write on several of the labels.

7. When the first person has completed his or her story, during which time colleagues have been recording their adjectives on the labels, he or she listens to the feedback from colleagues.

8. In turn, each colleague looks the storyteller in the eye and tells him or her what is written on each dot and alternately affixes it to the reverse side of the speaker's strength bombardment sheet. For example, "Mary, I see you as courageous because you stood up to your brother." In just a few minutes, Mary has many labels on her sheet that describe her character.

9. Repeat the process for each participant.

## ■ Debriefing

Ask the following questions:

1. What did you think, feel, or wonder while assessing your life?

2. What did you think, feel, or wonder while telling your story?

3. What was your reaction to the feedback you received in the two forms of communication: the verbal message and direct eye con-

tact from your colleagues and the label dots affixed to the reverse side of your sheet?

4. It never varies with this activity that someone will minimize the feedback from his or her colleagues. Some will indicate that their colleagues were generous. If this should occur, remind them that it was that person's story; the colleagues were only feeding back to that person what they were hearing.

    Let participants know that, yes, life is not always expressed in terms of positive feedback, but it sure does feel good when it occurs. Then continue with the following questions:

5. What did you think, feel, or wonder as you heard the stories of your group members?

6. What implications does this have for our work with students? With parents? With one another?

7. Invite participants to keep this sheet in a safe place so that someday in the future they can pull the sheet out and remind themselves of what people had to say to them on this day.

# 10 ⚜

# The Case:
# One Last Look

*Any real change implies the breakup of
the world, as one has always known it, the
loss of all that gave one an identity, the
end of safety.*

—James Baldwin

The cases used in this book are presented here in their entirety. In each chapter, you found a portion of the cases—at the beginning of the chapter, and sometimes integrated into the chapter—to illustrate points that we made. The people and their stories in the cases are people we have met and have worked with in school districts across the country. Although none of what you have read is fiction, all of the names are fictionalized. So if you think you recognize your name or the name of someone you know, please be sure that it is purely coincidental. We present the case here so that you can go further with your analysis of these two fictitious districts—comparing them to your own, identifying common responses to issues of diversity, honing your skills as you use the tools of cultural proficiency, and acknowledging that cultural proficiency is not an event but a process.

# Rolling Meadows School District

Rolling Meadows Unified School District has been getting some negative media coverage. One of the few African American parents in the district, Barbara Latimer, an attorney, has accused some of the high school teachers of racism. Superintendent Hermon Watson is concerned and privately incensed. He has provided leadership for this district for the past 15 years, and he is not happy to have this kind of press coverage so close to his retirement. One of the reasons people live in this bedroom community is that it has historically been a stable, safe, family-oriented neighborhood in which to raise kids. It has been a place people moved to because the schools are excellent and people don't have to deal with the issues commonly found in desegregated schools and neighborhoods.

The school district is currently experiencing a growth spurt. The district has 15,000 students enrolled in 15 elementary schools, three middle schools, two comprehensive high schools, a continuation high school, and an adult school. Ten years ago, 92% of the district's student population was European American, 4% African American, 2% Latino, 1% Asian and Pacific Islander, and 1% First Nations people. The current student population is 77% European American, 9% African American, 8% Latino, 5% Asian and Pacific Islander, and 1% First Nations. Ten years ago, the teaching population, which has remained relatively stable, was 94% European American; the current teaching force is 91% European American.

Last year, the district hired its first woman, and African American, high school principal. Dina Turner had served as an assistant principal in another state. In her first year, there was little evidence that anyone mentored her or showed her the Rolling Meadows way of doing business. She was also confronted with a new pressure in that the high school received only provisional accreditation from the regional accrediting agency, which proved to be a blow to the egos of faculty and the community. The report concluded that although the high school did an excellent job of preparing most kids academically to transition to college, it failed to fulfill a mission of adequately providing students with skills and knowledge to participate comfortably as citizens in the increasingly diverse country.

Although Rolling Meadows has its own business and civic center, the majority of the population makes a long commute into the urban center for work. The trade-off is a community that is not fraught with urban problems. Today's paper quoted one parent as saying, "We moved out here to get away from these people, and now they are all moving here and starting trouble." Hermon shudders as he imagines his board members reading this over their morning coffee.

Later that morning, as Hermon reviews the *Tribune* article with his cabinet, he says, "We've handled every single incident that has occurred in a fair but discreet manner. We don't have racist teachers and are certainly not a racist district. No one is perfect, and we have had only a few isolated incidents. My goal is that when we look at the faces in our classrooms, or out across the lunchrooms, we don't see colors, we just see kids."

Winston Alexander, the assistant superintendent for business, clears his throat. "I'm not sure, Hermon, but do you think that we should hire consultants? It might look good right now to bring in some outside experts so they can tell the press what a good job we are doing."

"That's a fabulous idea," exclaims Holly Kemp, the assistant superintend for curriculum and instruction. "We just finished the Regional Association of Schools and Colleges (RASC) accreditation review process, so the documents describing our programs and students are in order. We could hire consultants to provide a cultural accreditation of some sort. We are not bad people, surely they will know that."

"My cabinet rarely lets me down," Hermon muses. "That is why we have been honored as a national distinguished district three times in the past 10 years." Aloud, he says, "A cultural audit. Good idea. Winston and Holly, can the two of you put together a request for proposal (RFP) this week? Ask our attorney friend, Barbara Latimer, to give you a hand. That should quiet her down for a while, and it will let her know that we really mean to do well by her people. Winston, see what kind of money we can find for this effort. We may need to dig pretty deep in order to climb out of this hole."

Hermon recognizes that during his tenure, the demographics of the district have shifted from being almost totally white to more multiethnic and socioeconomically diverse. He has gathered data on student achievement, noted the interethnic fights at the high schools, and heard parents' complaints about the curriculum. The RFP that the staff prepares seeks consultants to conduct a yearlong cultural audit and needs assessment that taps into the views and beliefs of all sectors of the district—the educators, classified staff, students, and members of the community. Although he has only been introduced to the concept of cultural proficiency, he knows intuitively to move in this comprehensive direction and involve all layers of district and community so they will understand his vision.

As the cabinet reviews the proposals they have received in response to the RFP, they discover that they are learning a lot themselves. They note information that they glean from specific responses to the questions they have asked. They pay particular attention to the underlying values of one group of consultants. It is easy to discern what they believe and value from the way they present their ideas and the extra material that they have included. They are particularly impressed with the following two concepts:

1. No nation has ever sought to provide universal education for as broad a spectrum of social, class, and ethnic or racial groups as has the United States.
2. We are more successful at kindergarten through college education than any other nation in the world today, but our development of a de facto caste system has created great inequities in our educational system. We are at a point in history where we must heed the warning to avoid creating "two societies, separate and unequal" (Riot Commission, 1968).

The teachers at the high school have heard that the district is going to hire consultants to assess their cultural sensitivity. They are neither impressed nor pleased. Sitting in the teachers' lunchroom, they speak wistfully about when their own children attended district schools, failing to acknowledge that the shift in demographics has made a significant change in the type of district they have. Their comments about the children and the impending cultural audit reflect attitudes that range from culturally destructive to culturally proficient.

Many believe that the school can be organized to provide a high-quality education for all students. A smaller but very vocal group, however, continually decries any changes that appear to lower standards. They accuse the district administration of not supporting the school by failing to get tough with troublemakers. Members of this group believe that if the school returns to a well-defined tracking system that creates a vocational level for students who are not interested in learning, the needs of everyone will be served. They also believe that senior teachers should be given first choice for teaching upper-level courses. This vocal minority continues to protest that too many changes are occurring at the high school.

In one corner, Celeste, a teacher at the high school, impatiently circled "sex" on the needs assessment form sent out from the district office. Beside it, she wrote "as often as possible." Then she wrote "gender" on the form, carefully drew a small box next to it, wrote "female" beside the box and checked it. Further down on the form, she was asked to indicate her race or ethnicity. "Ayy," she groans, and turns to her friend Bobby, who was completing the same form. "I hate these forms. I am so tired of being forced into boxes that don't fit."

Bobby yawned. "Just fill out the form. It doesn't really matter. And besides, these are the categories that the U.S. Census uses."

"I don't care about the Census Bureau," said Celeste, "they are wrong! Where is the box for me on the chart? I am not African American. My cultural identity is Brazilian."

"Well, you are Black Hispanic, aren't you?" asks Bobby.

"No. I am a U.S. citizen of African descent. I was born in Boston and moved with my parents to Brazil when I was a baby. My first language is Portuguese. My father is Brazilian and my mother is from Panama; they met when they were studying at Tufts University. I speak Spanish, but I am not Hispanic because Spain did not colonize Brazil. I look black and I relate most strongly to people from Central and South America."

In another corner, we hear . . . "This is America, everyone should speak English; they should be adapting to us. This is reverse discrimination. We didn't do anything to those people, why do we have to change?"

"Our goal for examining our school policy on student grouping must be to enhance student achievement. If we get some good consultants in here, they can help us to disaggregate our test data. Then we can really understand our students' different needs."

"Why are we trying to fix something that's not broken? When I walk into my classroom, I do not see color or gender, I only see children."

"I believe that conflict is natural and normal; I'm glad we will be learning how to do things differently when conflict occurs."

Across the room, some teachers are discussing their students . . . "I didn't realize that his father was gay. He doesn't look gay to me."

"She catches and throws a baseball well for a girl."

"I can't believe my Japanese boys only scored in the 80th percentile on the state test!"

Over by the copier, some teachers are trying to be proactive . . . "We need a Korean vice principal to help us with the Korean students."

"We celebrate Cinco de Mayo and Martin Luther King's birthday. What holiday can we use for Native Americans?"

"Let's look at the school calendar to be sure that we don't schedule our potlucks during Ramadan, Ridvan, or Yom Kippur."

A few weeks later, Rolling Meadows High School Principal Dina Turner conducts a meeting with her site council. "We are at the midpoint of our year, and our plan specifies that we assess our progress by examining our benchmarks. As you recall, our goals for this year were for schoolwide academic improvement in reading and learning more about our interaction patterns with students."

Bobby, a consistently unhappy teacher, replies, "You know, I am all for academic improvement, but I still don't see how it is related to having another teacher observe in my classroom."

Another teacher, Celeste, speaks up in Dina's defense. "I am not sure I agree with you, Bobby. Since we have started the schoolwide focus on reading and our interactions with students, it's become easier for me to talk with some of my students about reading for fun."

Barbara Latimer, parent activist, adds, "That's a good point, Celeste. Just this week, my daughter asked if I didn't think that we watched way too much television while not reading enough. I hated to admit it, but she is right. I was just wondering how parents who are not members of this council feel. She also says that she has noticed that some of her teachers are easier to talk to."

Dina says, "Obviously, I am very supportive of our reading initiative. I am also deeply committed to our continued study of student-teacher interactions. Has anyone tried any of the teacher expectation behaviors in their classroom? These behaviors will benefit all students."

"I have," said Celeste. "You know, Bobby, I know I am a good teacher now, and these activities are helping me see some of my blind spots. I am beginning to see how my unintentional behaviors can have a negative effect on some students' learning!"

"What occurs to me," adds Dina, "is that if these unintentional behaviors occur between teachers and students, they may also occur among adults, too. It scares me to think about the damage we do to one another without even realizing it."

Barbara has an idea. "You know, we may want to consider some of that training for parents and community members. From what you are saying, it may be very enlightening, possibly a little uncomfortable, but very worthwhile."

"Most teachers are comfortable with the training process," Dina replies. "I believe if everyone sees themselves as students, and if we are all willing to commit the time and energy it takes to walk this path toward improvement, we can all grow and our kids will really benefit. And, I agree, it would be good for this group too. In fact, it would be an excellent topic for training all our parents."

Dina then asks Bobby, "How balanced do you see our curriculum? In other words, Bobby, what do you see as our strong points, and what are some of our omissions?"

After a moment of reflection, Bobby responds, "I want you to know that I don't know everything. For example, since the attack on the World

Trade Center, I've realized how little I know about the Middle East, the Muslim religion, or our country's policies that affect these issues. One of the things I see coming from this training is that even though our school has few Middle Easterners or Muslim students that I know of, it will be important for our curriculum to be inclusive of them."

"Yes, the new state standards for social studies," offer Dina, "are very explicit that our students be prepared to live and function in an interdependent world. I am sure, Bobby, that your concerns are shared by many of us. We need that kind of openness to do this work well."

The consultants are making a presentation to Superintendent Watson's cabinet, and Holly is not sure they really understand the situation at the high school because she hasn't seen most of the problems that they are identifying. They indicate that the social studies curriculum teaches students little or nothing about the class and caste systems in this country. Recent textbooks, however, have inserted some materials and lessons mentioning women and people of color, although these insertions have generally been few and they are frequently segregated into discrete units and not integrated into the totality of U.S. history.

They further note that the acknowledgment of African Americans in U.S. history is limited to brief lessons on slavery, the celebration of Dr. King's birthday, and observances of black history month in February. Lessons about First Nations often range from highlighting their nobility to underscoring their savagery; their only significant role was to attend the first Thanksgiving. Lessons about Latinos are frequently relegated to music, dance, and a lesson about Cesar Chavez or Che Guevara. They almost never are mentioned as existing outside of New York and the southwestern United States. Students learn about Asians and Pacific Islanders as the celebrants of Chinese New Year, the sneak attack at Pearl Harbor, and the reluctant recipients of U.S. "help" during the Korean and Vietnam wars. Lessons about women often resort to the "great woman approach," focusing on a few heroic individuals rather than on the historic and continuing role of women in the United States. These discrete lessons lead to the objectification and invisibility of girls and people of color. The contributions of Gay Men and Lesbians are totally omitted from the curriculum. Although there are many Gay Men and Lesbians involved in the growth and development of the United States, they are never mentioned by name in association with their achievements.

The consultants then direct the cabinet's attention to a chart with quotations gathered from the focus group that was conducted during the cultural audit:

"If we are celebrating diversity, why don't we have celebrations of European American history month?"

"A teacher wrote on my child's paper that she didn't understand the black inner-city experience and therefore couldn't grade her essay fairly. This child has never lived in the inner city! Her father is a chemist and I am vice president of the Red Cross. Her teacher knows we are a middle-class family."

"The immigrant students don't even have magazines and books in their homes. They are at a tremendous disadvantage when compared to the other students."

"Standard English is the official language of our country. It should be the only language permitted in our schools."

After giving the cabinet a chance to reflect on the impact of these statements, one of the consultants says, "Each of these comments assumes that students from the dominant culture, and the families of European American students, are the standard of measure for every other student. In the first comment, it is not recognized that most traditional school curricula celebrate the dominant culture daily. The second illustration shows the lack of awareness of the relationship of economic class and ethnic culture. The third quote reflects the assumption that the speaker knows what is in students' homes and that students in homes with books and magazines read them. The final quote fails to recognize the important connection between culture and language and their relationship to identity and self-concept."

# Coolidge Unified School District

On the other side of the county, Coolidge Unified School District serves the families that live in the urban center where many of the Rolling Meadows parents work. Historically, Coolidge High School was among the schools in the county that earned top academic honors. The advanced placement classes have less than 10% African American and Latino students. Over the past five years, the Title I population has increased from 10% to 55%. In that same time period, the English as a Second Language (ESL) classes have increased from serving 2% of the student population to serving slightly more than 35% of the students.

There have been two resulting effects of these trends. The first has been a decrease in the number of sections of honors classes and a dramatic increase in remedial and heterogeneous classes. The heterogeneous classes in English and social studies were created to overcome criticism about the negative effects of tracking; placement in mathematics and science classes, however, has hampered establishing true heterogeneous grouping in English and social studies.

The second effect of the demographic changes has been that the school's standardized test scores have steadily declined, and the local media have surmised that the quality of education has deteriorated. Teachers still have an interest in a traditional academic approach to curriculum. They also place a high value on a tracked system in which the highest achievers are allowed to move at an accelerated rate.

The extracurricular programs except for football tend to be associated with specific ethnic groups. Swimming and baseball are perceived to be European American sports, wresting a Latino sport, track and basketball are dominated by African Americans, and tennis has been given over to Asians and Pacific Islanders. Student government leaders represent the demographic profile of the school, but most clubs and other organizations are predominated by one ethnic group. Latino students tend to participate in smaller numbers in these activities than other ethnic groups do. In recent years, the level of tension has been rising between various groups. There have been some fights and retaliatory attacks that have received wide coverage by local media.

Bill Fayette, superintendent of the Coolidge district, arranged to have coffee with his colleague, Hermon Watson. Hermon was interested in discussing how the Coolidge district had approached their diversity issues with cultural proficiency and if they had experienced any successes. Bill shared the Coolidge experience with Hermon.

"Hermon, the first thing I did was ask Leatha Harp, my director of human resources, to gather a team of teachers and administrators to serve on employment interview panels to help select new administrators. The panel collected input from across the district regarding the qualities they wanted in new administrators. I was surprised at many of the responses." Bill then asks Leatha to come in and share the information that she has gathered. First, Leatha showed Hermon the list of fairly negative comments:

- What our district needs is a strict disciplinarian so the kids will know who is charge.
- The Latino kids need a Latino administrator so they can have a role model.
- Administrators come and go, but I will always be here.
- Our schools are too tough for women administrators.
- I want someone who has majored in my area so I can be fairly evaluated.

"Some of those comments are pretty personal and jaded," Hermon notes.

"You are right about that, and I have some others that are not nearly as bad. All of the comments tell us a lot about what people want in their leaders. This second list tells us a lot about where the informal leadership is in the district. These people hold no formal appointed leadership positions, yet they have gained power and influence. Barbara Latimer is on the board of the city's Human Relations Council. She doesn't have a formal title or position in the district, but she is highly respected and her input is valued and respected. Her daughter attends Rolling Meadows High School. She is frequently at the district office and attends many board meetings. Look at these other comments. They acknowledge other forms of informal leadership within the district."

- The secretary at the high school has trained seven principals!
- If you want to reach out to parents, just get the word to Mrs. Latimer. That woman is well respected throughout the community.
- The aide in room 7 at the middle school has the ear of the Latino community.
- The union representative is a very important member of the leadership council, but DeLois Winters, a teacher at the middle school, is the person to whom the others look for guidance.

Bill then says to Hermon, "We hired James Harris to provide cultural proficiency training for faculty. At the first staff development session, James explained the underlying principles that inform his approach to dealing with the issues that emerge in a diverse environment. He also explained that the responses to these issues fell within one of four categories." Bill then shares the categories with Hermon.

- *Right the Wrongs:* Some people are angry or have a strong sense of justice. If something is wrong, they think the wrongdoers need to be identified and punished.
- *The Golden Rule:* These people want everyone to just get along. They say, "If we all treat everyone equally, with courtesy and kindness, there wouldn't be a problem."
- *My Pain Equals Yours:* This group takes the position that "everyone has been discriminated against for some reason. I got over it; so should they. We need to forget about the past and move forward."
- *Oppression Olympics:* These people realize that every group has suffered some form of discrimination. They are, however, certain that their group has suffered the most and should not be mini-

mized by discussing everyone else's alleged experience of oppression.

"James pointed out that each of these perspectives has some serious drawbacks," says Bill, "and each one also is useful. If we diagrammed these positions as adjacent circles, we would place cultural proficiency in the center, slightly overlapping each circle. With cultural proficiency, we draw from the best of each of those positions, adding to it our understanding of the cultural proficiency tools so that we can make a positive difference for students, our colleagues, and the community."

James also had collected a number of comments from teachers and administrators in other districts:

"Doesn't focusing on differences just make it harder for us to get along?"

"I don't have a culture. I'm just a generic person, Heinz 57."

"He sure didn't sound black when we talked on the phone."

"I didn't know that there are Chinese people over six feet tall."

"You are different, however, we are comfortable with you. We would have more of your kind around if they were all just like you."

"Why do we have to have special programs like affirmative action and Title IX? I think everyone should be given the same attention and information. That's fair."

Bill points out that James used these quotes to illustrate the guiding principles of cultural proficiency. Bill then invites Hermon to visit Richard Diaz, who is the principal at one of Coolidge's middle schools. Richard provides Hermon with a detailed summary of some of the things that have happened at the middle school.

Richard tells how he decided to include the essential elements of cultural proficiency as standards for his teachers and students. He carefully studied the concepts and consulted with James Harris, and they determined that he should start with the element *assessing culture*. He made this choice because many of his staff members had fervently resisted any forms of change. Richard identified two teacher leaders, Derek and DeLois, who both valued diversity and were willing to serve as co-chairs of the school's diversity committee. The diversity committee conducted a needs assessment. One immediate need they identified was the barrier that was manifested by the growing number of Spanish-speaking students. The committee recommended that Spanish be offered to all students. This would provide all students with the opportunity to become bilingual. It also served as the bridge to increase understanding across cultural lines between and among Latino, African American, and European American students. It also tended to mitigate tensions and misunderstandings that occurred because of differences in culture and language.

Richard and the diversity committee continued to work to overcome the resistance to change. They built a strong case demonstrating how old language, attitudes, values, and behaviors could damage both students and the school's reputation. They indicated that proposed changes needed to become an integral part of the school's mission, not just a supplement to it. He is pleased to report that despite several false starts, teachers are now beginning to recognize behavior and attitudes that were at best precompetent. They created an environment in which the faculty and students experienced some immediate success with a few "feel good" cultural assemblies and fairs. They knew that this was superficial, but it created momentum and got the whole staff talking, supporters and resisters alike.

Superintendents Bill Fayette of Coolidge Unified School District and Hermon Watson continue to have conversations about cultural proficiency. At one of their meetings, Bill shared this story with Hermon.

"My middle school and elementary school administrators had noticed for several years that large numbers of Mexican and Mexican American students regularly visited their families in Mexico around Christmas and Easter. What made this a problem was that the children were often gone for three or four weeks at a time. Consequently, they missed a lot of classroom work and lagged behind the other students.

"The teachers and the administrators at each school implored the parents to respect the school calendar and have their children back when school resumed, but most did not comply. The teachers even developed homework packets that the children could take with them, but those efforts had only mixed results.

"Finally, it occurred to the leadership team that the school was organized around the living patterns of an agriculturally based community that had long ago become an urban center. They decided rather than demanding that the parents respect an anachronistic practice, they could demonstrate respect for the families at the schools by organizing the school calendar around their lifestyles, in much the same way the school leaders' predecessors had done in generations earlier. So now, the schools are closed for 4 weeks in late December and early January and for

2 weeks during the observance of Passion Week and Easter. We make up the days in the summer.

"You see," Bill concluded, "once people understood that the school calendar wasn't etched in stone, it was pretty easy to get our priorities in order and decide how we could best meet the needs of our students and their families."

At the end of one staff development session at his school, Richard writes on the board, "That [women] and men do not learn very much from the lessons of history is the most important of all the lessons that history has to teach" (Huxley, 1959).

"There he goes again," whispers Lane to Harvey, both of whom are social studies teachers. Richard has developed a mantra of change and a rallying cry for the new order of things he is trying to establish at Coolidge. He knows that one speech, one memo, or one training session will not do it. Every time the faculty and staff see him, he talks about change and what it will mean for whomever he is addressing as well as its potential impact on students and the community.

"These diversity sessions are a waste of time," Harvey continues. "No one's going to change. I've been here for 17 years, and I've seen it all. I have tenure, so I'll just sit tight. These administrators are only here long enough to get promoted. Each one brings his own program, and each program leaves with the administrator. If we wait long enough, we won't have to do a thing.

"Let me tell you what changes I have seen, Lane. When I first came here, this was a nice, stable, working-class community where the parents wanted their children to achieve more than they had. Then the population began to change. . . . Too many minority students began to come to our school."

"And?" Lane asks.

"What do you mean, 'And?'" Harvey was getting annoyed. "You know exactly 'and what.' That was precisely when our test scores dropped, drug problems rose, and the school started to become a ghetto nightmare. And I'm not a racist; these are just the facts."

Across the room, Derek and DeLois are eagerly taking notes. "I wish I had taken more history courses when I was in college," DeLois sighs. "I'm sure that I could be more effective if I had a stronger historical foundation for what we are doing."

"We're not here to teach history, we're here to teach kids," Derek retorts. "I wish he would just tell us more about this cultural proficiency model so I can figure out what I need to change in my classroom."

"You're probably right," sighs DeLois. "Richard and the consultant just need to mandate what changes they want to see. Understanding history is not going to change some of the bigots in this room."

At the next training session, James Harris overhears a conversation between Steve Petrossian, the elementary school principal, and Richard Diaz.

Steve says, "You know, this activity in determining how prejudice differs from racism or sexism gives me some new ideas to work with. I had never considered the concept of institutional power as an element of racism and sexism. It just never occurred to me. Let me ask you this. One of our African American coaches said that a certain student is 'a good athlete for a white boy.' Now, isn't that racism?"

Richard asks Steve, "Have you never thought about the institutional power that accrues to European American people in this country?"

Steve gets defensive. "Hey, why attack me? I'm being honest with you. Power is not something that I have ever thought about. Shoot, just because I'm white doesn't mean that I have power. Besides, you haven't answered my question. Isn't that story an example of racism?"

James, the consultant, responds to Steve. "No, it isn't racism. Your story illustrates an ethnocentric use of a stereotype, and it demonstrates cultural incapacity. Even though the coach is wrong, he lacks the ability to institutionalize his misguided beliefs. The term *racism* implies the power to act on one's bigotry or reflects the systems within our institutions that discriminate against people of color without their consent or even the conscious participation of the people within the institution or system."

James then addresses the whole group and uses Steve's story as an illustration of how people lack awareness of—as well as their wish to deny—their own entitlement. "The coach was not reinforcing or perpetuating institutional racism, which affects every person and has grave social consequences no matter whether it is recognized or acknowledged. More often than not, people who are not directly affected by institutional oppression fail to understand when ethnic groups speak out about their experiences. Members of the dominant group, whatever that group is, usually fail to notice their power or entitlement."

Richard speaks up, saying, "Yeah, they say, 'If I didn't experience the oppression, or witness it, then you must be overreacting.' Or they want to start talking about their own pain, and the Oppression Olympics begins. Culturally proficient listeners learn to hear with open, nonjudgmental mind-sets."

James continues addressing the group by sharing a personal story. "As a young European American teacher, I became aware of how ill equipped I was to fully meet the needs of the African American students I encountered when I began teaching in an urban district. I had a degree in history from a major midwestern university, but there were major gaps in my preparation. I began taking coursework on the history of the

U.S. Negro. My knowledge base was greatly expanded, and I quickly realized how valuable this new knowledge would be for *all* students. At the same time, I was a puzzle for many of my European American professors and colleagues. They did not understand why a bright, young, European American man with a fairly secure future would waste his time taking these classes. It was while taking these classes that I began to notice the degree that entitlement—white privilege—had affected my own perceptions. First, the courses in my bachelor's degree program had provided almost no information about black history, thereby rendering the history and the people almost invisible. My second insight was the degree to which I would be able to enrich the knowledge and lives of *all students*."

James continued, telling how he had lived in California for a while, where he taught students who were of Mexican and Portuguese descent for the first time. He experienced the same sense of inadequacy all over again. During a discussion about curricular content with his colleagues, he was shocked to learn that U.S. citizens of Japanese ancestry had been incarcerated in relocation camps (concentration camps) during World War II. "My shock and anger stem from two sources. First, I was angry and disappointed that my own country would do such a thing to its own citizens, and second, I had earned both a bachelor's and a master's degree from two reputable universities but had never encountered this event in any class."

After the training session, Harvey and DeLois are walking across the parking lot toward their cars. DeLois says to Harvey, "I am really enjoying these sessions."

Harvey, cynical as always, lashes back, "Are you for real? I would like this cultural expert to spend a day in the vice principal's office like I did last week. All day long, he deals with the scum of this school. If those kids were in your classroom, you would know why they are so far behind."

DeLois can't believe what she is hearing. "Let me tell you something," she hisses. "First, if you think that 'those students' are the scum of the school, you are in worse shape than you know. The true scum in this school are the educators who do not see students when they come into their classrooms. All they see is skin color and judge the kids and their families on this one factor."

The next day, Brittney, who teaches next door to DeLois, is looking at a framed list hanging on the wall near DeLois' desk. "What is this?" Brittney asks.

"When I was a child, my mom taught me how to make quilts, and quiltmaking taught me some life lessons that I try to remember for myself and I try to share with my students and my colleagues." This is what DeLois learned from her mother and quiltmaking:

- There is no rehearsal. It all counts.
- Sometimes you need the big picture before you can start.
- Don't skimp.
- Be patient with yourself.
- Try it out.
- Take it apart, start over.
- Nonconformity, although beautiful, is sometimes very disruptive.
- Stop when you are tired. It's better to have only three things to do when you are fresh than to have three things to do over when you are frustrated.
- Sometimes you won't know the best process to use until you have finished.
- Good work is not always transferable. What works well in one setting may be totally wrong in another.
- Perfection is perception.

## Going Further

Now that you have read the entire case, you may want to see how your analysis of it has changed from the portions of the case you read in each chapter. You may also want to use the case as a study tool. You and your colleagues may create new ways for using this case and those cases and vignettes that you develop. Let us hear from you so we can share your successes with others. Our e-mail address is **culturalproficiency@earthlink.net**.

1. With which characters in the two cases do you identify most strongly? Why?
2. Does your school or district resemble either of the districts?
3. After reading the case, what lessons do you take with you?
4. What will be the first step you take toward becoming culturally proficient?

# Reflection

_____

_____

_____

_____

_____

_____

_____

_____

_____

_____

_____

# Activities

The charts on the following pages organize the activities by topic, expertise of the facilitator, and readiness of the group. It is our hope that you will use these activities with your students and with your colleagues. Organizing the activities in this way will make it easier for you to choose one that is appropriate for your needs.

■ Activities Organized by Topic

■ Activities Organized by Expertise of Facilitator

■ Activities Organized by Readiness of Group

| Activities Organized by Topic | Expertise of Facilitator | Readiness of Group | Time Needed |
| --- | --- | --- | --- |
| **Getting Ready for Diversity** | | | |
| 1.1: Diversity Lifeline | Moderate | Intermediate | 90 minutes |
| 1.2: Identifying Shared Values for Diversity | Extensive | Intermediate | 1-2 hours |
| 1.3: Cultural Proficiency Consensus | Extensive | Intermediate | 45 minutes |
| 1.4: Journaling | Low | Beginning | flexible |
| **Telling Your Stories** | | | |
| 2.1: Storytelling | Low | Beginning | 20 minutes |
| 2.2: Simultaneous Storytelling | Moderate | Intermediate | 20 minutes |
| 2.3: Pick a Cell | Extensive | Intermediate | 45 minutes |
| 2.4: Discussion About U.S. History | Extensive | Intermediate | 60 minutes |
| 2.5: Cultural Perceptions | Extensive | Beginning | 20 minutes |
| 2.6: Circle of Stereotypes | Extensive | Intermediate | 40 minutes |
| 2.7: Personal Stereotypes | Extensive | Intermediate | 30 minutes |
| 2.8: Cultural Stereotypes | Extensive | Advanced | 60 minutes |
| 2.9: Ethnic Perceptions | Extensive | Advanced | 3 hours |
| 2.10: Group Stereotypes | Extensive | Intermediate | 60 minutes |
| **The Continuum** | | | |
| 3.1: The Cultural Proficiency Continuum | Moderate | Intermediate | 30 minutes |
| 3.2: Circle of History | Moderate | Beginning | 1-3 hours |
| 3.3: Human Relations Needs Assessment | Extensive | Beginning | flexible |
| **The Essential Elements** | | | |
| 4.1: Exploring Behaviors Along the Continuum | Moderate | Intermediate | 30-60 minutes |
| 4.2: Understanding the Essential Elements | Moderate | Beginning | 40 minutes |
| 4.3: Essential Elements of Cultural Proficiency | Moderate | Intermediate | 30 minutes |
| 4.4: Planning With the Five EssentialElements | Moderate | Intermediate | 90-120 minutes |
| 4.5: Performance Competencies and the Essential Elements | Extensive | Advanced | 90-120 minutes |
| 4.6: Intercultural Communication | Moderate | Intermediate | 2 hours |
| 4.7: Managing Conflict With Our Core Values | Extensive | Advanced | 60-90 minutes |
| **The Principles** | | | |
| 5.1: Guiding Principles Discussion Starters | Extensive | Intermediate | 60 minutes |
| 5.2: My Work Values | Low | Intermediate | 60-90 minutes |
| 5.3: Demographics | Moderate | Intermediate | 2 weeks |
| 5.4: Assessing Your School's Culture | Extensive | Intermediate | 3 hours |
| 5.5: Examining Your Organizational Values | Extensive | Advanced | 90-120 minutes |

## Activities Organized by Topic

| | Expertise of Facilitator | Readiness of Group | Time Needed |
|---|---|---|---|
| **Team Building** | | | |
| 6.1: The Great Egg Drop | Moderate | Beginning | 90 minutes |
| 6.2: Seven-Minute Day | Extensive | Intermediate | 2 hours |
| **Preparing for Change** | | | |
| 7.1: The Process of Personal Change | Moderate | Intermediate | 20 minutes |
| 7.2: Seven Dynamics of Change | Low | Beginning | 30 minutes |
| 7.3: Differences That Make a Difference | Moderate | Intermediate | 60 minutes |
| 7.4: Paradigms | Moderate | Intermediate | 60 minutes |
| **Power and Privilege** | | | |
| 8.1: Stand Up | Moderate | Beginning | 20 minutes |
| 8.2: Line of Privilege | Moderate | Intermediate | 30 minutes |
| 8.3: Entitlement Survey | Extensive | Advanced | 60 minutes |
| 8.4: Star Power | Moderate | Beginning | 2 hours |
| 8.5: Barriers to Cultural Proficiency | Low | Beginning | 45 minutes |
| **Getting to Know You** | | | |
| 9.1: Introductory Grid | Moderate | Intermediate | 10-20 minutes |
| 9.2: Totems or Crests—Getting to Know You | Low | Beginning | 30 minutes |
| 9.3: Name Five Things | Low | Beginning | 30 minutes |
| 9.4: Who Are You? | Low | Beginning | 30 minutes |
| 9.5: Who Am I? | Low | Beginning | 45 minutes |
| 9.6: Cultural Portrait | Moderate | Intermediate | 45-60 minutes |
| 9.7: Exploring Your Cultural Roots | Intermediate | Moderate | 60 minutes |
| 9.8: Observation | Moderate | Beginning | 2 hours |
| 9.9: Strength Bombardment | Moderate | Beginning | 60-90 minutes |

## Activities Organized by Expertise of Facilitator

| | Expertise of Facilitator | Readiness of Group | Time Needed |
|---|---|---|---|
| 1.4: Journaling | Low | Beginning | flexible |
| 2.1: Storytelling | Low | Beginning | 20 minutes |
| 5.2: My Work Values | Low | Intermediate | 60-90 minutes |
| 7.2: Seven Dynamics of Change | Low | Beginning | 30 minutes |

## Activities Organized by Expertise of Facilitator

| Activities Organized by Expertise of Facilitator | Expertise of Facilitator | Readiness of Group | Time Needed |
| --- | --- | --- | --- |
| 9.2: Totems or Crests—Getting to Know You | Low | Beginning | 30 minutes |
| 9.3: Name Five Things | Low | Beginning | 30 minutes |
| 9.4: Who Are You? | Low | Beginning | 30 minutes |
| 9.5: Who Am I? | Low | Beginning | 45 minutes |
| 1.1: Diversity Lifeline | Moderate | Intermediate | 90 minutes |
| 2.2: Simultaneous Storytelling | Moderate | Intermediate | 20 minutes |
| 3.1: The Cultural Proficiency Continuum | Moderate | Intermediate | 30 minutes |
| 3.2: Circle of History | Moderate | Beginning | 1-3 hours |
| 4.1: Exploring Behaviors Along the Continuum | Moderate | Intermediate | 30-60 minutes |
| 4.2: Understanding the Essential Elements | Moderate | Beginning | 40 minutes |
| 4.3: Essential Elements of Cultural Proficiency | Moderate | Intermediate | 30 minutes |
| 4.4: Planning With the Five Essential Elements | Moderate | Intermediate | 90-120 minutes |
| 4.6: Intercultural Communication | Moderate | Intermediate | 2 hours |
| 5.3: Demographics | Moderate | Intermediate | 2 weeks |
| 6.1: The Great Egg Drop | Moderate | Beginning | 90 minutes |
| 7.1: The Process of Personal Change | Moderate | Intermediate | 20 minutes |
| 7.3: Differences That Make a Difference | Moderate | Intermediate | 60 minutes |
| 7.4: Paradigms | Moderate | Intermediate | 60 minutes |
| 8.1: Stand Up | Moderate | Beginning | 20 minutes |
| 8.2: Line of Privilege | Moderate | Intermediate | 30 minutes |
| 8.4: Star Power | Moderate | Beginning | 2 hours |
| 8.5: Barriers to Cultural Proficiency | Moderate | Intermediate | 45 minutes |
| 9.1: Introductory Grid | Moderate | Intermediate | 10–20 minutes |
| 9.6: Cultural Portrait | Moderate | Intermediate | 45-60 minutes |
| 9.7: Exploring Your Cultural Roots | Moderate | Intermediate | 60 minutes |
| 9.8: Observation | Moderate | Beginning | 2 hours |
| 9.9: Strength Bombardment | Moderate | Beginning | 60-90 minutes |
| 1.2: Identifying Shared Values for Diversity | Extensive | Intermediate | 1-2 hours |
| 1.3: Cultural Proficiency Consensus | Extensive | Intermediate | 45 minutes |
| 2.3: Pick a Cell | Extensive | Intermediate | 45 minutes |
| 2.4: Discussion About U.S. History | Extensive | Intermediate | 60 minutes |
| 2.5: Cultural Perceptions | Extensive | Beginning | 20 minutes |

## Activities Organized by Expertise of Facilitator

| | | Expertise of Facilitator | Readiness of Group | Time Needed |
|---|---|---|---|---|
| 2.6: | Circle of Stereotypes | Extensive | Intermediate | 40 minutes |
| 2.7: | Personal Stereotypes | Extensive | Intermediate | 30 minutes |
| 2.10: | Group Stereotypes | Extensive | Intermediate | 60 minutes |
| 2.8: | Cultural Stereotypes | Extensive | Advanced | 60 minutes |
| 2.9: | Ethnic Perceptions | Extensive | Advanced | 3 hours |
| 3.3: | Human Relations Needs Assessment | Extensive | Beginning | flexible |
| 4.5: | Performance Competencies and the Essential Elements | Extensive | Advanced | 90-120 minutes |
| 4.7: | Managing Conflict With Our Core Values | Extensive | Advanced | 60-90 minutes |
| 5.1: | Guiding Principles Discussion Starters | Extensive | Intermediate | 60 minutes |
| 5.4: | Assessing Your School's Culture | Extensive | Intermediate | 3 hours |
| 5.5: | Examining Your Organizational Values | Extensive | Advanced | 90-120 minutes |
| 6.2: | Seven-Minute Day | Extensive | Intermediate | 2 hours |
| 8.3: | Entitlement Survey | Extensive | Advanced | 60 minutes |

## Activities Organized by Readiness of Group

| | | Expertise of Facilitator | Readiness of Group | Time Needed |
|---|---|---|---|---|
| 1.4: | Journaling | Low | Beginning | flexible |
| 2.1: | Storytelling | Low | Beginning | 20 minutes |
| 2.5: | Cultural Perceptions | Extensive | Beginning | 20 minutes |
| 3.2: | Circle of History | Moderate | Beginning | 1-3 hours |
| 3.3: | Human Relations Needs Assessment | Extensive | Beginning | flexible |
| 4.2: | Understanding the Essential Elements | Moderate | Beginning | 40 minutes |
| 6.1: | The Great Egg Drop | Moderate | Beginning | 90 minutes |
| 7.2: | Seven Dynamics of Change | Low | Beginning | 30 minutes |
| 8.1: | Stand Up | Moderate | Beginning | 20 minutes |
| 8.4: | Star Power | Moderate | Beginning | 2 hours |
| 9.2: | Totems or Crests—Getting to Know You | Low | Beginning | 30 minutes |
| 9.3: | Name Five Things | Low | Beginning | 30 minutes |
| 9.4: | Who Are You? | Low | Beginning | 30 minutes |
| 9.5: | Who Am I? | Low | Beginning | 45 minutes |
| 9.8: | Observation | Moderate | Beginning | 2 hours |
| 9.9: | Strength Bombardment | Moderate | Beginning | 60-90 minutes |

## Activities Organized by Readiness of Group

| Activities Organized by Readiness of Group | Expertise of Facilitator | Readiness of Group | Time Needed |
|---|---|---|---|
| 1.1: Diversity Lifeline | Moderate | Intermediate | 90 minutes |
| 1.2: Identifying Shared Values for Diversity | Extensive | Intermediate | 1-2 hours |
| 1.3: Cultural Proficiency Consensus | Extensive | Intermediate | 45 minutes |
| 2.2: Simultaneous Storytelling | Moderate | Intermediate | 20 minutes |
| 2.3: Pick a Cell | Extensive | Intermediate | 45 minutes |
| 2.4: Discussion About U.S. History | Extensive | Intermediate | 60 minutes |
| 2.6: Circle of Stereotypes | Extensive | Intermediate | 40 minutes |
| 2.7: Personal Stereotypes | Extensive | Intermediate | 30 minutes |
| 2.10: Group Stereotypes | Extensive | Intermediate | 60 minutes |
| 3.1: The Cultural Proficiency Continuum | Moderate | Intermediate | 30 minutes |
| 4.1: Exploring Behaviors Along the Continuum | Moderate | Intermediate | 30-60 minutes |
| 4.3: Essential Elements of Cultural Proficiency | Moderate | Intermediate | 30 minutes |
| 4.4: Planning With the Five Essential Elements | Moderate | Intermediate | 90-120 minutes |
| 4.6: Intercultural Communication | Moderate | Intermediate | 2 hours |
| 5.1: Guiding Principles Discussion Starters | Extensive | Intermediate | 60 minutes |
| 5.2: My Work Values | Low | Intermediate | 60-90 minutes |
| 5.3: Demographics | Moderate | Intermediate | 2 weeks |
| 5.4: Assessing Your School's Culture | Extensive | Intermediate | 3 hours |
| 6.2: Seven-Minute Day | Extensive | Intermediate | 2 hours |
| 7.1: The Process of Personal Change | Moderate | Intermediate | 20 minutes |
| 7.3: Differences That Make a Difference | Moderate | Intermediate | 60 minutes |
| 7.4: Paradigms | Moderate | Intermediate | 60 minutes |
| 8.2: Line of Privilege | Moderate | Intermediate | 30 minutes |
| 8.5: Barriers to Cultural Proficiency | Moderate | Intermediate | 45 minutes |
| 9.1: Introductory Grid | Moderate | Intermediate | 10-20 minutes |
| 9.6: Cultural Portrait | Moderate | Intermediate | 45-60 minutes |
| 9.7: Exploring Your Cultural Roots | Moderate | Intermediate | 60 minutes |
| 2.8: Cultural Stereotypes | Extensive | Advanced | 60 minutes |
| 2.9: Ethnic Perceptions | Extensive | Advanced | 3 hours |
| 4.5: Performance Competencies and the Essential Elements | Extensive | Advanced | 90-120 minutes |
| 4.7: Managing Conflict With Our Core Values | Extensive | Advanced | 60-90 minutes |
| 5.5: Examining Your Organizational Values | Extensive | Advanced | 90-120 minutes |
| 8.3: Entitlement Survey | Extensive | Advanced | 60 minutes |

# Bibliography

Adams, David Wallace. (1996). Fundamental considerations: The deep meaning of Native American schooling, 1880-1900. In T. Beauboeuf-Lafontant & D. S. Augustine (Eds.), *Facing racism in education* (2nd ed.). Cambridge, MA: Harvard University Press.

Alvesson, M., & Per Olof, Berg. (1992). *Corporate culture and organizational symbolism.* New York: De Gruyter.

Argyris, Chris. (1990). *Overcoming organizational defenses: Facilitating organizational learning.* Englewood Cliffs, NJ: Prentice Hall.

Armelagos, George. (1995, February 13). *Newsweek,* 68.

Armstrong, Thomas. (1994). *Multiple intelligences in the classroom.* Alexandria, VA: Association for Supervision and Curriculum Development.

Association of California School Administrators. (1991). Whites think black kids can't learn, pollster says. *Edcal, 21*(4), 1.

Baldwin, James. (1986). Blood, bread and poetry. In Adrienne Rich, *Blood, bread and poetry: Selected prose 1979-1985.* New York: W. W. Norton.

Ball, Edward. (1998). *Slaves in the family.* New York: Ballantine.

Banks, James. (1994). *Multiethnic education: Theory and practice.* Needham, MA: Allyn & Bacon.

Banks, James. (1999). *An introduction to multicultural education* (3rd ed.). Needham, MA: Allyn & Bacon.

Banks, James, & Banks, Cheryl McGee. (2001). *Multicultural education: Issues & perspectives: Strategies, issues and ideas for today's increasingly diverse classrooms* (4th ed.). New York: Wiley/Jossey-Bass.

Barker, Joel. (1989). *Discovering the future: The business of paradigms.* Lake Elmo, MN: Ili Press.

Barker, Joel (Producer). (1996). *Paradigm principles* [Motion picture]. (Available from Charthouse International Learning Corporation, Burnsville, MN)

Barth, F. (Ed.). (1991). *Ethnic groups and boundaries.* Boston: Little, Brown.

Beckhard, Richard, & Harris, Reuben. (1987). *Organizational transitions: Managing complex change* (2nd ed.). Reading, MA: Addison Wesley.

Beckhard, Richard, & Pritchard, Wendy. (1992). *Changing the essence: The art of creating and leading fundamental change in organizations.* San Francisco: Jossey-Bass.

Bennis, Warren, & Nanus, Bert. (1985). *Leaders: The strategies for taking charge.* New York: Harper & Row.

Berliner, David C. (1992, February). *Educational reform in an era of disinformation.* Paper presented to the American Association of Colleges for Teacher Education, San Antonio, TX.

Blank, Renee, & Slipp, Sandra. (1994). *Voices of diversity: Real people talk about problems and solutions in a workplace where everyone is not alike.* New York: American Management Association.

Block, Peter. (1989). *The empowered manager: Positive political skills at work.* San Francisco: Jossey-Bass.

Boaz, David, & Crane, Edward. (Eds.). (1985). *Beyond the status quo: Policy proposals for America.* Washington, DC: Cato Institute.

Bolman, Lee G., & Deal, Terrence E. (2001). *Leading with soul: An uncommon journey of spirit* (rev. ed.). New York: Wiley.

Bolman, Lee G., & Deal, Terrence E. (2002). *Reframing the path to school leadership.* Thousand Oaks, CA: Corwin.

Bothwell, Lin. (1983). *The art of leadership.* New York: Prentice Hall.

Boutte, Gloria S. (2001). *Resounding voices: School experiences of people from diverse backgrounds.* Boston: Allyn & Bacon.

Boyd, Malcolm. (1984). *Take off the masks.* Philadelphia: New Society.

Boyer, Ernest L. (1983). *High school: A report on secondary education in America.* New York: Harper & Row.

Boyer, Ernest L. (1995). *The basic school: A community for learning.* Menlo Park, CA: Carnegie Foundation.

Bracey, Gerald R. (1991). Why can't they be like we were? *Phi Delta Kappan, 73*(2), 104-117.

Branding, Ronice. (1998). *Fulfilling the dream.* St. Louis, MO: Chalice.

Bridges, William. (1980). *Transitions: Making sense of life's changes.* Reading, MA: Addison Wesley.

Bridges, William. (1991). *Managing transitions: Making the most of change.* Reading, MA: Addison Wesley.

Bridges, William. (2001). *The way of transition: Embracing life's most difficult moments.* Cambridge, MA: Perseus.

Brookover, W. (1982). *Creating effective schools: An inservice program for enhancing school learning climate and achievement.* Holmes Beach, FL: Learning Publications.

Brown, Susan C., & Kysilka, Marcella L. (2001). *Applying multicultural and global concepts in the classroom and beyond.* Boston: Allyn & Bacon.

Burns, James MacGregor. (1978). Prologue. In *Leadership.* New York: Harper & Row.

California Commission on Teacher Credentialing. (1995). *Standards of quality and effectiveness for administrative services credential programs.* Sacramento, CA: Author.

Callahan, Raymond E. (1962). *Education and the cult of efficiency.* Chicago: University of Chicago Press.

Campbell, David. (1984). *If I'm in charge here, why is everybody laughing?* Greensboro, NC: Center for Creative Leadership.

Capper, Coleen. (Ed.). (1993). *Educational administration in a pluralistic society.* Albany: State University of New York Press.

Carlson, C. C., Huelskamp, Robert M., & Woodall, T. D. (1991). *Perspectives on education in America, annotated briefing—third draft.* Alamogordo, NM: Sandia National Laboratories, Systems Analysis Department.

Carter, Thomas P. (1970). *Mexican Americans in school: A history of educational neglect.* New York: College Entrance Examination Board.

Cheek, Donald K. (1976). *Assertive blacks puzzled white.* San Luis Obispo, CA: Impact.

Chinn, Phillip, & Gollnick, Donna. (2002). *Multicultural education in a pluralistic society* (6th ed.). Upper Saddle River, NJ: Merrill Education/Prentice Hall.

Clark, Kenneth B., & Gordon, E. L. (1970). *Racism and American education: A dialogue and agenda for action.* New York: Harper & Row.

Collins, James, & Porras, Jerry. (1997). *Built to last: Successful habits of visionary companies.* New York: Harperbusiness.

Comer, James P. (1988). Educating poor and minority children. *Scientific American, 259*(5), 42-48.

Comer, James P., & Haynes, N. M. (1991). Parent involvement in schools: An ecological approach. *Elementary School Journal, 3,* 271-277.

Cose, Ellis. (1998). *Color-blind: Seeing beyond race in a race-obsessed world.* New York: Harper Perennial.

Cross, Elsie. (2000). *Managing diversity: The courage to lead.* Westport, CT: Quorum.

Cross, Terry. (1989). *Toward a culturally competent system of care.* Washington, DC: Georgetown University Child Development Program, Child and Adolescent Service System Program. (Cross is the executive director of the National Indian Child Welfare Association, Portland, Oregon.)

Cross, Terry L., Bazron, Barbara J., Dennis, Karl W., & Isaacs, Mareasa R. (1989). *Toward a culturally competent system of care.* Washington, DC: Georgetown University Child Development Program, Child and Adolescent Service System Program.

Cross, Terry L., Bazron, Barbara J., Dennis, Karl W., & Isaacs, Mareasa R. (1993). *Toward a culturally competent system of care* (Vol. 2). Washington, DC: Georgetown University Child Development Program, Child and Adolescent Service System Program.

Culbertson, J. A. (1988). A century's quest for a knowledge base. In N. J. Boyan (Ed.), *Handbook of research on educational administration.* White Plains, NY: Longman.

Cummins, Jim. (1988). From multicultural to anti-racist education: An analysis of programmes and practices in Ontario. In T. Skuttnabb-Kangas & J. Cummins (Eds.), *Minority education.* Philadelphia: Multilingual Matters.

Cummins, Jim. (1990). Empowering minority students. In N. M. Hidalgo, C. L. McDowell, & E. V. Siddle (Eds.), *Facing racism in education.* Cambridge, MA: Harvard University Press.

Davidman, Leonard, & Davidman, Patricia. (2000). *Teaching with a multicultural perspective* (3rd ed.). New York: Longman.

Davis, G., & Watson, C. (1985). *Black life in corporate America: Swimming in midstream.* Garden City, NY: Anchor.

Deal, Terrence, & Kennedy, Allen. (1982). *Corporate cultures: The rites and rituals of corporate life.* Reading, MA: Addison Wesley.

Deal, Terrence, & Peterson, Kent D. (1998). *Shaping school culture: The heart of leadership.* San Francisco: Jossey-Bass.

Delpit, Lisa. (1988). The silenced dialogue: Power and pedagogy in educating other people's children. *Harvard Educational Review, 58*(3), 280-298.

Delpit, Lisa. (1993). Silenced dialogue. In L. Weis & M. Fine (Eds.), *Beyond silenced voices: Class, race, and gender in United States schools.* Albany: State University of New York Press.

Delpit, Lisa, Levine, David, Lowe, Robert , Peterson, Bob, and Tenorio, Rita. (Eds.). (1995). Teachers, culture and power. In David Levine et al. (Eds.), *Rethinking schools: An agenda for change.* New York: New Press.

Deming, C. Edwards. (1986). *Out of the crisis: Productivity and competitive position.* Cambridge, UK: Cambridge University Press.

De Pree, Max. (1997). *Leading without power: Finding hope in serving community.* San Francisco: Jossey-Bass.

Derman-Sparks, Louise, Phillips, Carol Brunson, & Hilliard, Asa G., III. (1997). *Teaching/learning anti-racism: A developmental approach.* New York: Teachers College Press.

Dinnerstein, Leonard, Nichols, Roger L., & Reimers, David M. (1979). *Natives and strangers: Ethnic groups and the building of America.* New York: Oxford University Press.

Doyle, Denis P., & Pimentel, Susan. (1998). *Raising the standard: An eight-step action guide for schools and communities.* Thousand Oaks, CA: Corwin.

Drucker, Peter F. (1954). *The practice of management.* New York: Harper & Row.

Duchene, Marlys. (1990). Giant law, giant education, and ant: A story about racism and Native Americans. In N. M. Hidalgo, C. L. McDowell, & E. V. Siddle (Eds.), *Facing racism in education.* Cambridge, MA: Harvard University Press.

Eakin, Sybil, & Backler, Alan. (1993). *Every child can succeed: Readings for school improvement.* Bloomington, IN: Agency for Instructional Technology.

Edmonds, Ronald. (1979). Some schools work and more can. *Social Policy, 9*(5), 3.

Ellison, Ralph. (1952). *Invisible man.* New York: Random House.

El Sadat, Anwar. (1978). *In search of identity: An autobiography.* New York: HarperCollins.

Espinosa, Ruben W., & Ochoa, Alberto M. (1992). *The educational attainment of California youth: A public equity crisis.* San Diego, CA: San Diego State University, Department of Policy Studies in Language and Cross Cultural Education.

Fanon, Frantz. (1963). *The wretched of the earth.* New York: Grove.

Feldstein, S., & Costello, L. (Eds.). (1974). *The ordeal of assimilation: A documentary history of the white working class.* Garden City, NY: Anchor.

Fine, Michelle. (1993). Missing discourse of desire. In L. Weis & M. Fine (Eds.), *Beyond silenced voices: Class, race, and gender in United States schools.* Albany: State University of New York Press.

Flamholtz, Eric G., & Randle, Yvonne. (1987). *The inner game of management*. New York: American Management Association.

Foriska, Terry J. (1998). *Restructuring around standards: A practitioner's guide to design and implementation*. Thousand Oaks, CA: Corwin.

Francis, Dave, & Woodcock, Mike. (1990). *Unblocking organizational values*. Glenview, IL: Scott Foresman.

Franklin, John Hope. (1968). *Color and race*. Boston: Beacon.

Franklin, John Hope, & Moss, Alfred. A., Jr. (1988). *From slavery to freedom: A history of Negro Americans*. New York: Knopf.

Freire, Paolo. (1970). *Pedagogy of the oppressed* (Nyra Bergman Ramos, Trans.). New York: Seabury.

Fullan, Michael. (1991). *The new meaning of educational change*. New York: Teachers College Press.

Fullan, Michael. (2001). *Leading in a culture of change*. New York: Wiley.

Galbraith, John Kenneth. (1977). *The age of uncertainty*. New York: Houghton Mifflin.

Garcia, Eugene. (2001). *Hispanic education in the United States*. Lanham, MD: Rowman & Littlefield.

Gardner, Neely D. (1974). *Group leadership*. Washington, DC: National Training and Development Service Press.

Gilligan, Carol. (1983). *In a different voice*. Cambridge, MA: Harvard University Press.

Giroux, Henry. (1992a). *Border crossings: Cultural workers and the politics of education*. New York: Routledge.

Giroux, Henry A. (1992b). Educational leadership and the crisis of democratic government. *Educational Researcher, 21*(4), 411.

Gladwell, Malcolm. (2000). *The tipping point: How little things can make a big difference*. Boston: Little, Brown.

Goffman, Erving. (1959). *The presentation of self in everyday life*. New York: Doubleday.

Goodlad, John. (1983). *A place called school: Prospects for the future*. St. Louis, MO: McGraw-Hill.

Goodwin, Doris Kearns. (1994, 19 December). In Anthony Lewis, Leading from behind, *New York Times*.

Gordon, Milton M. (1964). *Assimilation in American life: The role of race, religion, and national origins*. New York: Oxford University Press.

Greer, Colin. (1972). *The great school legend: A revisionist interpretation of American public education*. New York: Viking.

Griffiths, Daniel E. (1988). Administrative theory. In N. J. Boyan (Ed.), *Handbook of research on educational administration*. White Plains, NY: Longman.

Guild, P., & Garger, S. (1985). *Marching to different drummers*. Alexandria, VA: Association for Supervision and Curriculum Development.

Hall, Edward T. (1959). *The silent language*. New York: Doubleday.

Hall, Edward T. (1966). *The hidden dimension*. New York: Anchor.

Hall, Edward T. (1981). *Beyond culture*. New York: Anchor.

Hall, Edward T. (1983). *The dance of life: The other dimension of time*. New York: Anchor Doubleday.

Hamada, Tomoko. (1994). *Anthropology and organizational culture*. New York: University Press of America.

Hanson, M. J., Lynch, E. W., & Wayman, K. I. (1990). Honoring the cultural diversity of families when gathering data. *Topics in Early Childhood Special Education, 10*(1), 112-131.

Harragan, Betty L. (1977). *Games Mother never taught you: Corporate gamesmanship for women*. New York: Warner.

Harrison, Barbara Schmidt. (1992). *Managing change in organizations*. Los Angeles: Baskin-Robbins International.

Harrison, Roger, & Stokes, H. (1992). *Diagnosing organizational culture*. San Diego, CA: Pfeiffer.

Hawley, Willis. (1983). *Strategies for effective desegregation: Lessons from research*. Lexington, MA: Lexington Books.

Henry, Jules. (1963). *Culture against man*. New York: Vintage.

Henze, Rosemary, Katz, Anne, Norte, Edmundo, Sather, Susan, Walker, Earnest, and Tsang, Sam-Lim. (2002). *Leading for diversity: How school leaders promote positive interethnic relations*. Thousand Oaks, CA: Corwin.

Hersey, Paul. (1984). *The situational leader*. Escondido, CA: Center for Leadership Studies.

Hersey, Paul, & Blanchard, Kenneth H. (1976). Leadership effectiveness and adaptability description. In J. W. Pfeiffer & J. E. Jones (Eds.), *1976 annual handbook for group facilitators*. San Diego, CA: University Associates.

Hessel, Karen, & Holloway, John. (2002). *A framework for school leaders: Linking the ISLLC standards to practice*. Princeton, NJ: Educational Testing Service.

Hilliard, Asa. (1991). Do we have the will to educate all children? *Educational Leadership, 40*(1), 31-36.

Hodgkinson, Harold. (1991). Reform versus reality. *Phi Delta Kappan, 73*(1), 8-16.

Hofstede, G. (1980). *Culture's consequences: International differences in work-related values*. Beverly Hills, CA: Sage.

Hord, Shirley M., Rutherford, William L., Huling-Austin, Leslie, & Hall, Gene E. (1987). *Taking charge of change*. Alexandria, VA: Association for Supervision and Curriculum Development.

Howard, G. R. (1993). Whites in multicultural education: Rethinking our role. *Phi Delta Kappan, 75*(1), 36-41.

Howe, Harold. (1991). America 2000: A bumpy ride on four trains. *Phi Delta Kappan, 73*(3), 193-203.

Huxley, Aldous Leonard. (1977). *The Human Situation: Lectures at Santa Barbara, 1959*. New York: HarperCollins.

Immegart, Gerald L. (1988). Leadership and leadership behavior. In N. J. Boyan (Ed.), *Handbook of research on educational administration*. White Plains, NY: Longman.

Kanter, Rosabeth Moss. (1977). *Men and women of the corporation*. New York: Basic Books.

Katz, Michael B. (1973). *Education in American history: Readings on the social issues.* New York: Praeger.

Keyes, Ken, Jr. (1985). *The 100th monkey.* Coos Bay, OR: Vision Books. This book is also available as an e-book through www.amazon.com.

Knowles, Louis L., & Prewitt, K. (1969). *Institutional racism in America.* Englewood Cliffs, NJ: Prentice Hall.

Kohn, Alfie. (1998). Only for my kid: How privileged parents undermine school reform. *Phi Delta Kappan, 79,* 568-579.

Kovel, Joel. (1984). *White racism: A psychohistory.* New York: Columbia University Press.

Kozol, Jonathan. (1991). *Savage inequalities: Children in America's schools.* New York: Harper Perennial.

Ladson-Billings, Gloria. (1994). *Dreamkeepers: Successful teachers of African American children.* San Francisco: Jossey-Bass.

Levin, Henry M. (1988). *Accelerated schools for at-risk students.* New Brunswick, NJ: Center for Policy Research in Education.

Lightfoot, Sara L. (1983). *The good high school: Portraits of character and culture.* New York: Basic Books.

Locust, Carol. (1996). Wounding the spirit: Discrimination and traditional American Indian beliefs. In T. Beauboeuf-Lafontant & D. S. Augustine (Eds.), *Facing racism in education* (2nd ed.). Cambridge, MA: Harvard University Press.

Loewen, James W. (1995). *Lies my teacher told me: Everything your American history textbook got wrong.* New York: New Press.

Maccoby, Michael. (1981). *The leader.* New York: Simon & Schuster.

Machiavelli, Niccolò. (1940). *The prince and the discourses* (trans. Luigi Ricci and Christian E. Detmold). New York: Modern Library.

Malinowski, Bronislaw. (1933). *A scientific theory of culture.* Chapel Hill: University of North Carolina Press.

Massey, Morris. (1979a). *The people puzzle: Understanding yourself and others.* Reston, VA: Reston.

Massey, Morris. (Producer). (1979b). *What you are is where you were when . . .* [Motion picture]. (Available from Morris Massey Associates, Boulder, CO)

McCarthy, Cameron. (1993). After the canon: Knowledge and ideological representation in the multicultural discourse on curriculum reform. In C. McCarthy & W. Crichlow (Eds.), *Race identity and representation in education.* New York: Routledge.

McDermott, D., & Stadler, H. A. (1988). Attitudes of counseling students in the United States toward minority clients. *International Journal for the Advancement of Counseling, 11*(1), 61-69.

McGregor, Douglas M. (1960). *The human side of enterprise.* New York: McGraw-Hill.

McIntosh, Peggy. (1988). *White privilege and male privilege: A personal account of coming to see correspondences through work in women's studies.* Wellesley, MA: Wellesley College.

Moore, Alexander. (1992). *Cultural anthropology: The field study of human beings.* San Diego, CA: Collegiate.

Naisbitt, John. (1984). *Megatrends: Ten new directions transforming our lives*. New York: Warner.

Naisbitt, John, & Aburdene, Patricia. (1990). *Megatrends 2000: Ten new directions for the 1990's*. New York: William Morrow.

National Association of Elementary School Principals. (2001). *Leading learning communities: Standards for what principals should know and be able to do*. Alexandria, VA: Author.

National Center for Educational Statistics. (1994). *Digest of Education Statistics, Institute of Education Sciences*. Washington, DC: U.S. Dept. of Education.

National Commission on Excellence in Education. (1983). *A nation at risk: The imperative for educational reform*. Washington, DC: Government Printing Office.

Nieto, Sonia. (2000). *Affirming diversity: The sociopolitical context of multicultural education* (3rd ed.). Reading, MA: Addison Wesley.

Nuri Robins, Kikanza, Lindsey, Randall B., Lindsey, Delores B., & Terrell, Raymond D. (2002). *Culturally proficient instruction: A guide for people who teach*. Thousand Oaks, CA: Corwin.

Oakes, Jeannie. (1985). *Keeping track: How schools structure inequality*. New Haven, CT: Yale University Press.

Oakes, Jeannie, & Lipton, Martin. (1990). *Making the best of school*. New Haven, CT: Yale University Press.

Obiakor, Festus. (2001). *It even happens in "good" schools: Responding to cultural diversity in today's classrooms*. Thousand Oaks, CA: Corwin.

Ogbu, John U. (1978). *Minority education and caste: The American system in cross-cultural perspective*. New York: Academic Press.

Ogbu, John U. (1992). Understanding cultural diversity and learning. *Educational Researcher, 21*(8), 5-14.

Ogbu, John U., & Matute-Bianchi, M. E. (1990). Understanding sociocultural factors: Knowledge, identity, and school adjustment. In Charles Leyba (Ed.), *Beyond language: Social and cultural factors in schooling language minority students*. Los Angeles: California State University Press.

Ouchi, William G., & Wilkins, A. L. (1985). Organizational culture. *Annual Review of Sociology, 11*, 457-483.

Owens, Robert G. (1991). *Organizational behavior in education*. Englewood Cliffs, NJ: Prentice Hall.

Owens, Robert G. (1995). *Organizational behavior in education* (5th ed.). Boston: Allyn & Bacon.

Pate, Gerald S. (1988). Research on reducing prejudice. *Social Education, 52*(4), 287-289.

Peters, Thomas J., & Waterman, R. H. (1982). *In search of excellence: Lessons from America's best-run companies*. New York: Harper & Row.

Peterson, Kent, & Deal, Terrence. (1998). *Shaping school culture*. San Francisco: Jossey-Bass.

Pfeiffer, J. William. (1987-1994). *Annuals: Developing human resources*. San Diego, CA: University Associates.

Pfeiffer, J. William, & Goodstein, L. D. (1982-1986). *Annuals for facilitators, trainers, and consultants*. San Diego, CA: University Associates.

Pfeiffer, J. William, & Jones, John E. (1972-1981). *Annual handbooks for group facilitators*. San Diego, CA: University Associates.

Pignatelli, Frank, & Pflaum, Susanna W. (1994). *Experiencing diversity: Toward educational equity*. Thousand Oaks, CA: Corwin.

Ponterotto, J. G. (1988). Racial consciousness development among white counselor trainees: A stage model. *Journal of Multicultural Counseling, 16*, 146-156.

Pritchett, Price. (1994). *The employee handbook of new work habits for a radically changing world: Thirteen ground rules for job success in the information age*. Dallas, TX: Pritchett & Associates.

Pritchett, Price. (1995). *Culture shift: The employee handbook for changing corporate culture*. Dallas, TX: Pritchett & Associates.

Pritchett, Price, & Pound, Ron. (1990). *The employee handbook for organizational change*. Dallas, TX: Pritchett & Associates.

Pritchett, Price, & Pound, Ron. (1991). *High velocity culture change: A handbook for managers*. Dallas, TX: Pritchett & Associates.

Pritchett, Price, & Pound, Ron. (1995). *A survival guide to the stress of organizational change*. Dallas, TX: Pritchett & Associates.

Reddin, William J. (1970). *Managerial effectiveness*. New York: McGraw-Hill.

Rendon, Laura I., Hope, Richard O., & Associates. (1995). *Educating a new majority*. San Francisco: Jossey-Bass.

Richardson, Ken, & Spears, David. (1972). *Race and intelligence: The fallacies behind the race-IQ controversy*. Baltimore: Penguin.

Riot Commission. (1968). *Report of the National Advisory Commission on Civil Disorders*. Washington, DC: Government Printing Office.

Roberts, Wess. (1987). *Leadership secrets of Attila the Hun*. New York: Warner.

Rosenfeld, G. (1976). Shut those thick lips! Can't you behave like a human being? In Joan Roberts & Sherrie K. Akinsanya (Eds.), *Schooling in the cultural context*. New York: David McKay.

Rosenthal, Robert, & Jacobsen, L. (1966). Teacher expectations: Determinants of pupils' IQ gains. *Psychological Abstracts, 19*, 115-118.

Ryan, William. (1976). *Blaming the victim*. New York: Vintage.

Sadker, Myra, & Sadker, David. (1994). *Failing at fairness: How America's schools cheat girls*. New York: Charles Scribner's Sons.

Sapon-Shevin, Mara. (1993). Gifted education. In L. Weis & M. Fine (Eds.), *Beyond silenced voices: Class, race, and gender in United States schools*. Albany: State University of New York Press.

Sargent, Alice G. (1983). *The androgynous manager*. New York: American Management Association.

Sashkin, Marshal. (1981). An overview of ten management and organizational theorists. In W. Pfeiffer & J. Jones (Eds.), *The 1981 annual handbook for group facilitators*. San Diego, CA: University Associates.

Schein, Edgar H. (1985). *Organizational culture and leadership: A dynamic view*. San Francisco: Jossey-Bass.

Scott, Cynthia D., & Jaffe, Dennis T. (1995). *Managing change at work*. Menlo Park, CA: Crisp Learning.

Senge, Peter, et al. (1994). *The fifth discipline fieldbook: Strategies and tools for building a learning organization*. New York: Doubleday.

Senge, Peter M., Kleiner, Art, Roberts, Charlotte, Roth, George, Ross, Rick, & Smith, Bryan. (1999). *The dance of change: The challenges to sustaining momentum in learning organizations*. New York: Doubleday.

Senge, Peter M., McCabe, Nelda, Cambron, H., Lucas, Timothy, Kleiner, Art, Dutton, Janis, & Smith, Bryan. (Eds.). (2000). *Schools that learn: A fifth discipline fieldbook for educators, parents, and everyone who cares about education*. New York: Doubleday.

Sergiovanni, Thomas J. (1991). *The principalship: A reflective practice perspective*. Boston: Allyn & Bacon.

Sergiovanni, Thomas J., & Corbally, J. E. (Eds.). (1984). *Leadership and organizational culture*. Urbana: University of Illinois Press.

Shieve, Linda T., & Schoenheit, Marian B. (1987). Leadership: Examining the elusive. In *1987 yearbook of the Association for Supervision and Curriculum Development*. Alexandria, VA: Association for Supervision and Curriculum Development.

Shirrts, R. Garry. (1969). *Starpower*. Del Mar, CA: Simile II.

Sizemore, Barbara A. (1983). *An abashing anomaly: The high achieving predominately black elementary school*. Pittsburgh, PA: University of Pittsburgh, Department of Black Community Education, Research and Development.

Sizer, Theodore R. (1985). *Horace's compromise: The dilemma of the American high school*. Boston: Houghton Mifflin.

Slavin, Robert. (1990). *Cooperative learning: Theory, research and practice*. Englewood Cliffs, NJ: Prentice Hall.

Slavin, Robert. (1996). *Every child, every school: Success for all*. Thousand Oaks, CA: Corwin.

Sleeter, Christine E. (Ed.). (1991). *Empowerment through multicultural education*. Albany: State University of New York Press.

Sleeter, Christine E., & Grant, Carl A. (1991). Mapping terrains of power: Student cultural knowledge versus classroom knowledge. In C. E. Sleeter (Ed.), *Empowerment through multicultural education*. Albany: State University of New York Press.

Smitherman, Geneva. (1977). *Talkin and testifyin*. Boston: Houghton Mifflin.

Sparks, Dennis. (1997). Maintaining the faith in teachers' ability to grow: An interview with Asa Hilliard. *Journal of Staff Development, 18*, 24-25.

Spring, Joel H. (2000). *Deculturalization and the struggle for equality: A brief history of the education of dominated cultures in the United States* (3rd ed.). New York: McGraw-Hill.

Suzuki, Bob. (1987). *Cultural diversity: Achieving equity through diversity*. (ERIC Document Reproduction Service No. ED303527)

Terry, Robert W. (1970). *For whites only*. Grand Rapids, MI: Eerdmans.

Thomas, Roosevelt, R. Jr. (1991). *Beyond race and gender: Unleashing the power of your total work force by managing diversity.* New York: American Management Association.

Tiedt, Iris, & Tiedt, Pam. (2001). *Multicultural teaching: A handbook of activities, information, and resources* (6th ed.). Boston: Allyn & Bacon.

Tyack, David B. (1974). *The one best system: A history of American urban education.* Cambridge, MA: Harvard University Press.

U.S. Bureau of the Census. (1997). *Census updates, 1997.* Washington, DC: Author.

Valverde, Leonard A., & Brown, Frank. (1988). Influences on leadership development among racial and ethnic minorities. In N. J. Boyan (Ed.), *Handbook of research on educational administration.* White Plains, NY: Longman.

Vigil, J. Diego. (1980). *From Indians to Chicanos: A sociocultural history.* St. Louis, MO: Mosby.

Vroom, V. H., & Yetton, P. W. (1973). *Leadership and decision making.* Pittsburgh, PA: University of Pittsburgh Press.

Warren, David R. (1978). *History, education, and public policy.* Berkeley, CA: McCutchan.

Wartell, Michael A., & Huelskamp, Robert M. (1991, July 18). Testimony of Michael A. Wartell & Robert M. Huelskamp, Sandia National Laboratories, Before Subcommittee on Elementary, Secondary, and Vocational Education, Committee on Education and Labor, U.S. House of Representatives.

Weiss, Andrea, & Schiller, Greta. (1988). *Before Stonewall: The making of a gay and lesbian community.* Tallahassee, FL: Naiad.

West, Cornel. (1993). The new cultural politics of difference. In C. McCarthy & W. Crichlow (Eds.), *Race identity and representation in education.* New York: Routledge.

Wheatley, Margaret J. (1992). *Leadership and the new science.* San Francisco: Berrett-Koehler.

Wheelock, Anne. (1992). *Crossing the tracks: How "untracking" can save America's schools.* New York: New Press.

Wiggins, Grant. (1989). A true test: Toward more authentic and equitable assessment. *Phi Delta Kappan, 71,* 703-719.

Willis, Arlette Ingram. (1996). Reading the world of school literacy: Contextualizing the experience of a young African American male. In T. Beauboeuf-Lafontant & D. S. Augustine (Eds.), *Facing racism in education* (2nd ed.). Cambridge, MA: Harvard University Press.

Wright, Richard. (1940). *Native son.* New York: Harper & Row.

# Index

Abraham Lincoln, 90
Activism, 52
Activities
  context for, 21–22
  organized by
    expertise of facilitator, 337–339
    readiness of group, 339–340
    topic, 336–337
  purpose for, 20–21
  response sheets and, 24
Activities to Reinforce the Essential
    Elements of Cultural Proficiency
    (Response Sheet 4.2.2), 133–136
Adams, David Wallace, 49
Adapting to diversity, changing for
    the differences
  activities to reinforce, 135
  behavioral competencies for, 113,
    117, 127
African Americans
  civil rights movement and, 52
  cultural
    assimilation of, 201
    blindness of, 89
    destructiveness of, 87
    incapacity of, 89
  education of, 47–48, 190, 202–203,
    259–260
  immigrant *versus* caste status, 249–
    251, 252, 253, 254
  labels of inferiority and, 46–47
  language of entitlement and, 256–
    259
  name preferences of, 45
Age issues, 12
Aged. *See* Older Americans
Alienation, feelings of, 46, 49
American Society for Training and
    Development (ASTD), 22
Analyzing the Great Egg Drop
    (Response Sheet 6.1.2), 210

Answers and Commentary (Response
    Sheet 2.4.2), 66
Argyris, Chris, 118, 188, 177, 200, 198
Armelagos, George, 88 43-44
Asians
  cultural
    assimilation of, 201
    incapacity of, 88
  education of, 202–203
  labels of inferiority and, 47
  name preferences of, 45
Assertiveness continuum, 86
Assessing culture
  activities to reinforce, 133
  behavioral competencies for, 112,
    114–115, 126
Assessing the Culture of Your School
    (Response Sheet 5.4.1), 179–180
Assessing Your Paradigms (Response
    Sheet 7.4.1), 243
Assessing Your School's Culture
    (Activity 5.4), 177-178
Assimilation, cultural, 12, 49, 87, 201,
    237
Attendance laws, compulsory, 88, 201
Automobile sector, 12

Baldwin, James, 318
Ball, Edward, 245
Banking sector, 12
Banks, James, 52, 118, 188
Barker, Joel, 48, 219
Barriers, to cultural proficiency, 84,
    121
  presumption of entitlement, 7, 218,
    245–246
    caste status and
      illustrative story, 254–255
      immigrant status *versus* caste,
        249, 250t

oppression in U. S. history,
248–249, 251–254
teaching of history, 253–256
dynamics of, 247–248
educational practices of
educator expectations, 266–
267
illustrative story, 266–267
systems of tracking, 47–48,
202–203, 265–266
going further, questions for, 271
illustrative story, 244–245
manifestations of
illustrative story, 262–265
in education, 261–265
language, 256–259, 258*t*
power, 261–262
thingification, 258–261
racial consciousness, stages of,
267–271, 270*t*
reflection (form), 272
the activities
8.5 Barriers to Cultural Proficiency, 283–284
8.3 Entitlement Survey, 277–
278
8.2 Line of Privilege, 275–276
8.1 Stand Up, 273–274
8.4 Starpower, 281–282
the response sheets
8.5.1 Barriers to Cultural
Proficiency
8.3.1 A Survey of Privilege
and Entitlement, 279–280
unawareness of the need to adapt,
7, 218–219
change process
illustrative story, 226–228
myths about, 219–220, 221*t*
paradigm settlers, 226
paradigm shifters, 219
phases in the, 220, 222–224,
223*t*
resilience and, 225–226
resistance to, overcoming,
220, 224–225
seven dynamics of, 222, 224
going further, questions for
organizational change, 229

personal change, 228–229
resilience, 229
illustrative story, 8, 217–218
the activities
7.3 Differences That Make a
Difference, 238–240
7.4 Paradigms, 241–242
7.2 Seven Dynamics of
Change, 234–236
7.1 The Process of Personal
Change, 231–232
the response sheets
7.4.1 Assessing Your Paradigms, 243
7.2.1 Seven Dynamics of
Change, 237
7.1.1 The Process of Personal
Change, 233
*See also* Tools, of cultural
proficiency
Barriers to Cultural Proficiency
(Activity 8.5), 283
Barriers to Cultural Proficiency
(Response Sheet 8.5.1), 285
Bazron, Barbara J., 14
Behavioral competencies, cultural
going further, questions for, 122
illustrative story, 110–111, 113–114
reflection (form), 123
school leadership, analyzing, 118–
122, 119–120*t*, 188–189
standards for, 6, 13, 111–112
adapting to diversity, 113, 117,
127
assessing culture, 112, 114–115,
126
institutionalizing cultural
knowledge, 113, 117–118, 127
managing the dynamics of difference, 112–113, 116, 126–127
valuing diversity, 112, 115–116,
126
the activities
4.8 Cultural Competence Self
Assessment, 152–153
4.3 Essential Elements of Cultural Proficiency, 137–138
4.1 Exploring behaviors Along
the Continuum, 124–125

4.6 Intercultural Communication, 146–147
4.7 Managing Conflict with Our Core Values, 148–149
4.5 Performance Competencies and the Essential Elements, 141–143
4.4 Planning with the Five Essential Elements, 139–140
4.2 Understanding the Essential Elements, 129–130
the response sheets
4.2.2 Activities to Reinforce the Essential Elements of Cultural Proficiency, 133–136
4.1.2 Behaviors Along the Continuum, 128
4.8.1 Cultural Competence Self-Assessment, 154–156
4.2.1 Culturally Proficient Practices, 131–132
4.1.1 Essential Elements of Cultural Proficiency, 126–127
4.7.2 Examining Your Core Values, 151
4.7.1 Managing Conflict With Our Core Values—Example, 150
4.5.1 Performance Competencies and the Essential Elements, 144
4.5.2 Words to Describe Oppressed and Entitled Groups, 145
*See also* Tools, of cultural proficiency
Behaviors Along the Continuum (Response Sheet 4.1.2), 128
Biculturality, 50–51, 161, 162
Biological traits, 44
Biracial, 44
Bisexuals. *See* GLBT
Black History Month, 90–91
Boaz, David, 203
Boyd, Malcolm, 49
Bridges, William, 220
Brown, Frank, 199
Brown v. Topeka Board of Education, 10–11, 253

Bureau of Indian Affairs schools, 87
Burns, James MacGregor, 187
Business, historical changes in, 202–204
Business community, effective responses to, 15

California Commission on Teacher Credentialing, 197–198
Case study, 16–17, 318
Coolidge Unified School District
analysis of, 325–333
descriptive overview of, 18–19
going further, questions for, 333–334
reflection (form), 334
Rolling Meadows School District
analysis of, 319–325
descriptive overview of, 17–18
Caste status, 249
Caste system
educational practices and, 190
illustrative story, 254–255
immigrant *versus* caste status, 249, 250*t*
oppression in U. S. history and, 248–249, 251–254
teaching of history and, 253–256
Change process
illustrative story, 226–228
myths about, 219–220, 221*t*
paradigm settlers, 226
paradigm shifters, 219
phases of the, 220, 222–224, 223*t*
resilience and, 225–226
resistance to, overcoming, 220, 224–225
seven dynamics of, 222, 223
*See also* Barriers, to cultural proficiency
Cheek, Robert, 247
Chinese Exclusion Acts, 10
Cinco de Mayo, 90
Circle of History (Activity 3.2), 102–104
Circle of Stereotypes (Activity 2.6), 70
Citizenship, responsible, 267–268
Civil Rights Acts, 52, 253

Civil rights movement, historical perspective on, 11–12, 52, 253, 254–255
Class differences, 163–164
    See also Caste system
Classical scientific management period, 199, 200–202, 200
Classroom teachers, 122
Coaching, systems of, 197–198
Collegial leadership, 192–193
Collins, James, 165
Comer, James P., 13, 270
Commitment, to cultural proficiency
    an moral imperative, 294–295
    foundations for, 39, 40, 117, 290–294
    going further, questions for, 295
    illustrative story, 289–290
    reflection (form), 296
    the activities
        9.6 Cultural Portrait, 308–309
        9.7 Exploring Your Cultural Roots, 310–311
        9.1 Introductory Grid, 297–299
        9.3 Name Five Things, 302–303
        9.8 Observation Activity, 312–313
        9.9 Strength Bombardment, 315–317
        9.2 Totems or Crests—Getting To Know You, 300–301
        9.5 Who Am I?, 306–307
        9.4 Who Are You?, 304–305
    the response sheets
        9.8.1 Observation Questions, 314
Community participation, effective responses to, 16
Compulsory attendance laws, 87, 200–201
Conflict, strategies for resolving. See Difference, managing the dynamics of
Continuum, for developing cultural competence, 5–6, 111
    descriptive language, 84–86
    cultural
        blindness, 86-87, 89–90, 98
        competence, 87, 90–91, 99
        destructiveness, 86, 87–88, 97

incapacity, 86, 88–89, 98
precompetence, 87, 90–91, 99
proficiency, 87, 91–92, 100
illustrative story, 89
going further, questions for, 91–92
illustrative story, 83–84
reflection (form), 93
the activities
    3.2 Circle of History, 102–104
    3.3 Human Relations Needs Assessment, 105–106
    3.1 The Cultural Proficiency Continuum, 94–96
the response sheets
    3.3.1 Human Relations Needs Assessment Instrument, 107–109
    3.1.1 The Cultural Proficiency Continuum, 97–100
    3.1.2 The Cultural Proficiency Continuum Chart, 101
Coolidge Unified School District, case study
    analysis of, 318, 325–333
    descriptive overview of, 18–20
Cose, Ellis, 244
Crane, Edward, 203
Creator leaders, 196
Cross, Terry, 4, 5, 14, 110, 218
Cultural bias, 88–89, 160
Cultural blindness
    defining, 85, 86–87
    examples of, 89–90
    looking at differences, 98
Cultural competence
    defining, 85, 87
    examples of, 90–91
    looking at differences, 99
Cultural Competence Self Assessment (Activity 4.8), 152–153
Cultural Competence Self-Assessment (Response Sheet 4.8.1), 154–156
Cultural destructiveness
    defining, 85, 86
    examples of, 87–88
    looking at differences, 97
Cultural expectations
    as criteria for success, 161–162
    in educators, 266–267

norms for, 42, 116
paradigms of, 219
values and, 41, 98
Cultural groups
  defining, 14, 41–42
  discrimination, response to, 49–51
  illustrative story, 42–43
  labels of inferiority and, 46–48
  language of entitlement and, 256–259, 258t
  power, response to, 261–262
  racial terminology and, 44–45
Cultural incapacity
  defining, 85, 86
  examples of, 88–89
  illustrative story, 89
  looking at differences, 98
Cultural knowledge, institutionalized
  training about differences
    activities to reinforce, 136
    behavioral competencies for, 113, 117–118, 127
Cultural Perceptions (Activity 2.5), 67
Cultural Perceptions (Response Sheet 2.5.1), 69
Cultural Portrait (Activity 9.6), 308–309
Cultural precompetence
  defining, 85, 87
  examples of, 90–91
  looking at differences, 99
Cultural proficiency approach, understanding, 3–37
  "the next wave" in diversity training, 7–8
  basic tenets of, 13
  case study
    analysis of, 318, 319–333
    descriptive overview of, 16–20
    going further, questions for, 333–334
  commitment to, making the, 39, 40, 117, 294–295
  diversity issues, effective responses to, 14–16
    community participation, 16
    learning and teaching effectively, 15
    living in a global community, 15

    providing leadership, 16
  foundations to, 4–5, 290–294
  going further, questions for, 22
  historical perspective to, 9–14, 46–52
  illustrative story, 3–4
  reflection (form), 23
  the activities, 20–21, 24
    1.3 Cultural Proficiency Consensus, 31–32
    1.1 Diversity Lifeline, 2627
    1.2 Identifying Shared Values for Diversity, 28–29
    1.4 Journaling, 36–37
  the response sheets, 24
    1.3.1 Culturally Proficiency Consensus, 33
    1.3.2 Cultural Proficiency Consensus Preferred Responses, 34–35
    1.0.1 Culturally Proficient Professional, 25
    1.2.1 Definitions for Shared Values, 30
  the text, context for, 21–22
  tools for developing cultural competence
    the barriers, 7–8, 84, 121
    the continuum, 5–6, 84–86, 111
    the essential elements, 6, 13, 84, 111–113
    the guiding principles, 6–7, 84, 159–165, 233
Cultural Proficiency Consensus (Activity 1.3), 31–32
Cultural Proficiency Continuum (Activity 3.1), 94–96
Cultural Proficiency Continuum Chart (Response Sheet 3.1.2), 101
Cultural Proficiency Continuum (Response Sheet 3.1.1), 97–100
Cultural Proficiency Discussion Starters (Response Sheet 5.1.2), 170
Cultural Proficiency Consensus Preferred Responses (Response Sheet 1.3.2), 34–35
Cultural Proficiency Consensus (Response Sheet 1.3.1), 33

Cultural Stereotypes (Activity 2.8), 74
Culturally Proficient Instruction, 122
Culturally Proficient Practices
    (Response Sheet 4.2.1), 131–132
Culturally Proficient Professional
    (Response Sheet 1.0.1), 25
Culture
    as a predominant force, 160–161,
      169
    defining, 13–14, 41–42
    illustrative story, 42–43
Cummins, Jim, 50, 271
Curricula, 262–263

Darwin, Charles, 252
Darwinism, social, 41, 46, 252
*De facto* segregation, 11
Deconstruction leaders, 196–197
Deficient persons, 47, 90, 258
Definitions for Shared Values
    (Response Sheet 1.2.1), 30
Delpit, Lisa, 50, 259–260, 262
Deming, C. Edwards, 202–203
Demographics (Activity 5.3), 175–176
Dennis, Karl W., 14
Deprived, 258
Descriptive language, cultural
    going further, questions for, 91–92
    illustrative story, 89
    reflection (form), 93
    the activities
        3.2 Circle of History, 102–104
        3.3 Human Relations Needs
           Assessment, 105–106
        3.1 The Cultural Proficiency
           Continuum, 94–96
    the continuum for, 5–6, 84–86, 111
      cultural blindness, 86–87, 89–
        90, 98
      cultural competence, 87, 90–
        91, 99
      cultural destructiveness, 86, 87–
        88, 97
      cultural incapacity, 86, 88–89, 98
      cultural precompetence, 87, 90–
        91, 99
      cultural proficiency, 87, 91–92,
        100

the response sheets
    3.3.1 Human Relations Needs
      Assessment Instrument, 107–
      109
    3.1.1 The Cultural Proficiency
      Continuum, 97–100
    3.1.2 The Cultural Proficiency
      Continuum Chart, 101
    *See also* Tools, of cultural
      proficiency
Desegregation, 10–11
Developer leaders, 196
Difference, managing the dynamics of
    reframing the differences
      activities to reinforce, 133–136
      behavioral competencies for,
        112–113, 116
Differences, looking at
    the continuum, cultural
      blindness, 98
      competence, 99
      destructiveness, 97
      incapacity, 98
      precompetence, 99
      proficiency, 100
    *See also* Continuum, for developing
      cultural competence
Differences That Make a Difference
    (Activity 7.3), 238–240
Differently abled, 45, 46
Disability issues, 12
Discrimination, effects of, 49–51
Discussion Questions About U. S.
    History (Activity 2.4), 62–63
Discussion Questions About U. S.
    History (Response Sheet 2.4.1),
    64–65
Diversity, within cultures, 163–164,
    169
Diversity Lifeline (Activity 1.1), 26–27
Diversity training, historical perspec-
    tive on, 7–8, 12
Domestic revolutions, 11
Dominant culture
    assimilation and, goal of, 12, 49,
      87–88, 201
    caste system and
      illustrative story, 254–255

immigrant *versus* caste status, 249, 250*t*
   oppression in U. S. history, 248–249, 251–254
   teaching of history, 253–256
criteria for success, 161–162
discrimination and, effects of, 49–51
giving of names, 45
presumption of entitlement, 245–246
   dynamics of, 247–248
   educational practices of
      educator expectations, 266–267
      illustrative story, 262–265, 266–267
      recognizing entitlement, 261–265
      systems of tracking, 47–48, 202–203, 265–266
   power of, 46, 261–262
   the language used, 256–259, 258*t*
   thingification process, 258–261
superiority of, belief in, 87–88
Drucker, Peter F., 202–203
Dualism, sense of, 50–51
Duchene, Marlys, 50

Economic classes, 249
Education system
   contemporary trends in, 13
   entitlement and oppression in
      educator expectations, 266–267
      illustrative story, 262–265, 266–267
      recognizing entitlement, 261–265
      systems of tracking, 47–48, 202–203, 265–266
   learning and teaching effectively, 15
   school leadership and
      analyzing, 118–122, 119–120*t*
      changing styles of, 194
      collegial leaders, 192–193
      formal and nonformal qualities, 188–189

      historical changes in, 51, 199, 200–202, 200*t*
      illustrative story, 189
      shared vision, achieving, 197–199
      two-tiered policies, 190–191
   standardized testing, 201–202
   systems of grouping, 266
   *See also* Leadership, culturally proficient
Educational leaders. *See* Leadership, culturally proficient
Educator expectations, 266–267
Einstein, Albert, 165
Elementary and Secondary Education Act, 11
Ellison, Ralph, 259–260
Emergency School Assistance Act, 11
Emerging minority issues
   biculturality, 161
   cultural incapacity, 88
   discrimination, effects of, 49–51
   education, 199
   labels of inferiority and, 46–48
   model minority syndrome, 162
En la Kech, 48
English-only policies, 87–88
Entitlement and oppression, historical perspective on, 7, 218, 245–246
   caste status and
      illustrative story, 254–255
      immigrant status *versus* caste, 249, 250*t*
      oppression in U. S. history, 248–249, 251–254
      teaching of history, 253–256
   dynamics of, 247–248
   educational practices of
      educator expectations, 266–267
      illustrative story, 262–265, 266–267
      recognizing entitlement in, 261–265
      systems of tracking, 47–48, 202–203, 265–266
   illustrative story, 244–245
   power, response to, 261–262
   the language used, 256–259, 258*t*
   thingification process, 258–261

*See also* Barriers, to cultural proficiency
Entitlement programs, 11–12
Entitlement Survey (Activity 8.3), 277–278
Equal access, integration for historical perspective on, 11–12, 48, 50, 52
Equal benefits, 12
Equal rights, integration for historical perspective, 11–12, 48, 50, 52
Essential elements, of cultural proficiency, 6, 13, 84, 111–113
  behavioral competencies
    adapting to diversity, 113, 117, 127
    assessing culture, 112, 114–115, 126
    institutionalizing cultural knowledge, 113, 117–118, 127
    managing the dynamics of difference, 112–113, 116, 126–127
    valuing diversity, 112, 115–116, 126
  going further, questions for, 122
  illustrative story, 110–111, 113–114
  reflection (form), 123
  school leadership, analyzing, 118–122, 119–120*t*, 188–189
  the activities
    4.8 Cultural Competence Self- Assessment, 152–153
    4.3 Essential Elements of Cultural Proficiency, 137–138
    4.1 Exploring Behaviors Along the Continuum, 124–125
    4.6 Intercultural Communication, 146–147
    4.7 Managing Conflict with Our Core Values, 148–149
    4.5 Performance Competencies and the Essential Elements, 141–143
    4.4 Planning with the Five Essential Elements, 139–140
    4.2 Understanding the Essential Elements, 129–130
  the response sheets

    4.2.2 Activities to Reinforce the Essential Elements of Cultural Proficiency, 133–136
    4.1.2 Behaviors Along the Continuum, 128
    4.8.1 Cultural Competence Self-Assessment, 154–156
    4.2.1 Culturally Proficient Practices, 131–132
    4.7.2 Examining Your Core Values, 151
    4.7.1 Managing Conflict With Our Core Values—Example, 150
    4.5.1 Performance Competencies and the Essential Elements, 144
    4.1.1 The Essential Elements of Cultural Proficiency, 126–127
    4.5.2 Words to Describe Oppressed and Entitled Groups, 145
Essential Elements of Cultural Proficiency (Activity 4.3), 137–138
Essential Elements of Cultural Proficiency (Response Sheet 4.1.1), 126–127
Ethnic cleansings, 87-88
Ethnic cultures, defining, 42, 43
Ethnic groups
  caste system and
    illustrative story, 254–255
    immigrant *versus* caste status, 249, 250*t*
    oppression in U. S. history, 248–249, 251–254
    teaching of history, 253–256
  defining, 14, 41, 44
  diversity within, 163–164, 169
  language of entitlement and, 256–259, 258*t*
  racial terminology for, 44–45
Ethnic Perceptions (Activity 2.9), 76
Ethnicity, defining, 44
Ethnocentrism, 248–249, 237
European Americans, 10, 40, 45, 237
Evolution of Equity Policies (Response Sheet 2.3.1), 61

Examining Our Organizational Values (Response Sheet 5.5.1), 183–184
Examining Your Core Values (Response Sheet 4.7.2), 151
Examining Your Organizational Values (Activity 5.5), 181–182
Executive Order 9066, 10
Expertise levels, 21–22
Exploring Behaviors Along the Continuum (Activity 4.1), 124–125
Exploring Your Cultural Roots (Activity 9.7), 310–311

Facilitator skills, 21–22
Feminist movement, 52
Fifteenth Amendment, 252
Fine, Michelle, 50
Formal leaders. *See* Leadership, culturally proficient
Fourteenth Amendment, 252
Franklin, John Hope, 254–255
Freire, Paolo, 190, 191, 246
Fullan, Michael, 189, 246

Galbraith, John Kenneth, 83
Gay men. *See* GLBT
Gay Pride movement, 52
Gender issues
    cultural blindness and, 89–90
    culture and, 42, 191
    discrimination and, 49
General Instructions (Response Sheet 6.2.2), 215
Genocide, cultural, 87
Gilligan, Carol, 49, 189, 191, 247, 259–260
Giroux, Henry A., 118, 246, 259–260
Gladwell, Malcolm, 7
GLBT (Gay Men, Lesbians, Bisexual, & Transgendered people), historical perspective
    discrimination, effects of, 49, 51
    dualism experience, 50
    education of, 199
    labels of inferiority and, 46
    name preferences, 45

thingification of, 259–260
Global community, effective responses to, 15
Goodwin, Doris Kearns, 3
Great Egg Drop (Activity 6.1), 206–208
Great Egg Drop (Response Sheet 6.1.1), 209
Group identity, acknowledgment of, 162–163, 169
Group Stereotypes (Activity 2.10), 79
Group systems, 266
Guiding principles, of cultural proficiency, 6–7, 84, 233
    going further, questions for, 165
    illustrative story, 157–159, 158*f*
    making it count, 164–165
    mission statements, 159–160
    reflection (form), 166
    the activities
        5.4 Assessing Your School's Culture, 177–178
        5.3 Demographics, 175–176
        5.5 Examining Your Organizational Values, 181–182
        5.1 Guiding Principles Discussion Starters, 167–168
        5.2.1 My Work Values, 173–174
    the response sheets
        5.4.1 Assessing the Culture of Your School, 179–180
        5.1.2 Cultural Proficiency Discussion Starters, 170
        5.5.1 Examining Our Organizational Values, 183–184
        5.1.3 Guiding Principles Discussions, 171–172
        5.1.1 The Guiding Principles of Cultural Proficiency, 169–170
    underlying values of
        acknowledge the group identity of individuals, 162–163, 169
        culture is a predominant force, 160–161, 169
        diversity within cultures, 163–164, 169
        people are served in varying degrees by the dominant culture, 161–162, 169

respect unique cultural needs,
164, 169
*See also* Tools, of cultural
proficiency
Guiding Principles Discussion Starters
(Activity 5.1), 167–168
Guiding Principles Discussions
(Response Sheet 5.1.3), 171–172
Guiding Principles of Cultural Pro-
ficiency (Response Sheet 5.1.1),
169–170

Hall, Edward T., 157
Harris, Louis, 258–259
Hate speeches, 89
Hawley, Willis, 11
Heterosexism, 248–249
Hiring practices, discriminatory, 88, 98
Hispanic groups
cultural blindness of, 89–90
labels of inferiority and, 47, 48
name preferences of, 45
Historical context, for cultural
proficiency
as inside-out approach, 39–40, 114,
118, 292
beyond political correctness, 13–14
culture types
defining, 13–14, 41–42
illustrative story, 42–43
going further, questions for, 53
illustrative story, 38–39
oppressed groups, historically
caste system and
illustrative story, 254–255
immigrants *versus* caste status, 249, 250*t*
oppression in U. S. history,
248–249, 251–254
teaching of history, 253–256
discrimination, effects of, 49–51
entitlement and, 245–246
dynamics of, 247–248
educational practices of
educator expectations,
266–267
illustrative story, 262–265,
266–267

recognizing entitlement,
261–265
systems of tracking, 47–48,
202–203, 265–266
power of, 261–262
the language of, 256–259,
258*t*
thingification process, 258–
261
illustrative story, 48
labels for, 46–48
race and, 43–45
reflection (form), 54
reforms in
business, 202–204
school leadership, 51, 199, 200–
202, 200*t*
social impetus and motivation,
51–52
societal response, to diversity, 9–14
cultural competence and
proficiency (1990s and
beyond), 13
desegregation (1950s), 10–11
diversity (1980s), 12
equal benefits and multiculturalism (1970s), 12, 51, 52
integration for equal access
and rights (1960s), 11–12, 48,
50, 52
labels of inferiority, 46–48
segregation (prior to 1950s),
9–10, 46, 49
the activities
2.4 Discussion Questions About
U. S. History, 62–63
2.3 Pick a Cell, 59–60
2.2 Simultaneous Storytelling,
57–58
2.1 Storytelling, 55–56
the response sheets
2.4.2 Answers and Commen-
tary, 66
2.4.1 Discussion Questions
About U. S. History, 64–65
2.3.1 Evolution of Equity
Policies, 61
Hodgkinson, Harold, 201, 203
Holocausts, 87–88

Howard, G. R., 255–256
Human Relations Needs Assessment
    (Activity 3.3), 105–106
Human Relations Needs Assessment
    Instrument (Response Sheet
    3.3.1), 107–109
Human relations period, 202–203

Identifying Shared Values for Diver-
    sity (Activity 1.2), 28—29
Ignorance, characteristic of, 89
Immigrant minorities
    cast system and
        caste *versus* immigrant status,
            249, 250*t*
        oppression in U. S. history, 248–
            249, 251–254
        teaching of history, 253–256
    cultural assimilation of, 12, 49, 87–
        88, 201
Inside-out approach, 39–40, 114, 118,
    292
Institutionalized cultural knowledge,
    training about differences
    activities to reinforce, 136
    behavioral competencies for, 113,
        117–118, 127
Institutionalized oppression, 246
Integration, for equal access and equal
    rights
    historical perspective on, 11–12, 48,
        50, 52
Intercultural Communication (Activ-
    ity 4.6), 146–147
Intracultural differences, 163–164
Introductory Grid (Activity 9.1), 297–
    299
Isaacs, Mareasa R., 14

Jacksonian democracy, 261–262
Jacobsen, L., 266
Jim Crow laws, 9, 46, 88, 251
Johnson, Lyndon, 253
Journaling (Activity 1.4), 36–37

Kerner, Otto, 253

Kerner Report, 253
Keyes, Ken Jr., 7
Kovel, Joel, 49, 252, 258–259, 259–260
Kozol, Jonathan, 201

Labeling, 46–48
    *See also* Language, of entitlement
Labor unions, pressures from, 202–203
Language, of entitlement, 256–259
Latino/Latina Americans, historical
    perspective
    cultural
        assimilation of, 201
        blindness of, 89
        incapacity of, 88
    educational practices and, 48, 190,
        202–203
    effects of
        desegregation, 10–11
        discrimination, 50
    immigrant *versus* caste status, 240
    labels of inferiority and, 47
    name preferences of, 45
Leadership, culturally proficient
    analyzing school leadership, 118–
        122, 119–120*t*
    choosing effective leaders, 194–195
    demographic profiles and, 188–189,
        191
    educator expectations, 266–267
    formal and nonformal leaders
        changing styles of, 194
        collegial, 192–193
        illustrative story, 189, 192–193
        personal attributes of, 189–191
        qualities of, 188–189
        support systems for, 197–198
    going further, questions for, 204
    historical perspective, 51
        business reforms, 202–204
        educational reforms, 51, 199,
            200–202, 200*t*
    illustrative story, 187–188
    leadership styles, 195–197
        descriptions of
            creators, 196
            deconstructors, 196–197
            developers, 196

reconstructors, 196
situational, 195
sustainers, 196
illustrative story, 198–199
reflection (form), 205
shared vision, achieving, 197–199
the activities
6.2 Seven-Minute Day, 211–213
6.1 The Great Egg Drop, 206–208
the response sheets
6.1.2 Analyzing the Great Egg
Drop, 210
6.2.2 General Instructions, 215
6.2.3 Seven-Minute Day Data
Sheet, 216
6.2.1 Seven-Minute Day Roles,
214
6.1.1 The Great Egg Drop, 209
See also Barriers, to cultural
proficiency
Leadership, process of, 189–190
Leadership styles
descriptions of, 195–197
illustrative story, 198–199
Learned helplessness, 88
Learning and teaching, effective
responses to, 15
Lesbians. See GLBT
Levin, Henry M., 13, 270
Liang, Zhuge, 289
Line of Privilege (Activity 8.2), 275–
276
Lipton, Martin, 189, 265, 266
Locust, Carol, 49
Louis Harris poll, 258–259

Machiavelli, Niccolò, 217
Managing Conflict with Our Core
Values (Activity 4.7), 148–149
Managing Conflict With Our Core
Values—Example (Response
Sheet 4.7.1), 150
Managing Transitions: Making the
Most of Change (Bridges), 220
Marginality, 50–51
Massey, Morris, 190
Matute-Bianchi, M. E., 202–203, 249,
237

McCarthy, Cameron, 49, 51
McGregor, Douglas M., 202–203
McIntoch, Peggy, 247, 268, 269
Melting pot theory, 12, 49, 87–88, 201
Mentoring, systems of, 197–198
Mexican Americans, 47
Mexican Cession of 1848, 10
Military desegregation, 10
Mission and value statements, 159–
160
Mixed-race, 44
Model minority syndrome, 162
Modern organizational period, 202–
204
Moral imperative, 294–295
See also Commitment, to cultural
proficiency
Morally deficient, 90
Moss, Alfred A., 254–255
Multiculturalism, 12, 51, 52
Multiracial groups, 44
My Work Values (Activity 5.2.1), 173–
174
Myths about change, 219–220, 221t

Name Five Things (Activity 9.3), 302–
303
Naming ceremonies, 44–45
National Association for the Advance-
ment of Colored People
(NAACP), 253
National Center for Educational
Statistics, 188
National Indian Child Welfare Associ-
ation, 4
National Organizational Development
Network (NODN), 22
National Training Labs (NTL), 22
Native Americans, 10
See also People of the First Nations
Nazi exterminations, 87–88
Need to adapt, unawareness of the.
See Change process
Nineteenth Amendment, 252–253
Noble savage, 47
Nonformal leaders. See Leadership,
culturally proficient

Oaks, Jeannie, 189, 201, 265, 266
Observation Activity (Activity 9.8), 312–313
Observation Questions (Response Sheet 9.8.1), 314
Occupational cultures, 41
Ogbu, John U., 49, 189, 190, 191, 202–203, 249, 249
Older Americans, 45, 46
Oppressed groups, historical perspective on
 caste system and
  illustrative story, 254–255
  immigrants *versus* caste status, 249, 250*t*
  oppression in U. S. history, 248–249, 251–254
  teaching of history, 253–256
 discrimination, effects of, 49–51
 entitlement and, 245–246
  dynamics of, 247–248
  educational practices of
   educator expectations, 266–267
   illustrative story, 262–265, 266–267
   recognizing entitlement, 261–265
   systems of tracking, 47–48, 202–203, 265–266
  power of, 261–262
  the language of, 256–259, 258*t*
  thingification process, 258–261
 illustrative story, 48
 labels for, 46–48
Organizational behavior period, 202–203
Organizational cultures, 41, 42
Oriental Exclusion Acts, 88
Owens, Robert G., 189, 194, 246

Pacific Islanders
 cultural
  assimilation of, 201
  incapacity of, 88
 name preferences, 45
Paradigm resisters, 219
Paradigm shifters, 219

Paradigms (Activity 7.4), 241–242
People of color, historical perspective
 caste system and
  illustrative story, 254–255
  immigrant *versus* caste status, 249, 250*t*
  oppression in U. S. history, 248–249, 251–254
  teaching of history, 253–256
 effects of
  desegregation, 10–11
  discrimination, 49
  segregation, 10
 entitlement and, 245–246
  dynamics of, 247–248
  the language of, 256–259
 labels of inferiority, 46
People of the First Nations, historical perspective
 cultural
  assimilation of, 201
  destructiveness of, 87
 education of, 190, 202–203
 effects of
  discrimination, 50
  segregation, 10
 immigrant *versus* caste status, 251–252
 labels of inferiority, 46–47
 name preferences, 45
Performance Competencies and the Essential Elements (Activity 4.5), 141–143
Performance Competencies and the Essential Elements (Response Sheet 4.5.1), 144
Personal identity, acknowledging, 162–163
Personal Stereotypes (Activity 2.7), 72
Personality problems, 163
Personnel polices, values and, 159–160
Perucca, Kirk, 8
Peterson, Kent, 165
Physical appearance, of humans, 41, 43, 44, 49
Physically challenged, 45
Pick a Cell (Activity 2.3), 59–60
Planning with the Five Essential Elements (Activity 4.4), 139–140

Polices, perspective for examining.
    *See* Continuum, for developing
    cultural competence
Political correctness, 13
Ponterotto, J. G., 269
Porras, Jerry, 165
Pound, Ron, 220
Poverty, 190
Power, of entitlement, 261–262
Pritchett, Price, 220
Process of Personal Change (Activity
    7.1), 231–232
Process of Personal Change (Response
    Sheet 7.1.1), 233
Professional cultures, 42
Project Equality, 8

Race
    defining, 41, 43–44
Race riots, 253, 254–255
Racial consciousness, stages of, 267–
    271, 270*t*
Racial groups
    definition of, 41, 42
    historical perspective
        desegregation of, 10–11
        integration for equal access and
            rights, 11–12, 48, 50, 52
        segregation of, 9–10, 46, 49
Racial prejudice, roots of, 252
Racial terminology, 44–45
Racism
    components of, 248–249, 251
    defining, 44
Readiness levels, 21–22
Reconstruction leaders, 196
Report of the National Advisory Com-
    mission on Civil Disorders, 253
Response sheets, 24
Revolutionary War, 254–255
Riot Commission, 253
Rite of passage, 45
Rituals, naming, 44–45
Rolling Meadows Unified School Dis-
    trict, case study
    analysis of, 318, 319–325
    descriptive overview of, 17–18
Roosevelt, Franklin D., 10

Rosenfeld, G., 258–259
Rosenthal, Robert, 266

Sadat, Anwar El, 38
Sadker, David, 270
Sadker, Myra, 270
Sapon-Shevin, Mara, 50
Schiller, Greta, 49
School culture, defining, 42
School desegregation, 10–11
School efficiency movement, 201
School leadership
    analyzing, 118–122, 119–120*t*
    changing styles of, 194
    collegial leaders, 192–193
    formal and nonformal qualities,
        188–189
    historical changes in, 51, 199, 200–
        202, 200*t*
    illustrative story, 189
    shared vision, achieving, 197–199
    *See also* Leadership, culturally
        proficient
Segregation, 9–10, 46, 49
Senge, Peter M., 118, 188, 194
Seven Dynamics of Change (Activity
    7.2), 234–236
Seven Dynamics of Change (Response
    Sheet 7.2.1), 237
Seven-Minute Day (Activity 6.2), 211–
    213
Seven-Minute Day Data Sheet
    (Response Sheet 6.2.3), 216
Seven-Minute Day Roles (Response
    Sheet 6.2.1), 214
Sexism, 248, 269
Sexual orientation, historical perspec-
    tive on, 12, 41, 42, 49
Simultaneous Storytelling (Activity
    2.2), 57–58
Situational leaders, 195
Sizer, Theodore R., 13, 189, 270
Skilled workers, need for, 202–203
Slavery, 9, 46, 252
Slavin, Robert, 13
Sleeter, Christine E., 271
Social class, 249
Social cultures, 41, 42

Societal response, to diversity, 9–14
 beyond politically correctness,
  13–14
 historical perspective
  cultural competence and
   proficiency (1990s and
   beyond), 13
  desegregation (1950s), 10–11
  diversity (1980s), 12
  equal benefits and multiculturalism (1970s), 12, 51, 52
  integration for equal access
   and rights (1960s), 11–12, 48,
   50, 52
  labels of inferiority, 46–48
  segregation (prior to 1950s), 9–
   10, 46, 49
 impetus for motivation and, 51–52
Socioeconomic status (SES), historical
  perspective, 87–88, 163–164, 190,
  258
Stand Up (Activity 8.1), 273–274
Standardized testing, 201–202
Starpower (Activity 8.4), 262, 281–282
Statements, mission and value, 159–
  160
Stereotypes, 88, 98
Storytelling (Activity 2.1), 55–56
Strength Bombardment (Activity 9.9),
  315–317
Student cultures, 42
Student leadership, 193
Survey of Privilege and Entitlement
  (Response Sheet 8.3.1), 279–280
Sustainer leaders, 196

Teaching and learning, effective
  responses to, 15
Technology sector, 12
Terminology, racial, 44–45
Terry, Robert W., 253, 261–262
Textbooks, recognizing entitlement in,
  264
100th Monkey: A Story About Social
  Change (Keyes), 7
Thirteenth Amendment, 252
Tipping Point (Gladwell), 7
Title I programs, 11

Tocqueville, de Alexis, 252
Tokenism, 88
Tolerance, 115
Tools, of cultural proficiency, 5
 the barriers, 84, 121
  presumption of entitlement, 7,
   218, 245–246
   caste status and
    illustrative story, 254–255
    immigrant status versus
     caste, 249, 250t
    oppression in U. S. his-
     tory, 248–249, 251–254
    teaching of history, 253–
     256
   dynamics of, 247–248
   educational practices of
    educator expectations,
     266–267
    illustrative story, 262–265,
     266–267
    recognizing entitlement,
     261–265
    systems of tracking, 47–48,
     202–203, 265–266
   going further, questions for,
    271
   illustrative story, 244–245
   power of, 261–262
   racial consciousness, stages
    of, 267–271, 256t
   reflection (form), 272
   the activities
    8.3 Entitlement Survey,
     277–278
    8.2 Line of Privilege, 275–
     276
    8.1 Stand Up, 273–274
    8.4 Starpower, 281–282
   the language used, 256–257,
    258t
   the response sheets
    8.3.1 A Survey of Privilege
     and Entitlement, 279–
     280
   thingification process, 258–
    261
  unawareness of the need to
   adapt, 7, 218–219

change process
  illustrative story, 226–228
  myths about, 219–220,
    221t
  paradigm settlers, 226
  paradigm shifters, 219
  phases of the, 220, 222–
    224, 223t
  resilience and, 225–226
  resistance to, overcoming,
    220, 224–225
  seven dynamics of, 222,
    224
going further, questions for
  organizational change, 229
  personal change, 228–229
  resilience, 229
illustrative story, 8, 217–218
the activities
  7.3 Differences That Make
    a Difference, 238–240
  7.4 Paradigms, 241–242
  7.2 Seven Dynamics of
    Change, 234–236
  7.1 The Process of Per-
    sonal Change, 231–232
the response sheets
  7.4.1 Assessing Your
    Paradigms, 243
  7.2.1 Seven Dynamics of
    Change, 237
  7.1.1 The Process of
    Personal Change, 233
the continuum, 5–6, 111
  descriptive language of, 84–86
    cultural competence, 87, 90–
      91, 99
    cultural destructiveness, 86,
      87–88, 97
    cultural incapacity, 86, 87–88,
      98
    cultural precompetence, 87,
      90–91, 99
    cultural proficiency, 87, 91–
      92, 100
    illustrative story, 89
  going further, questions for,
    91–92
  illustrative story, 83–84

reflection (form), 93
the activities
  3.2 Circle of History, 102–104
  3.3 Human Relations Needs
    Assessment, 105–106
  3.1 The Cultural Proficiency
    Continuum, 94–96
the response sheets
  3.3.1 Human Relations Needs
    Assessment Instrument,
    107–109
  3.1.1 The Cultural Proficiency
    Continuum, 97–100
  3.1.2 The Cultural Proficiency
    Continuum Chart, 101
the essential elements, 6, 13, 84,
  111–113
behavioral competencies of
  adapting to diversity, 113,
    117, 127
  assessing culture, 112, 114–
    115, 126
  institutionalizing cultural
    knowledge, 113, 117–118,
    127
  managing the dynamics of
    difference, 112–113, 116,
    126–127
  valuing diversity, 112, 115–
    116, 126
going further, questions for, 122
illustrative story, 110–111, 113–
  114
reflection (form), 123
school leadership, analyzing,
  118–122, 119–120t, 188–189
the activities
  4.8 Cultural Competence Self
    Assessment, 152–153
  4.3 Essential Elements of Cul-
    tural Proficiency, 137–138
  4.1 Exploring Behaviors
    Along the Continuum,
    124–125
  4.6 Intercultural Communica-
    tion, 146–147
  4.7 Managing Conflict with
    Our Core Values, 148–149

4.5 Performance Competencies and the Essential Elements, 141–143
4.4 Planning with the Five Essential Elements, 139–140
4.2 Understanding the Essential Elements, 129–130
the response sheets
    4.2.2 Activities to Reinforce the Essential Elements of Cultural Proficiency, 133–136
    4.1.2 Behaviors Along the Continuum, 128
    4.8.1 Cultural Competence Self-Assessment, 154–156
    4.2.1 Culturally Proficient Practices, 131–132
    4.7.2 Examining Your Core Values, 151
    4.7.1 Managing Conflict With Our Core Values—Example, 150
    4.5.1 Performance Competencies and the Essential Elements, 144
    4.1.1 The Essential Elements of Cultural Proficiency, 126–127
    4.5.2 Words to Describe Oppressed and Entitled Groups, 145
the guiding principles, 6–7, 84, 233
going further, questions for, 165
illustrative story, 157–159, 158f
making it count, 164–165
mission statements, 159–160
reflection (form), 166
the activities
    5.4 Assessing Your School's Culture, 177–178
    5.3 Demographics, 175–176
    5.5 Examining Your Organizational Values, 181–182
    5.1 Guiding Principles Discussion Starters, 167–168
    5.2.1 My Work Values, 173–174

the response sheets
    5.4.1 Assessing the Culture of Your School, 179–180
    5.1.2 Cultural Proficiency Discussion Starters, 170
    5.5.1 Examining Our Organizational Values, 183–184
    5.1.3 Guiding Principles Discussions, 171–172
    5.1.1 The Guiding Principles of Cultural Proficiency, 169–170
underlying values of
    acknowledge the group identity of individuals, 162–163, 169
    culture is a predominant force, 160–161, 169
    diversity within cultures, 163–164, 169
    people are served in varying degrees by the dominant culture, 161–162, 169
    respect unique cultural needs, 164, 169
    See also Leadership, culturally proficient
Top-down organization structures, 189
Totems or Crests—Getting To Know You (Activity 9.2), 300–301
Toward a Culturally Competent System of Care (Cross), 4, 291
Tracking, systems of
    entitlement and oppression in, 47–48, 202–203, 265–266
Transgendered people. See GLBT
Transitions: Making Sense of Life's Changes (Bridges), 220
Trends, societal
    in diversity training, 7–8
    in education, 13
Truman, Harry S., 10
Turkish exterminations, 87–88

U. S. Congress, 10
U. S. Constitution, 252, 253
U. S. Supreme Court, 10, 253

Understanding the Essential Elements (Activity 4.2), 129–130

Values, underlying
   illustrative story, 157–159, 158*f*
   making it count, 164–165
   mission statements, 159–160
   of cultural proficiency, guiding
      principles, 6–7, 84, 247
      acknowledge the group identity
        of individuals, 162–163, 169
      culture is a predominant force,
        160–161, 169
      diversity within cultures, 163–
        164, 169
      people are served in varying
        degrees by the dominant
        culture, 161–162, 169
      respect unique cultural needs,
        164, 169
   *See also* Guiding principles, of
      cultural proficiency
Valuing diversity, claiming your
   identity
   activities to reinforce, 134
   behavioral competencies for, 112,
      115–116, 126
Valverde, Leonard A., 199

Vigil, J. Diego, 247
Voting Rights Act of 1965, 253

Weiss, Andrea, 49
West, Cornel, 51
Wheatley, Margaret J., 118, 188, 189,
   194
Wheelock, Anne, 265, 266
White people. *See* European
   Americans
Who Am I? (Activity 9.5), 306–307
Who Are You? (Activity 9.4), 304–305
Wiggins, Grant, 201
Willis, Arlette Ingram, 51
Women's issues, historical perspec-
   tive on
   caste status, 252
   discrimination, effects of, 49
   education, 199
   labels of inferiority, 46
   multiculturalism, 12
   teaching of history, 253–256
   thingification, 259–260
Words Used to Describe Oppressed
   and Entitled Groups (Response
   Sheet 4.5.2), 145
World War II, 10, 254
Wright, Richard, 259–260

## CORWIN
## PRESS

The Corwin Press logo—a raven striding across an open book—represents the happy union of courage and learning. We are a professional-level publisher of books and journals for K–12 educators, and we are committed to creating and providing resources that embody these qualities. Corwin's motto is "Success for All Learners."